THE DOMINANT IDEOLOGY THESIS

The Dominant Ideology Thesis

NICHOLAS ABERCROMBIE
Senior Lecturer in Sociology, University of Lancaster

STEPHEN HILL
*Reader in Sociology, London School of Economics
and Political Science*

BRYAN S. TURNER
*Professor of Sociology, The Flinders University
of South Australia*

London
GEORGE ALLEN & UNWIN
Boston   Sydney

George Allen & Unwin (Publishers) Ltd,
40 Museum Street, London WC1A 1LU, UK

George Allen & Unwin (Publishers) Ltd,
Park Lane, Hemel Hempstead, Herts HP2 4TE, UK

Allen & Unwin Inc.,
9 Winchester Terrace, Winchester, Mass 01890, USA

George Allen & Unwin Australia Pty Ltd,
8 Napier Street, North Sydney, NSW 2060, Australia

First published in 1980
This edition first published 1984
Second impression 1985

British Library Cataloguing in Publication Data

Abercrombie, Nicholas
    The dominant ideology thesis.
1. Ideology
I. Title   II. Hill, Stephen   III. Turner,
Bryan Stanley
301.2′1   HM213   80–40546
ISBN 0–04–301117–9 cased
ISBN 0–04–301181–0 paperback

Set in 10 on 11 point Times by Grove Graphics, Tring
and printed in Great Britain
by Billing and Sons Ltd., Guildford, London and Worcester

Contents

Acknowledgements

We would like to thank Leigh Beier, Pendalis Glavanis, Mick Mann, John Martin, Larry Ray, John Urry and John Walton for their help at various stages of the preparation of this book; Tom Bottomore for kindly agreeing to write a foreword; and Brenda Wright for her patience in typing and retyping the manuscript. None of these people is responsible for errors which remain in our text.

Foreword

This book makes an important contribution to the current debate about the functions of ideology in social life. The authors set out to contest the view, widely diffused among present-day Marxists, that modern capitalist society, in particular, maintains and reproduces itself through the effects of a 'dominant ideology' which successfully incorporates the working class into the existing social system, thereby perpetuating its subordination. This thesis itself is directed against 'economism'; that is to say, against the view that the crucial element in the subordination of one class to another is always to be found in the organisation of social production.

The authors espouse this latter view, arguing broadly that the maintenance and reproduction of a given form of class society – or in other terms, its cohesion – is not to be explained by the influence of a 'dominant ideology', but principally by what Marx called the 'dull compulsion of economic relations'. They develop their argument initially through a theoretical analysis of the conceptions propounded by a number of modern Marxist thinkers – especially Gramsci, Habermas and Althusser – which they then compare, in a very illuminating way, with the theories of a 'common culture' formulated by the sociological functionalists.

Having thus shown that there *is* a 'dominant ideology thesis', widely accepted among Marxists, and that this thesis, like the theories of a 'common culture', is open to fundamental theoretical criticism, the authors set out to demonstrate, by means of three substantial case studies, that the thesis is empirically false. In feudal society, they argue, it was not religion but primogeniture which played the major part in maintaining class domination; in early capitalism there was nothing like a complete assimilation of the working class, and an explanation of mid-Victorian stability in Britain, for example, should be sought rather in political repression, successful reformism and internal divisions in the working class than in ideological indoctrination; finally, in late capitalism, although the mechanisms for transmitting ideology are highly developed, a 'dominant ideology' is less well defined, or even perhaps non-existent, so that it cannot possibly bear the burden of explanation that is placed upon it.

It will be seen that the authors formulate their counter thesis in very strong terms. The only important function they are willing to assign to a dominant ideology is that of binding together the dominant class itself, and even then not in all instances, as their account of late capitalism shows. But here it could be argued, I think, that the disintegration of the dominant ideology (if such is the case) both expresses, and is a significant factor in, the historical decline of a ruling class. The value of setting out the contrast between the 'dominant ideology thesis' and their own conception in such stark terms is that in this way attention is focused sharply upon a crucial issue in the general orientation of Marxist social theory; namely, whether it should be quite so preoccupied as it has been in recent years with cultural analysis, or whether it should now be redirected toward a more systematic investigation of economic and political trends.

But we must be careful not to throw the baby out with the bath water. If the 'dominant ideology thesis' in its strong version should be rejected – as I am persuaded that it should – this does not imply that there is no virtue at all in a weaker version of the thesis, asserting what I would describe as the negative influence of a dominant ideology. By this I mean the capacity of such an ideology, not to bring about social integration, or even to reinforce the cohesion of a dominant class (these would be positive functions), but to inhibit and confuse the development of the counter ideology of a subordinate class. It is not difficult to think of examples of such negative influence. One is to be found in the impact of nationalism upon socialism, analysed in Otto Bauer's classic study *Die Nationalitäten-frage und die Sozialdemokratie*, and from another aspect in his essay on fascism. Another, discussed by the authors in their chapter on late capitalism, is the 'ideology of achievement', which Claus Offe, in *Industry and Inequality*, has subjected to a comprehensive critical analysis as a major legitimating concept in present-day capitalist society.

In neither of these cases do we have to claim that the ideology – nationalism, or the achievement principle – produces, either alone or pre-eminently, a cohesive society, or even that it is the only negative influence which inhibits the clear expression of a radical counter ideology. Indeed, in their concluding chapter the authors suggest a variety of other influences. But it is hard to believe that such ideologies have no effect at all; and in so far as they are influential, then the critique of ideology must remain an integral part of a Marxist sociology. It is just this question, concerning the scope and importance of different forms of Marxist analysis, which the authors illumine so clearly and, through their trenchant formulation of the alternatives, establish as a major ground of future debate.

TOM BOTTOMORE

Introduction

The attempt to explain why societies cohere or collapse has been central to sociological theory since the term 'sociology' first emerged in the 1830s. It has often been suggested that the sociological emphasis on common culture as the ultimate root of social stability arose originally as a response to the instability which followed from the rapid industrialisation of European society. The analytical issues surrounding the so-called 'Hobbesian problem of order' (Parsons, 1937) are not, however, peculiar to the sociological tradition of Weber and Durkheim, since Marxists are also clearly concerned with the nature of social coherence and social collapse. From the revolutions of 1848 to the Paris Commune of 1871, Marx and Engels attempted to produce an account of the reproduction of capitalist relations and of how that reproduction might be interrupted by class struggle. The coherence of capitalist society was, for Marx and Engels, explained by the subordination of the labourer by economic and political means.

The apparent success of capitalism in surviving periodic crises and the absence of violent revolutionary struggle of the Western working class against the exploitative conditions of modern industrial production have led a variety of Marxist writers to argue that, especially in late capitalism, the coherence of industrial society is to be explained primarily by the *ideological* incorporation of the labour force. There exists a widespread agreement among Marxists, such as Habermas, Marcuse, Miliband and Poulantzas, that there is a powerful, effective, dominant ideology in contemporary capitalist societies and that this dominant ideology creates an acceptance of capitalism in the working class. It is with this dominant ideology thesis that our book is concerned. We argue that some version of this thesis is present in almost all forms of modern Marxism and that it is empirically false and theoretically unwarranted. We provide an alternative theory which explains the principal characteristics of capitalist society in economic and political terms without recourse to the notion of the ideological incorporation of social classes.

The major conceptual components of the dominant ideology thesis can be summarised in the following terms. The thesis argues that in all societies based on class divisions there is a dominant class which enjoys control of both the means of material production and the means of mental production. Through its control of ideological production, the dominant class is able to supervise the con struction of a set of coherent beliefs. These dominant beliefs of the dominant class are more powerful, dense and coherent than those of subordinate classes. The dominant ideology penetrates and infects the consciousness of the working class, because the working class comes to see and to experience reality through the conceptual categories of the dominant class. The dominant ideology functions to incorporate the working class within a system which is, in fact, operating against the material interests of labour. This incorporation in turn explains the coherence and integration of capitalist society.

Although this book is primarily a critique of Marxist versions of the dominant ideology thesis, we also wish to illustrate a number of clear analytical parallels between Marxist accounts of ideology and functionalist theories of common culture in sociology. If a social system is to exist, then there must be, according to Parsonian functionalism, a shared set of values and beliefs. This common culture is reproduced across different generations by the process of socialisation within primary groups such as the family. As these values are internalised, the individual experiences a psychological reward for his acceptance of existing social arrangements. The social control of the individual and the integration of the social system are thereby explained in terms of a dominant culture which inhibits instability and conflict within society. In Chapters 1 and 2 we formulate the principal assumptions of the dominant ideology thesis and the theory of common culture, comparing and contrasting their analytical problems. In Chapter 1 we show that Marx, unlike modern Marxists, did not treat ideological incorporation of the working class as a serious issue. In Chapter 2 we show that Durkheim, unlike Parsons, did not regard common culture as a necessary or essential feature of industrial society. The outcome of these two parallel arguments is that there is a form of convergence between the 'economic sociology' of Marx, Weber and Durkheim which distinguishes them from the 'superstructural sociology' of modern theorists.

Any dominant ideology thesis has to provide solutions to four basic questions. Briefly stated, these questions may be presented as a simple list.

(1) What is the dominant ideology?
(2) What effect does the dominant ideology have on the dominant class?
(3) What effect does the dominant ideology have on subordinate classes?
(4) What is the apparatus that transmits the dominant ideology in society?

In many versions of the dominant ideology thesis these elementary questions are not clearly separated and not precisely identified. Because the existence of a dominant ideology is often taken for granted, it is assumed that somehow this ideology is easily identified as a system of beliefs which is obvious, consistent and widely prevalent in society. The dominant ideology thesis is frequently couched in terms of one class *doing* something to a subordinate class. Thus, class relationships are analysed by reference to the dominant class which, through ideology, incorporates or mystifies or lulls the subordinate class into an acceptance of the legitimacy of modern society. The thesis of ideological incorporation thereby fails to ask what the effects of the dominant ideology are on the dominant class. Although we wish to suggest that political and economic control of the working class is far more important than ideological incorporation, we attempt to show that dominant ideologies do have, in feudalism and early capitalism, important functions in the conservation of property within dominant families. In general, ideology has importance in explaining the coherence of the dominant class but not in the explanation of the coherence of a society as a whole. Finally, the dominant ideology thesis has failed to distinguish between control of the means of mental production and the apparatus by which dominant beliefs can be transmitted and distributed. By contrast with feudal societies, the apparatus for transmitting beliefs and values in late capitalism has been greatly extended and refined. The effects of the apparatus may also be variable. As a general rule, historical studies of the dominant classes of feudal and capitalist societies suggest that the dominant class was more exposed and more receptive to the dominant ideology than subordinate classes. We do not assert that there has *never* been a dominant ideology; we simply argue that the importance of ideology has been greatly exaggerated by Marxists and sociologists, and that ideologies do not have the consequences which are attributed to them by the dominant ideology thesis.

While we have numerous *theoretical* criticisms of theories of the dominant ideology and theories of the common culture, the central thrust of objection to these theories is presented in the *empirical* analyses of ideology in Chapters 3, 4 and 5. These chapters deal respectively with feudalism and early and late capitalism. The point of the chapters on feudalism and early capitalism is to consider historical data in order to produce theoretical criticisms of sociological problems. Such a project clearly raises a range of serious difficulties relating to questions of evidence and methodology. Certain aspects of the problems facing the sociology of beliefs in general have been tackled elsewhere (Abercrombie, 1980), but there are a number of specific issues confronting a book of this nature. First, in defining 'the dominant ideology' of a particular period, we often produce a list of possible belief systems or aspects of belief in order to show that the list did not function as a dominant ideology. This characterisation of ideology in terms of an ostensive list might appear naive, but we adopt this tactic because the dominant ideology thesis itself tends to proceed as if ideology were a self-evident list of items. Thus, accounts of the dominant ideology of late capitalism, in Westergaard and Resler (1975), for example, often present the dominant ideology in the form of a list, including beliefs about private property, opportunities, rewards, management and consumption. The implication of *our* employment of lists of beliefs is that such an approach is unsatisfactory because the beliefs which could be added to the list are infinite.

Secondly, in presenting the historical evidence we are forced to summarise and compress complex historical arguments and detailed historical research. We do not enter into historical debates which are implicit in the way in which we have divided our argument into sections. For example, we do not raise the whole problem of how feudalism can be divided into early and late phases; we do not raise the issue of whether indeed 'feudalism' is the appropriate designation of the pre-capitalist period which we consider.

Thirdly, this problem of historical characterisation is closely related to the form of periodisation which is indicated by these central, empirical chapters. In Chapter 3, which examines the nature of religious ideologies in feudal society, the argument is focused on historical evidence which is drawn predominantly from the period 1200–1400. Some aspects of the argument, however, cite evidence from research into the eighth and ninth centuries. In Chapter 4, where we discuss early capitalism, the historical period under examination is 1780–1880, although the principal argument considers the nature of the dominant ideology from 1820 to 1870. In Chapter 5 our analysis of late capitalism centres on the changed structure of capitalism in the period after the Second World War. We appear, consequently, to ignore two interesting and important periods in British history, namely, the transition from the dominance of the feudal mode to the dominance of the capitalist mode of production in the seventeenth and eighteenth centuries, and the reorganisation of private, competitive capitalism in the first half of the twentieth century. Our argument is, thus, directed at periods when a particular mode of production is dominant rather than at periods of transition. The explanation for this focus is that we have set out to falsify the dominant ideology thesis, which assumes that dominant ideologies flourish in mature modes of production but not in periods of transition. A dominant feudal ideology cannot be identified in a period of transition when the counter ideology of the bourgeois class is opposed to that of the feudal aristocracy. The ideologies of transitional periods are obviously interesting for sociology, but consideration of these ideologies does not bear directly on our central task.

Fourthly, most of our examples are taken from British society. In the feudalism chapter our evidence comes equally from English and French examples. The inclusion of French illustrations can be easily justified on the ground that these two societies were united by a common political structure. After the Norman Conquest it is difficult in the feudal period to refer to France and England as separate nation-states, and there developed important linkages between the dominant classes of France and England in the period before the Tudor and Stuart kings. The use of French and English evidence to support our claims about the nature of primogeniture as a strategy for conserving property and power is not an unreasonable mixing of cases. In Chapters 4 and 5 we concentrate exclusively on British illustrations so that we make no explicit claims about the relevance of our argument to other capitalist societies. We would, however, be surprised if our argument had *no* relevance to capitalist societies in Europe and North America. In Chapter 5, for example, we show how changes in the ideology of the dominant class are related to changes in the form of capitalism with the increasing intervention of the state in the economy, the separation of economic ownership and control, the increasing scale of industrial activity, the decline of the private investor, and so forth. Since these changes are not peculiar to modern Britain, we would expect that certain aspects of our argument in that chapter on modern British society would have more general applicability. Our more theoretical discussion of the apparatus of transmission of beliefs, the end of ideology thesis and managerialism, for example, does not have these temporal and geographical restrictions.

On the basis of this historical and contemporary evidence, we conclude that the dominant ideology thesis is false in both its sociological and its Marxist versions. While our rejection of the thesis has required, at least in Chapters 3 and 4, the support of historical research, this book is for sociologists rather than for historians. The latter will not find anything new and will, no doubt, be suspicious of our sweeping generalisations and compressed historical characterisation. With respect to history and historians, we might suitably quote a sociologist who, in employing a very specialist literature to make a sociological point, created a controversy in the historical analysis of capitalism (Weber, 1930, pp. 28–9).

The specialist

will of course find no facts unknown to him. We only hope that
he will find nothing definitely wrong in points that are essential
. . . But however objectionable it may be, such trespassing on
other special fields cannot be avoided in comparative work.

Having acknowledged that we are trespassing on a specialist terrain,
we would emphasise the fact that our study of ideology sets out
with the aim of understanding modern capitalist society, not historical
pre-capitalist societies. The critique of the dominant ideology thesis
provides us with the conceptual vehicle for arriving at the specific
characteristics of British capitalist society. Again, much of the
inspiration for this project is Weberian since 'The type of social
science in which we are interested is an empirical science of concrete reality. Our aim is the understanding of the characteristic
uniqueness of the reality in which we move' (Weber, 1949, p. 72).
Thus in Chapter 6 we argue that in stressing the importance of a
dominant ideology there is a tendency for Marxists and sociologists to overemphasise the degree of coherence, integration and
stability of British society. By contrast, we stress the conflictual,
unstable quality of modern capitalism and argue that the subordinate
classes are controlled by what Marx referred to as 'the dull compulsion' of economic relationships, by the integrative effects of the
division of labour, by the coercive nature of law and politics. We
arrive at this perspective, not by creating an opposition between
Marx, Weber and Durkheim, but by drawing together their principal theoretical frameworks.

This book arose out of our earlier discussions of the dominant
ideology and the ideologies of subordinate classes (Hill, 1976;
Abercrombie and Turner, 1978). While these earlier analyses
indicated the range of theoretical and methodological problems,
the present study substantially changes our previous standpoint,
especially in our treatment of Marx's own view of 'the ruling ideas'.
Some of the technical issues which are germane to the analysis of
ideology are considered in the theoretical appendix to the book
where we outline some components of recent perspectives on
ideology as a set of beliefs or as a collection of practices.

Chapter 1

Theories of the Dominant Ideology

Within Marxism, the kind of view which, in the Introduction, we have characterised as the dominant ideology thesis has its origins in the *German Ideology*. We quote at length (Marx and Engels, 1965, p. 61):

> The ideas of the ruling class are in every epoch the ruling ideas: i.e., the class which is the ruling material force of society, is at the same time its ruling intellectual force. The class which has the means of material production at its disposal, has control at the same time over the means of mental production, so that thereby, generally speaking, the ideas of those who lack the means of mental production are subject to it. The ruling ideas are nothing more than the ideal expression of the dominant material relationships, the dominant material relationships grasped as ideas; hence of the relationships which make the one class the ruling one, therefore, the ideas of its dominance. The individuals composing the ruling class possess among other things consciousness, and therefore think. Insofar, therefore, as they rule as a class and determine the extent and compass of an epoch, it is self-evident that they do this in its whole range, hence among other things rule also as thinkers, as producers of ideas, and regulate the production and distribution of the idea of their age: thus their ideas are the ruling ideas of the epoch.

There are three preliminary points to be made about this very familiar passage. First, Marx and Engels, in speaking of the means of mental production, place what we shall call the apparatus of the transmission of ideology at the centre of their analysis. The ruling class has a grip over the mental life of a society, because it controls this apparatus. Secondly, Marx and Engels speak of a ruling *class* producing ruling ideas. The imagery is very much of one class *doing* something to another; members of the ruling class *rule* also as thinkers. We may call this view a class-theoretical account of the way in which the dominant ideology works. Thirdly, it is possible to formulate *two* interpretations of the passage, one stronger than the other. In the weak version, Marx and Engels can be interpreted as saying that the intellectual life of a society is dominated by the ruling class, so that an observer will necessarily perceive only the ruling ideas and will not be able to apprehend the culture of subordinate classes simply because that culture does not have institutions to give it public expression. More strongly, it can be argued that the command exercised by the ruling class over the apparatus of intellectual production means that there cannot be any subordinate culture, for all classes are incorporated within the same intellectual universe, that of the ruling class. So, in the first interpretation there are a variety of cultures present in a society, but only one is ever publicly noticeable, while in the second there is only one dominant culture, in which all classes share.

In the *German Ideology* it is not clear which interpretation Marx and Engels favoured. In fact, both make an appearance in the text. However, from their other work it is clear that they did not adopt a fully fledged theory of incorporation, and the notion of class struggle, at the ideological as well as at the economic and political levels, plays a central role. For example, Engels said in his *The Condition of the Working Class in England in 1844*: 'The bourgeoisie has more in common with every other nation of the earth than with the workers in whose midst it lives. The workers speak other dialects, have other thoughts and ideals, other customs and moral principles, a different religion and other politics than those of the bourgeoisie' (Engels, 1968, p. 124). In Volume 1 of *Capital*, Marx was at pains to show that the working class was engaged in a struggle with the bourgeoisie over the length of the working day. This struggle was partly won by the working class in that legislation was passed restricting the length of the working day (Marx, 1970, ch. 10). Marx made it clear that the struggle started as a purely economic phenomenon, but was generalised into a political movement (Marx's letter to F. Bolte in Marx and Engels, 1968). However, there was also an ideological conflict involved in the economic and political struggle which concerned the rights and wrongs of child labour, methods of work and the length of the working day, amongst other things.

We contend, therefore, that Marx and Engels did *not* adopt an incorporation theory. However, this is not true of their recent followers, many of whom have stressed the stronger interpretation of the *German Ideology* as a basis for their own theories of the ideological incorporation of the working class in capitalist societies.

In the last fifty years or so many Marxists have been impressed by the apparent stability of capitalist societies and the lack of a radical working-class consciousness. They have looked for an explanation of these phenomena in the ideological control of the working class by the capitalist ruling class, such that the working class has come to identify its interests with those of capitalism rather than with a revolutionary movement. Further, in very recent works of Marxist theory there has been a tendency, not only to stress the importance of compliance through ideological control in *capitalist* societies, but also to elevate the theoretical importance of the concept of ideology by comparison with that of the economy (Althusser, 1969, 1977; Hindess and Hirst, 1975; Cutler *et al.*, 1977). It is the central argument of this book that such a tendency exaggerates the importance of ideology.

In the early phase of the development of Marxist thought, from Marx's death up to the beginning of the First World War, there was an emphasis on the elaboration of Marx's economics. The belief was that an account of the laws of motion of the capitalist mode of production would show clearly how the system would break down. The social could simply be read off from the economic. Connected with this emphasis was the use of a particular scientific method, namely, a crude positivism. That is, Marxist analyses were to take the form of law-like propositions expressing causal connections between the economy and other social phenomena. The combination of the emphasis on the economy and the adoption of a positivist method produced a firm belief in the inevitable collapse of capitalism through its own contradictions (Bottomore, 1975, ch. 1).

Bernstein was an early dissentient from this economic reductionism and since the early 1920s the bulk of Marxist thought has reacted against the earlier texts. This reaction has taken three main forms. First, as has often been pointed out (P. Anderson, 1976), these later theorists were essentially academics, not activists. Not only were their working lives remote from working-class struggles, their writing was often of a technical nature, not likely to appeal to a wide audience. Secondly, there was an increasing emphasis on the *method* of Marxism and on Marxist philosophy. This often took the form of an objection to positivism and an emphasis on the importance of human agency and 'subjective' elements. Thirdly, the Marxist response to 'Second International Marxism' took the form of a relatively greater interest in superstructural questions of politics and ideology, and relatively less interest in analyses of the economy. The supposition was that the hidden secrets of capitalist society could not be discovered merely in the economy. Rather, the opportunities for progress, both political and theoretical, lay in the detailed analysis of the superstructure, on the assumption that it was relatively independent of the economy.

The renewed interest in the superstructure is, from the perspective of this book, the major point of interest in the revival of Marxist theory after the First World War. It has three separable elements. First, there is a concern with superstructure *in general*. In this respect emphases differ as between different writers. The Frankfurt school, for example, emphasised the independent role of culture, while Gramsci was primarily a theorist of politics. Althusser, however, sums up the spirit of reaction when he says:

> But History 'asserts itself' through the multiform world of the superstructures, from local traditions to international circumstance . . . In History, these instances, the superstructures, etc. – are never seen to step respectfully aside when their work is done or, when the time comes, as his pure phenomena, to scatter before His Majesty the Economy as he strides along the royal road of the Dialectic.

These are confident words even though 'the theory of the specific effectivity of the superstructures and other "circumstances" largely remains to be elaborated' (Althusser, 1969, pp. 112–13).

Secondly, there has been a continuing specific interest in the sphere of *ideology* and culture. Adler sums up this theme well when he says 'it cannot be said that ideology, in the Marxist sense, is something inessential and ineffective in historical development, [it] is a substantial and essential element in the lawfulness of the social process' (Adler, 1978, pp. 256, 261). However, more specifically, it is not only ideology *per se* which commands interest, but its particular effects. Thus, it is often argued that one of the main reasons for the relative quiescence of the working class, and the consequent stability of capitalism, is the independent power of ideological incorporation, an outcome intended and produced by the intellectual activities of the ruling class. As Marcuse says, 'One-dimensional thought is systematically promoted by the makers of politics and their purveyors of mass information. Their universe of discourse is populated by self-validating hypotheses which, incessantly and monopolistically repeated, become hypnotic definitions or dictations' (1964, p. 14).

Of course, the various themes in the renewed interest in the superstructure are closely related. A remoteness from working-class struggle produced both an academic interest in philosophy and art and a pessimism, a belief in the essential stability of capitalism. Given the conviction that capitalism will no longer collapse of its

Robert BATES, (ed)

Towards a Political Eco
of development

He a good essay on
property in South and S. East
Asia — related to our model

MALABAR HILL INDIA CUI
145 E MAIN ST
ELMSFORD, NY 10523
914-347-7890

DATE:06/13/93   TIME: 14:00:56 PM

ITEM: 002   PA   001
INVOICE: 00000012
ACCT: 4114410148071737 EXP DATE: 9404
RESP: APPROVED: 013875

SUB-TOTAL : $ 22.31
GRATUITY :
TOTAL   : $22.31

I AGREE TO PAY ABOVE TOTAL AMOUNT
ACCORDING TO THE CARD ISSUER AGREEMENT

X _____
SIGNATURE

RETAIN THIS COPY FOR YOUR RECORDS

own internal contradictions, the only way forward for socialism is the assertion of the human will to overcome a massive social reality. Hence the interest in recent Marxist theory in voluntarism and humanism (Bottomore, 1975; P. Anderson, 1976).

We do not intend to review the history of Marxist thought in any detail. However, in order to illustrate these tendencies within recent Marxism, we will discuss the views of three Marxist writers of very different theoretical persuasions: Gramsci, Habermas and Althusser.

Gramsci

Gramsci's work is very much directed by his opposition to any form of economism, which involves 'The iron conviction that there exist objective laws of historical development similar in kind to natural laws, together with a belief in a predetermined teleology like that of a religion' (Gramsci, 1971, p. 168). Similarly, 'The claim, presented as an essential postulate of historical materialism, that every fluctuation of politics and ideology can be presented and expounded as an immediate expression of the structure, must be contested in theory as primitive infantilism and combated in practice with the authentic testimony of Marx . . .' (Gramsci, 1971, p. 407). Bukharin, on whom a good deal of the *Prison Notebooks* is lavished, is a favourite target. Ironically, Gramsci cites Croce's critique of Bukharin's economism in which technique is made the supreme cause of economic and social development. Croce holds that Marx did not reduce everything to the 'mere technical instrument' and his work was, in any case, not a pursuit of 'ultimate causes'.

For Gramsci, the rejection of economic reductionism is an acceptance of the relative importance of superstructures, a point of view which he believes is faithful to Marx. He is pre-eminently a theorist of politics, particularly of the state and of political parties. However, he is also concerned with the ideological sphere and would not in any case have regarded the separation of politics and ideology as at all valuable. He takes the cultural differences between societies, or parts of societies, seriously in that they have important social, political and economic effects; they cannot be treated as mere epiphenomena (Gramsci, 1971, pp. 93 ff.). His concern with ideology and politics is also connected with an emphasis on the creative possibilities of the individual as against a determining social structure. For Gramsci, since 'the will and initiative of men themselves cannot be left out of account', not only can Marxism not be a science which formulates general laws, but politics and ideology themselves must be autonomous practices, the outcome of the triumph of the human will.

In sum, Gramsci expresses a general antipathy to economism and a wish to establish theoretically the autonomy of political and ideological practice. This orientation produces the concept of hegemony, a concept crucial in the history of Marxism since the First World War and aptly illustrative of our argument of the central tendency of Marxist theory.

The concept of hegemony expresses the notion of leadership which is as much ideological as political or repressive, although, in fact, Gramsci's use of the term varies considerably (P. Anderson, 1976/7). Further, a number of commentators on Gramsci have rendered the concept entirely in terms of ideological control. Despite these divergencies, it seems to us not only a fair interpretation of Gramsci but also a theoretically sensible usage to treat hegemony as fusing all the elements of leadership together, particularly control by repression with control by ideological persuasion. For example, Gramsci says (1971, pp. 57–8):

> The methodological contention on which our own study must be based is the following: that the supremacy of a social group manifests itself in two ways, as 'domination' and as 'intellectual and moral leadership'. A social group dominates antagonistic groups, which it tends to 'liquidate', or to subjugate perhaps even by armed force; it leads kindred and allied groups. A social group can, and indeed must, already exercise 'leadership' before winning governmental power . . . it subsequently becomes dominant when it exercises power, but even if it holds it firmly in its grasp, it must continue to 'lead' as well.

Hegemony, then, cannot be seen as a purely ideological notion. However, it is also true that Gramsci's distinctive contribution is his insistence on the importance of 'intellectual and moral leadership' and that is certainly how he is often interpreted (see, for example, Bates, 1975; Femia, 1975).

Hegemony, then, critically involves ideological domination. However, the balance between coercion and consent in the exercise of hegemony varies historically. Generally, the weaker the engineering of consent, the stronger the repression exercised by the state has to be. For example, Gramsci contrasts Russia, in which repression is the main weapon, with the West, in which there is a combination of repression and consent, and incidentally implies that the West is the stronger for combining the two.

Gramsci is careful to point out that one cannot take consent for granted; obedience is not automatic but has to be produced. There has, therefore, to be some analysis of the machinery by which ideological domination is effected. Some indication of Gramsci's solution to this question is provided by his distinction between civil society and political society or state. Again, Gramsci's usage is variable. As Anderson argues, there are at least three senses of the terms themselves and of the relationships between them (1976/7). One of the senses, however, dominates Gramsci's writing and is the one for which he is best known. In this interpretation of the terms, Gramsci argues that civil society and the state are separate structures or sets of institutions within society. Civil society is made up of 'private' institutions like the church, trade unions and schools, while the state is made up of public institutions like the government, courts, police and the army. The distinction between civil society and the state runs together with that between force and consent discussed earlier. Civil society is the site of the engineering of consent while the state represents the apparatus of repression. Confusingly, Gramsci also equates the concept of hegemony both with civil society and with the generation of consent, and the concept of 'domination' with political society and the use of force. However, as we have already indicated, it is better to reserve the term hegemony for the leadership of one group based on a fusion of repression and consent, even if the balance between these two varies. At other points in his work Gramsci takes a rather different view of the relationship of state and civil society. Here he argues that the state in modern capitalist societies is not purely an instrument of repression but has important ideological functions, particularly in respect of the institution of parliamentary democracy. Although a minority view in Gramsci's work as a whole, this is a significant point and we will return to it later in the discussion of Althusser's views.

Within civil society, the site of the ideological unity of a society, intellectuals have an important role. For Gramsci, 'every relationship of "hegemony" is necessarily an educational relationship' and it is the intellectual stratum that directly educates. In his view everyone is an intellectual in some sense in that everyone works out some conception of the world. Besides that, any task, however menial, requires intellectual activity of some kind. However, 'All men are intellectuals, one could therefore say: but not all men have in society the function of intellectuals' (Gramsci, 1971, p. 9). There are therefore specialised groups of intellectuals, specialised by the function that they perform, and intellectual only in the sense that they have made a profession of a quality inherent in all men and women. There is no such thing, for Gramsci, as an autonomous intellectual stratum. All intellectuals are attached to a social class and perform the function of articulating the view of the social world appropriate to 'their' social class. As far as the ruling class is concerned, it is an intellectual stratum that refines and presents its world-view and thus provides an important part of the apparatus whereby the ideological component of ruling-class hegemony is preserved and transmitted.

As far as the arguments in this book are concerned, Gramsci's conceptions of hegemony, and of ideology as cementing and unifying, are important in that he has, probably more than any other theorist, contributed to the contemporary dominant ideology thesis. As Anderson says (1976/7, p. 26):

> In other words, the preponderance of civil society over the state in the West can be equated with the predominance of 'hegemony' over 'coercion' as the fundamental mode of bourgeois power in advanced capitalism. Since hegemony pertains to civil society, and civil society prevails over the State, it is the cultural ascendency of the ruling class that essentially ensures the stability of the capitalist order. For in Gramsci's usage here, hegemony means the ideological subordination of the working class by the bourgeoisie, which enables it to rule by consent.

Nevertheless, even if Gramsci does see capitalist societies as founded on the ideological subordination of the working class, and even if he is thus very much in the mainstream of modern Marxist theory, it would be dangerous to provide an over-integrationist interpretation of his work, like that advanced by Poulantzas (1973). Gramsci does not believe that the working class is completely subordinated any more than Marx did. He is no idealist. Although he opposes reduction to the economic structure, he is not an ideological reductionist. Indeed, for Gramsci the economy is of prime importance. Thus, Gramsci echoes Marx in saying that 'no social formation disappears as long as the productive forces which have developed within it still find room for further forward movement' (1971, p. 106).

More specifically, Gramsci does not argue that subordinate classes uniformly have a consciousness imposed on them by dominant classes. If anything, the working class has a dual consciousness. As we have already said, Gramsci argues that everybody is an intellectual in that everybody has *some* conception of the world. In the case of subordinate classes in capitalist society, this conception of the world is at the level of common sense. The most fundamental characteristic of common sense is that it is 'fragmentary, incoherent and inconsequential, in conformity with the social and cultural position of those masses whose philosophy it is' (Gramsci, 1971, p. 419). Furthermore, the working class has no *self*-consciousness within the common-sense conception. None the less, common sense is still a distinct working-class consciousness founded in the real practical activity and economic situation of the class. As such it is at variance with the conceptions of the dominant class which, as we have seen, are so important in the continued subordination of the working class. The result is that the worker has a dual consciousness and 'One might almost say that he has two theoretical consciousnesses (or one contradictory consciousness): one which is implicit in his activity and which in reality unites him with all his fellow-workers in the practical transformation of the real world; and one, super-ficially explicit or verbal, which he has inherited from the past and uncritically absorbed' (Gramsci, 1971, p. 333).

The critical point for Gramsci is that despite the fact that there is a working-class consciousness at some level its incorporation with-in a dominant ideology tends to produce 'moral and political passivity'. Development of working-class consciousness to a state of self-awareness and political activity is a result of struggle encouraged by a mass political party. In turn the success of a mass party in the struggle depends partly on the party's intellectuals who are important in the formation of a coherent and self-aware conscious-ness. Indeed, for Gramsci the intellectual preparation of the work-ing class is of critical significance in capitalist societies, for it is precisely those societies whose stability depends on ideological domination, and whose downfall will largely be produced by ideological struggle.

Habermas

Although Habermas is not a Marxist in the same sense as Althusser and Gramsci, and he certainly is no party militant, his work employs the vocabulary and often the theory of Marxism. Habermas is a part of, and has contributed to, the trend in modern Marxist theory that we describe in this chapter. Like Althusser and Gramsci, he decisively rejects economism and elevates the importance of super-structural elements. For Habermas, only in early capitalism does the economy have primacy. In *late* capitalism, however, politics and economics are literally inseparable (1971, p. 101):

A point of view that methodically isolates the economic laws of motion of society can claim to grasp the overall structure of social life in its essential categories only as long as politics depends on the economic base. It becomes inapplicable when the 'base' has to be comprehended as in itself a function of govern-mental activity and political conflicts.

Again, ideology is conceived as a relatively autonomous sphere with its own laws of motion. Indeed, for Habermas the origins of the crisis of contemporary capitalist society lie within the ideological sphere rather than in the economy directly.

The concept employed by Habermas that is of relevance to our arguments is that of *legitimation*. In Habermas's view, there has to be some process which legitimates social systems. Legitimation, the acceptance of social systems by actors, is a functional requirement. It is a complex process, potentially made up of numbers of very different elements, and different societies will rely on very different forms of legitimation. However, the legitimation process is not *reducible* to categories of consciousness. That is, Habermas does not argue that the only mechanism of legitimation is an implantation of certain beliefs in the minds of social actors so that they 'believe' in a particular set of social arrangements. The concept of legitimation is not, therefore, merely equivalent to ideology, as ideas in people's heads. For example, Habermas talks of legitimation being achieved by steadily increasing the level of material rewards. Again, the institution and practices of formal parliamentary democracy are important sources of legitimation, as is the tendency to make political decision-making into a technical and bureaucratic exercise. These are all forms of legitimation that are not reducible to people's beliefs about the practices concerned. In theory, for example, people could have any set of beliefs about parliamentary democracy; it is their *participation* in the institution that produces legitimation.

None the less, despite some discussion of legitimation as involving practices which are not *reducible* to categories of consciousness, Habermas does in fact largely refer to legitimation as involving beliefs, particularly as held by subordinate classes, in the reasonableness of current social arrangements. For example, he often refers to the effects of bourgeois ideologies of justice. Again, he speaks of the technocracy thesis as 'a background ideology that penetrates into the consciousness of the depoliticized mass of the population, where it can take on legitimating power' (1971, p. 105). Furthermore, legitimation, conceived of as beliefs, can be associated in Habermas's discussion with manipulation or propaganda, as when he talks of the public 'as engineered for purposes of legitimation' (1973, p. 657).

We would argue, therefore, that Habermas's concept of legitimation critically, but not exclusively, involves the generation and acceptance of certain positive beliefs on the part of a population about the social structure. It is convenient to discuss his views about the content of these beliefs in two parts, which are represented by his two publications, *Toward a Rational Society* (1971) and *Legiti-*

mation Crisis (1976). It is not precisely that he changes his mind, but rather that he discusses different aspects of the problem in different theoretical contexts. However, before going on to discuss these two works, it would be helpful to clarify a distinction which is important to Habermas's work in both publications.

Habermas makes a clear distinction between early and late capitalism, a distinction visible not only in different economic, political and social structures but also in very different requirements for legitimation. The differences are so marked that it is possible to say that the 'organising principles' of the two forms of capitalism are quite distinct. In particular, in late capitalism the state intervenes substantially in the economy, complementing and partially replacing the market mechanism, by a whole variety of processes from global economic planning to the improvement of the material and immaterial infrastructure (1976, pp. 34–5). The class conflict of early capitalism is replaced in late capitalism by class compromise. This important development, involving the loss of class identity and the fragmentation of class consciousness, has arisen from the manner in which wages are negotiated. Wage negotiations, particularly in the monopolistic and public sectors of the economy, are effectively *political* compromises between capital and labour represented by unions.

In *Toward a Rational Society* (1971), Habermas makes a further distinction between traditional and capitalist societies. The salient difference from our point of view is that traditional societies are legitimated by a central world-view, typically a religion. Again, Habermas is arguing that legitimation is founded in belief: 'The expression "traditional society" refers to the circumstance that the institutional framework is grounded in the unquestionable under-pinning of legitimation constituted by mythical, religious or meta-physical interpretations of reality . . .' (1971, p. 95). However, capitalism calls into question this form of legitimation, replacing it by another form. Legitimation in early capitalism does not take the form of an over-arching cultural tradition, but is instead based on reciprocal exchanges in a market. Capitalism is based on markets which are necessarily mechanisms that make exchanges fair and equal and that promise 'that exchange relations will be and are just owing to equivalence' (1971, p. 97). The legitimation of capitalism thus comes upwards from the very basis of economic life rather than downwards from some cultural superstructure.

However, as we have noted above, there is also a distinction between early and late capitalism. As far as forms of legitimation are concerned (rather than the structural differences between the two stages of capitalism), the critical point is that 'the root ideology

of just exchange', founded in the market mechanism that characterised early capitalism, has collapsed in contemporary capitalism. The
only way in which capitalism could be sustained was by government intervention. Politics thus directly enters economics and the
'institutional framework of society was repoliticized' (1971, p. 101).
A new form of legitimation which depends on the justification of
the state is now required. Such a form will be rather like that
needed in traditional society in which legitimation was 'direct', and
founded in an over-arching system of values rather than arising
from the economy itself. The state has to intervene in the economy
and preserve its particular capitalist form. As Habermas says, quite
consciously stressing some of the features of the dominant ideology
thesis: 'what is needed to this end is latitude for manipulation by
state interventions that, at the cost of limiting the institutions of
private law, secure the private form of capital utilization *and bind
the masses' loyalty to this form*' (1971, p. 102, original italics). The
form of legitimation that meets this need is a depoliticisation of
the mass of the population, so that the activities of the state that
are so necessary in late capitalism appear not as political decisions
between alternative courses of action but as *technical* solutions to
agreed problems. Furthermore, with the increased role of science
and technology, it seems as though the development of capitalist
societies is determined by the impersonal forces of science rather
than by the political and economic decisions of men. The net effect
of these developments is clearly put by Habermas (1971, p. 105,
original italics):

> Thus arises a perspective in which the development of the social
> system *seems* to be determined by the logic of scientific-technical
> progress. The immanent law of this progress seems to produce
> objective exigencies, which must be obeyed by any politics
> oriented toward functional needs. But when this semblance
> has taken root effectively, then propaganda can refer to the role
> of technology and science in order to explain and legitimate why
> in modern societies the process of decision-making about practical
> problems loses its function and 'must' be replaced by plebiscitory
> decisions about alternative sets of leaders of administrative
> personnel.

If the argument in *Toward a Rational Society* is overtly directed
towards the role of 'technocratic consciousness' in the legitimation
of late capitalist societies, that of *Legitimation Crisis* is only indirectly so, since it is ostensibly about the genesis of crisis. None
the less, it presents a further elaboration of Habermas's views about

legitimation in that it essentially argues that there is a *requirement* for legitimation. In a similar way to functionalist theorists of ideology, Habermas effectively suggests that system strains demand ideological solutions (see, for example, Geertz, 1964).

In *Legitimation Crisis*, Habermas again emphasises the distinction between early and late capitalism. He argues that while Marx's account of the essential nature of capitalism applies very well to early capitalism, it is less useful for the analysis of late capitalism. Specifically, the legitimations that served for the capitalism of Marx's day will no longer suffice since the dysfunctions of the market mechanism are all too obvious. Since the state has intervened to correct those dysfunctions, that intervention must be legitimated. It cannot be done by a reversion to pre-capitalist legitimations of autocratic state power, since the 'universalistic value systems of bourgeois ideology' have made civil rights universal. Habermas suggests that the problem is resolved through the mechanism of formal democracy.

The institution of parliamentary democracy is a 'legitimation process that elicits mass loyalty but avoids participation'. That is, it guarantees legitimation through the illusion of participation in political decision-making. It cannot be genuine participation since that would reveal the realities of state intervention. These are an amelioration of the worst effects of capitalism, together with the preservation of its essential form, the unequal private appropriation of value.

The legitimation requirement of advanced capitalism takes the form of an episodic and partial political commitment through voting. The population must be 'passive citizens' characterised by 'civil privatism'. However, this essential civil privatism is itself undermined by the spread of the government intervention so characteristic of late capitalism. Planning destroys traditional social life and politicises and makes public realms that were traditionally private. The contradiction between civil privatism and administrative planning makes for a potential crisis in the legitimation process. However, this contradiction will only *actually* issue in a crisis if there is a failure in the motivation system. 'This development must therefore be based on a motivation crisis – i.e. a discrepancy between the need for motives that the state and the occupational system announce and the supply of motivation offered by the sociocultural system' (Habermas, 1973, p. 660). The most important aspect of the motivational system is 'familial-vocational' privatism analogous to civil privatism. In brief, Habermas argues that familial-vocational privatism is being undermined in late capitalism by a variety of forces intrinsic to capitalism and that there is therefore a fair probability of a legitimation crisis (McCarthy, 1978, pp. 369 ff.).

There is one final point to make in discussing the relationship of Habermas's account of legitimation to the dominant ideology thesis. One distinctive feature of the latter, particularly as it appears in the *German Ideology*, is the relationship of the ideologies concerned to the class structure. The dominant ideology thesis is often presented as a question of one class imposing its beliefs on another class. It is not altogether clear what Habermas's position is on this point. On the one hand, he clearly rejects the 'traditional' model of the class struggle: 'The interests bearing on the maintenance of the mode of production can no longer be "clearly localized" in the social system as class interests. For the power structure, aimed as it is at avoiding changes to the system, precisely excludes "domination" . . . exercised in such a manner that one class subject confronts another as an identifiable group' (Habermas, 1971, p. 109). On the other hand, Habermas can also write that the 'glassy background ideology' of the technocratic consciousness 'not only justifies a particular class's interest in domination and represses another class's partial need for emancipation, but affects the human race's emancipatory interest as such' (1971, p. 111). Habermas does suggest that class antagonisms have not altogether died away and that they have become latent. However, he fails to elucidate the mechanism connecting forms of belief with social forces, especially classes. If there are ideologies which arise from within a ruling class (unconsciously), or alternatively from the very structure of society itself, and then come to serve the interests of that class by the ideological subordination of other classes, one must know how these ideologies come to perform that function. We return to this question at the end of this chapter.

Althusser

There are several good summaries of Althusser's views on ideology and its effects and we will concentrate our discussion on showing how his work fits into our argument (see, for example, Callinicos, 1976; Hirst, 1976; McLennan *et al.*, 1977). As with the other writers reviewed in this chapter, Althusser's major target is economism. He dislikes the base–superstructure metaphor which, for him, has too much of the notion of a determinant base, however much it is hedged about with qualifications. It conveys the notion of a social totality which is simply the expression of a single element; it is an *expressive totality*. Althusser takes a view of the social totality as an entity 'whose unity, far from being the expressive of "spiritual" of Leibniz's or Hegel's whole, is constituted by a certain type of complexity, the unity of a structured whole containing what can be

called levels or instances which are distinct and "relatively autonomous", and co-exist within this complex structural unity, articulated
with one another according to specific determinations, fixed in the
last instance by the level or instance of the economy' (1970, p. 97).

For Althusser, therefore, the social whole is a totality of instances,
relatively interdependent and relatively autonomous. It is not
possible to consider any one instance in isolation from the rest. In
particular, there is never a moment when the economy is somehow
'pure'; it is always associated with, and is literally inconceivable
without, political and ideological structures. At the same time
politics and ideology are not deducible from the economy. As
Althusser says, 'relations of production presuppose the existence
of a legal-political and ideological superstructure as a condition of
their peculiar existence . . . the relations of production cannot
therefore be thought in their concept while abstracting from their
specific superstructural conditions of existence' (1970, p. 177).
Althusser therefore proposes a fairly strong relationship between
ideology and politics on the one hand and the economy on the
other. The former are *conditions of existence* of the latter. It is
not a view of the simple interaction of the elements but one in
which the economy *must* have superstructural elements. For
example, Althusser argues that a legal system is a condition of
existence of a capitalist economy: 'The whole of the economic
structure of the capitalist mode of production from the immediate
process of production to circulation and the distribution of the social
product, presupposes the existence of a *legal system*, the basic
elements of which are the law of property and the law of contract'
(1970, p. 230, original emphasis).

Clearly ideology occupies a central place in Althusser's scheme.
As we have seen, however, he also speaks of the economy being
determinant in the last instance. This does not mean that eventually
everything is determined by the economy. Instead the economy is
determinant in that it establishes which other structure is to be
dominant. That is, the economy in certain modes of production
requires, as a condition of its existence, that some other structure
dominate. Marx, for example, argues that in the Middle Ages
ideology, in the form of Catholicism, dominated, while in ancient
societies it was politics that was dominant. In this conception of the
economy as determinant in the last instance, Althusser attempts to
reconcile the critical importance of superstructures, while preserving
some notion of the primacy of the economy. He suggests that this
was also Marx's project. 'Marx has at least given us the "two ends
of the chain" and has told us to find out what goes on between
them; on the one hand, determination in the last instance by the

economic . . . on the other, the relative autonomy of the super-structures and their specific effectivity' (1969, p. 111).

In Althusser's account, ideology acts specifically as a condition of existence, differently in each mode of production. However, it also has the general function of relating men to their conditions of existence and, in this sense, it is a necessary component of any society: 'ideology (as a system of mass representations) is indispens-able in any society if men are to be formed, transformed and equipped to respond to the demands of their conditions of existence' (Althusser, 1969, p. 235). Ideology is a 'lived relation' between men and their world, not merely a system of beliefs. It achieves its effect by placing and adapting men to their roles as bearers of the structures of social relations by constituting individuals as 'subjects'. Althusser points out that 'subject' has a double meaning, both as a 'centre of initiatives' and as 'a subjected being'. For him, therefore, ideology works by constituting individuals as subjects *of* the social structure, as subjects which bear functions within that structure, while apparently giving a unique individuality to each subject: 'the individual *is interpellated as a (free) subject in order that he shall submit freely to the commandments of the Subject i.e. in order that he shall freely accept his subjection* (Althusser, 1977, p. 169, original emphasis). In sum, ideology functions by moulding individuals as particular subjects and placing them in the structure, while at the same time concealing from them their role as agents of the struc-ture. As such, ideology is necessarily an illusory representation of the world. 'In ideology, the real relation is mentally invested in the imaginary relation, a relation that expresses a will . . . a hope or a nostalgia, rather than describing a reality' (Althusser, 1969, p. 235).

In Althusser's analysis, ideology is an *objective* form which arises out of the structures of the mode of production. He quite deliberately rejects any notion that it is generated by one *class* for the consumption by, and subordination of, other classes. However, he also holds that the illusions of ideology do have consequences for class relations. Thus he says that in class societies 'ideology is the relay whereby . . . the relation between men and their conditions of existence is settled to the profit of the ruling class' (1969, pp. 235–6). As with Habermas, Althusser has to explain how ideology produced 'objectively', independently of specific class interests, comes to have consequences for those interests. Part of an answer is provided by his essay 'Ideology and ideological state apparatuses' (1977).

In this essay Althusser starts from the common-sense position that every economic system must make provision for its own reproduction over time. This involves the reproduction of both the relations of production and the productive forces. The reproduction of the latter involves not only the replacement of physical means of production such as machinery or buildings, but also the reproduction of labour-power. In turn, the reproduction of labour-power is a function, not only of the provision of food, clothing, shelter, and so on, but also of skill. In contemporary capitalism, the labour-force has to be educated and trained, usually in schools and colleges, and training of this kind frequently has to be renewed. However, 'the reproduction of labour power requires not only a reproduction of its skills, but also, at the same time, a reproduction of its submission to the rules of the established order, i.e. a reproduction of submission to the ruling ideology for the workers, and a reproduction of the ability to manipulate the ruling ideology correctly for the agents of exploitation and repression, so that they, too, will provide for the domination of the ruling class "in words" ' (Althusser, 1977, pp. 127–8).

The reproduction of the relations of production and of skills and the submission to the ruling ideology is secured by the 'legal-political and ideological superstructure'. In particular, it is secured by the institutions of the Repressive State Apparatus (RSA) and the Ideological State Apparatus (ISA). These two apparatuses of the state are defined essentially by the institutions of which they are composed. Thus the RSA consists of the government, the civil service, the army, the police, the judiciary and the prisons. The ISA is made up of religious and educational institutions, the apparatuses of political parties and trade unions, radio, television and the press, artistic and recreational institutions and the family. Properly speaking, there is only one RSA, whose elements are centrally organised by the state, but a multiplicity of ISAs, which are relatively autonomous of one another. ISAs do, however, acquire some unity by virtue of the fact that they all discharge the same function 'beneath the ruling ideology'. This unity is to some extent threatened by the fact that ISAs, unlike the RSA, are the site of class struggle.

Societies will differ from one another in the relationships between RSA and ISAs and in the kinds of ISA present. For example, in the pre-capitalist period there was one dominant ISA, namely, the church, which included within its functions educational and cultural elements which have since become separated out into other ISAs. In capitalist societies, however, the educational system is the overwhelmingly dominant ISA. 'It takes children from every class at infant-school age, and then for years . . . it drums into them . . . a certain amount of "know-how" wrapped in the ruling ideology' (1977, p. 147).

Although ISAs function largely by ideology, they will also use repression in certain circumstances as when, for example, the church or the school uses punishment, or the press uses censorship. Similarly the RSA functions primarily by repression, although it also can use ideology, as when the police or army require ideological cohesion.

It is clear from Althusser's account that ideology is of crucial significance in the reproduction of the relations of production. In capitalism, it is the ISAs which 'largely secure the reproduction specifically of the relations of production behind a "shield" provided by the repressive state apparatus. It is here that the role of the ruling ideology is heavily concentrated . . .' (1977, p. 142). Indeed, in his essay 'Ideology and ideological state apparatuses' Althusser is moving to the conventional statement of the dominant ideology thesis. Thus he refers to the way that the bourgeoisie provides a dominant ideology via the ISAs (1977, p. 145), and to the way that subordinate classes absorb it in such a way that the current relations of production are preserved (1977, p. 147). This position is summarised well in Althusser's own words: 'To my knowledge, *no class can hold State power over a long period without at the same time exercising its hegemony over and in the State Ideological Apparatuses*' (1977, p. 139, original emphasis).

The Dominant Ideology and the Dominant Class

In the passage in which the dominant ideology thesis receives its classic statement, Marx says: 'The ideas of the ruling class are in every epoch the ruling ideas: i.e., the class which is the ruling *material* force of society, is at the same time its ruling *intellectual* force' (Marx and Engels, 1965, p. 61, original emphasis). We have argued that this sentiment has been interpreted strongly as suggesting that the ideological incorporation of subordinate classes is one of the major causes of working-class political quiescence. In an extreme form, proponents of a dominant ideology thesis will argue that a ruling class generates a form of belief which it imposes on other classes. This carries with it the suggestion that ideology is an *instrument* in the hands of the ruling class. Such an instrumentalist theory has important similarities with instrumentalist theories of the state. Miliband (1969, p. 265), for example, argues that there is, in contemporary capitalism, an 'economically dominant class' which is also dominant in politics.

The most important political fact about advanced capitalist societies . . . is the continued existence in them of private and ever more concentrated economic power. As a result of that power, the men – owners and controllers – in whose hands it lies enjoy a massive preponderance in society, in the political system, and in the determination of the state's policies and actions.

The result is that the state is a political instrument which advances and protects the dominant economic interests: 'Its "real" purpose and mission is to ensure their continued predominance, not to prevent it' (1969, pp. 265–6). The superiority of these dominant economic interests is primarily maintained by ideological control, a form of control intended to 'foster acceptance of a *capitalist* social order'. The processes involved here are so profound that Miliband refers to them as 'massive indoctrination'. Furthermore, the dominant classes use cultural control *on purpose* to preserve their overall economic dominance.

Miliband's account of the role of ideology in capitalist societies is too instrumentalist. In effect, he is describing the mechanism by which a dominant ideology achieves its effect as one *class* indoctrinating another. Weaker formulations might try to avoid the instrumentalism, while still retaining the idea that the stability of capitalist societies is largely due to the ideological incorporation of the working class. In either form, the dominant ideology thesis is based on the assumption that classes are the origins of knowledge, belief or ideology. The same assumption is at the root of conventional Mannheimian sociology of knowledge, which claims that social classes constitute the origins of ideology in the sense that they form the environment in which beliefs are acquired. Beliefs are formulated in accordance with class interests and, generally, the sociologist analyses systems of belief by showing to which class (or social group) they are appropriate. This 'class-theoretical' method of analysing ideology is one that informs many accounts of dominant ideologies (Abercrombie, 1980).

A number of more recent theories of ideology attempt to avoid tying ideologies to class formations directly by arguing that ideologies arise out of the structure of capitalist social relations and not out of the activities of identifiable groups of social actors. As we have demonstrated, this is an important aspect of Althusser's earlier work in which he suggests that ideology serves a necessary function in relating men to their conditions of existence. However, he has been accused of thereby neglecting what for many Marxists are the central issues of the role of classes and class struggle. His essay 'Ideology and ideological state apparatuses' can be read as an attempt to correct this neglect by providing some account of the mechanisms by which ideology is produced and by which it relates to both dominant and dominated classes. However, in solving this problem Althusser comes very close to providing an instrumentalist theory of the dominant ideology. Indeed, he almost returns to the economism of which he is so critical. In Hirst's judgement, 'Althusser's position in the ISAs represents a failure to break with economism and essentialism' (Hirst, 1976, p. 387).

Similar problems attend the work of Poulantzas who in many essential respects follows Althusser. For Poulantzas (1973), ideology's function is to ensure that individuals perform their tasks in supporting the social structure. Its general function is therefore to provide *cohesion*, which is achieved 'by establishing at the level of agents' experience relations which are obvious but false' (1973, p. 207). However, this function of ideology does not derive from 'some kind of genetic relation to a class-subject and its class-consciousness' (1973, p. 207). Instead it is derived from, or rather is part of, the *structure* of social relations, which is not deducible from the activities of social actors.

Such a position poses a difficulty for Poulantzas for he still has to answer the crucial question which is endemic in discussions of this issue: if one cannot conceive of social classes as the origin of ideology, what is the relationship between class and ideology? The problem is all the more acute for Poulantzas since he insists that there are dominant classes and that ideology is one of the mechanisms by which their dominance is assured. Furthermore, he continuously employs the category of 'dominant ideology'. Thus a way of rephrasing the crucial question is to ask what is the relation of *ideology*, as a form of social cement, to *dominant ideology*, which has crucial functions for relationships between classes. Poulantzas is clearly aware of this problem (1973, p. 209).

The correspondence between the dominant ideology and the politically dominant class is not due . . . to some kind of historico-genetic relation. It is due to the fact that the ideological (i.e. a given ideology) is constituted as a regional instance within the unity of the structure; and this structure has the domination of a given class as its effect in the field of the class struggle. The dominant ideology, by assuring the practical insertion of agents in the social structure, aims at the maintenance (the cohesion) of this structure, and this means *above all* class domination and exploitation.

Disappointingly, however, this proposal is really no more than a restatement of the problem. We still have no idea of the *specific* character of the dominant ideology. More important, by making the dominance of a class the *effect* of the structure, we have no adequate account of the *generation* of appropriate ideology.

The Althusserian account of ideology and its effects depends on the notion of 'inserting agents into their places'. There is another type of theory that also argues that the dominant ideology arises from the structure of capitalist social relations and not from the specific interest of social classes, but at the same time does not trade on the conception of the insertion of agents. This is the theory of commodity fetishism, largely derived from Marx's comments in Volume 1 of *Capital* (see also Geras, 1971; Mepham, 1972; Rose, 1977).

The conventional theory of commodity fetishism depends on the notion of commodity employed by Marx in *Capital*. A man can produce, by his own labour, certain objects for his own use; these objects have a *use-value*. Such objects are defined as commodities, however, when they are produced for exchange, for use by other people, in which case they have *exchange-value*. As soon as commodities are being produced for exchange, the labour-power involved assumes a social character. But since the producers do not come into contact with each other until they actually exchange their products, the social character of each producer's labour only shows itself in the act of exchange. Therefore 'the social character of men's labour appears to them as an objective character stamped upon the product of that labour; because the relation of the producers to the sum total of their own labour is presented to them as a social relation, existing not between themselves, but between the products of their labour . . . There it is a definite social relation between men, that assumes, in their eyes, the fantastic form of a relation between things' (Marx, 1970, p. 72). Men's thinking about the social relations involved in their work is characterised by a fetishism whereby beliefs about the physical products of labour and their exchange substitute for, and mask the social relations themselves. Since the tendency to fetishistic thinking only arises when objects are produced for exchange, the more a society is dominated by commodity production, the more it will be characterised by fetishism.

The theory is actually a good deal more complex than our simple presentation allows (Abercrombie, 1980) and there are three further points that we should make. First, the theory is effectively based on the limiting assumption that societies are comprised of independent producers who do exchange commodities with each other. It is not clear how it would apply to contemporary capitalist societies in which the more usual situation involves workers selling their labour-power to an employer. Secondly, it is important to be clear that Marx does not see commodity fetishism as representing an *illusion*. For him capitalism *is* an exchange of things, of commodities. Thus he says: 'The relations connecting the labour of one individual with that of the rest appear, not as direct social relations between individuals at work, but as what they really are, material relations between persons and social relations between things' (Marx, 1970, p. 73). However, although fetishism is not exactly illusory, it does nevertheless conceal, for the thing-like character of exchanges in capitalism masks the exploitative nature of capitalist social relations. Thirdly, the theory of fetishism does avoid the notion of ideological domination as 'one class doing something to another'. Fetishism is not an ideological form imposed by one class on another, although it does have the effect of concealing real social relations. Instead, it arises out of a *relation*, the exchange relation characteristic of capitalist societies.

In our opinion, the theory of commodity fetishism has a number of faults and its advantages as a theory of ideology are greatly exaggerated. From the point of view of the immediate argument, however, what is of interest is the relationship between commodity fetishism as a form which arises out of the structure of capitalist relations of exchange on the one hand, and social classes on the other. There is a critical theoretical gap between class domination and the generation of fetishistic forms. A number of specific questions arise out of this. For example, there is a great deal of difference between the relatively specific claim that commodity fetishism arises out of the production of goods for exchange and the more general assertion that fetishistic thinking is characteristic of society as a whole. To move from one to the other requires some explanation of how fetishism is distributed or amplified. For example, one needs to know how it is that those not involved in the production of commodities are nevertheless enmeshed in fetishised forms.

We have argued in this chapter that there is a tension, which is only occasionally recognised, between two positions in recent theories of the way that ideology conceals real social relations. On the one hand, there is a wish to avoid instrumentalism and to ground ideology in structures of relations rather than in class subjects. This position tends to a teleological mode of explanation in which ideology produces itself, and generally fails to specify the institutional mechanisms involved. On the other hand, in order to avoid the difficulties of the first position, one can restore the concepts of class and class struggle to the centre of theory about the dominant ideology. In turn, this introduces the danger of instrumentalism. The task is, then, to explain the origin of a dominant ideology while showing that it has determinate effects on class relations, without lapsing into instrumentalist explanations which reduce dominant ideology to a form of indoctrination generated within the dominant class.

Our argument is that there has been an increased emphasis on the autonomy and causal efficacy of superstructural elements, and of ideology in particular, in modern Marxism. One of the main reasons for this tendency has been the perceived stability of capitalism. If capitalism does not collapse because of its economic contradictions, then it must be stabilised by its superstructure, and ideology has a significant role in this process. This emphasis on ideology amounts to advocacy of what we have called the dominant ideology thesis. The main elements of this thesis are as follows:

(1) There is a dominant ideology, the precise content of which is not always carefully specified. Neither is it clear what scientific procedures would establish whether any given ideology is dominant.

(2) Dominant classes 'benefit' from the effects of the dominant ideology, although not necessarily through their own deliberate activities. There is generally little investigation of the impact of the dominant ideology on the dominant classes.

(3) The dominant ideology does incorporate the subordinate classes, making them politically quiescent, though there is considerable disagreement as to the degree of incorporation and the consequent degree of social stability. The effect of ideology is to conceal social relations.

(4) The mechanisms by which ideology is transmitted have to be powerful enough to overcome the contradictions within the structure of capitalist society.

There is not, of course, a uniform presentation of the thesis within modern Marxism. On the question of the incorporation of subordinate classes, for example, Gramsci emphasises the role of class struggle and working-class resistance more than either Habermas or Althusser does. Despite these undoubtedly important differences, versions of the dominant ideology thesis, whether their inspiration lies in the doctrine of commodity fetishism or in the class-theoretical theses of the *German Ideology*, dominate Marxist discussion of capitalist societies.

Chapter 2

Theories of the Common Culture

In Chapter 1 we established that modern Marxism advances a dominant ideology thesis. Our argument in this chapter is that, within classical sociology, similar theoretical assumptions are made about the role of ideology, values, knowledge and culture. One group of sociological theories, namely, the sociology of knowledge tradition of Weber and Mannheim, attempts to show how beliefs can be reduced to social groups. A second position explains social order by reference to common values and culture, particularly the case in the work of Parsons and other structural-functionalists.

There are a number of grounds for supposing that the distinctiveness of sociological and Marxist analyses has been greatly overdrawn. In the first place, the sociology of knowledge which tries to develop a non-Marxist theory of ideology in fact arrives at similar class-theoretical conclusions to the dominant ideology tradition within Marxism. Secondly, the sociology of common culture and beliefs, although it provides a different account of the subject-matter, does not surmount the difficulty that the dominant ideology thesis faces in establishing that there *is* a pervasive, dominant ideology which has the function of incorporation, which in this case takes the form of a difficulty in demonstrating the presence of a common culture which functions to integrate the social system. There are, indeed, significant points of similarity in the structure of the dominant ideology and common culture arguments. For example, there is a parallel between the notion that ritual practices embody the beliefs of a given society and the argument in Poulantzas that ideology can only be properly understood as *ideological practice*. The agencies of socialisation and internalisation of dominant values are sociologically parallel to the ideological state apparatus in Althusserian Marxism. The sociology of beliefs, therefore, is not an obvious alternative to Marxism because the concepts of 'dominant culture' or 'shared value system' are duplicated by those of 'hegemonic culture' or 'dominant ideology'. Neither version in fact provides an adequate account of order in industrial society.

In order to establish this somewhat controversial argument for the similarity of these approaches, we put forward an even more radical claim – one that involves us in the reinterpretation of the conventional views about the development of sociological theory, namely, that Weber and Durkheim in fact stand in a closer relationship to Marx than they do to the functionalist sociology of Parsons and the neo-Durkheimian school. Another line of argument is that the sort of sociology which emerged after the publication of Parsons's *The Structure of Social Action* (1937) underestimated the importance of Weber's and Durkheim's explanations of industrial society in terms of the centrality of economic structures and compulsion, which did not rely primarily on beliefs and culture. Contemporary sociological interpretations have 'Parsonianised' Weber and Durkheim in the same way that Lukács and Korsch 'Hegelianised' Marx, with the result that in both neo-Durkheimian sociology and neo-Marxism the superstructure of values and beliefs is emphasised at the expense of economic structure. What at first sight may appear as a simple inquiry into the relationship between the sociology of culture and Marxist analyses of dominant ideologies takes us into a complicated rewriting of the conventional picture of the theoretical development of sociology.

The Sociology of Knowledge Tradition

In many conventional textbooks on the sociology of knowledge the writings of Marx and Engels are treated as the springboard for the basic sociological notion that all beliefs have an existential location in the social processes of social classes or social groups. For example, Robert Merton in *Social Theory and Social Structure* treats the thesis that beliefs have an 'existential basis' in social processes as the basis of the sociology of knowledge and asserts that 'Marxism is the storm-center of *Wissenssoziologie*' (Merton, 1951, p. 462). Max Weber and Karl Mannheim responded to that 'storm-center' in the sociology of knowledge, not by providing an alternative, but by raising detailed questions about the causal links between social groups and beliefs. This view of Weber and Mannheim as critical figures *within* rather than outside the broad tradition of Marxist *Wissenssoziologie* is supported by Kurt H. Wolff who observes that Mannheim was 'rooted in the Marxist tradition' (Gross, 1959, p. 508). A similar claim has been made more recently by Remmling who notes that although Mannheim rejected certain aspects of Marx's causal analysis of the relation between beliefs and material processes in favour of 'relationalism', Mannheim's sociology of knowledge was firmly rooted in the Marxist tradition (1975, p. 44). These general observations on the historical relationship between Marx and Engels's original formulation of the existential basis of knowledge and subsequent conceptual developments in the sociologies of Weber and Mannheim require more precise elaboration within our presentation of theories of ideology.

Modern Marxist writers have predominantly taken the view that Weber's epistemology, theoretical perspective and ethico-political standpoint differ sharply and decisively from the theoretical analyses which Marx presented in *Capital*. This categorical separation of Marx from Weber is particularly characteristic of those Marxist authors who adhere to some variety of Althusserian epistemology (Hindess, 1977). There is clearly much to be said for the view that Weber intended to produce a sociology in which the subjective orientations of social actors were central to ideographic causal explanations, while in the later Marx we find causal explanations in terms of objective structural conditions existing independently of subjective consciousness. While Weber is neo-Kantian, Marx's political economy emerges from his theoretical confrontation with Hegelian philosophy and British utilitarianism. These contrasts are conventionally illustrated by reference to *The Protestant Ethic and the Spirit of Capitalism*, to Weber's taxonomy of power relations in *Economy and Society* and to Weber's more politically motivated lectures on socialism and bureaucracy (Runciman, 1978). It is well known that many aspects of Weber's comparative sociology of pre-capitalist, agrarian societies depend heavily on Marx's view of the collapse of slavery and feudalism (B. S. Turner, 1974; Weber, 1976). Rather than attempting to summarise the general connection between Weberian sociology and Marxism, it is more apposite from the point of view of providing a theory of ideology to concentrate on Weber's analysis of social systems of belief, especially religious beliefs.

At one level, Weber appears to reject the notion that beliefs can be reduced in any simple fashion to an economic class interest. Weber rejected Nietzsche's argument that Christian moral values could be understood solely in terms of the cosmological resentment of the poor. Similarly Weber in *Ancient Judaism*, by arguing that the Jewish prophets were not spokesmen of an anti-Jerusalemite peasantry, criticised Kautsky's presentation of Old Testament prophecy as an expression of the class struggle (Kautsky, 1925). However, although Weber clearly rejects vulgar Marxist reductions of belief directly to the class position of social actors, he typically provides a more complex explanation of beliefs in terms of the interests of social strata and social classes. It is sometimes suggested that Weber's treatment of 'class', 'status' and 'power' as three separate dimensions of domination cuts him off from the Marxist tradition which has a unitary analysis of economic relations of production. This simplistic view of Weber and Marx on social classes will no longer, of course, suffice to distinguish these two sociologies of class because of the enormous refinement in theoretical under-standing of Marx's view of 'social classes' as effects of complex political, ideological and economic structures (Poulantzas, 1973). Furthermore, even when Weber appears to be arguing that the material and ideal interests of social status groups (as opposed to the economic interests of classes) determine the development of religious beliefs because certain status groups act as the 'carriers' of salvational beliefs, Weber's arguments in *The Sociology of Religion* do in fact reduce religious beliefs to class position. In general, Weber makes a sharp distinction between the religious needs of the rich and those of the poor. The privileged develop a theodicy of legitimacy which justifies their position in the class structure, whereas the disprivileged urban proletariat requires a theodicy of compensation. A religion of future compensation in the next world is based on 'class hatred' only in certain exceptional circumstances relating to the role of 'pariah-groups' (B. S. Turner, 1977b). By contrast, the rural peasantry is rarely affected by the ethical content of world religions and knights as a class have been specifically hostile to the Christian doctrine of humility and sinful-ness. Thus Weber, regardless of the constant reminders about status differences, in practice operates with a basic dichotomy between upper and lower classes with their own quasi-psychological religious needs.

The effect of Weber's analysis of social classes and their religious proclivities is to produce a theory of religious culture which is parallel to a Marxist approach to dominant ideologies. We can summarise this implicit Weberian argument by saying that each society has a dominant religious tradition (Christian, Islamic, Hindu, and so on) and, out of that tradition, each social class by a process of 'elective affinity' between belief and interest selects a particular motif which gives expression to the social and psychological needs of class members. Weber is also aware, as contemporary Marxists have been, of the problems of contradictory class locations. For example, the urban merchants and other petty bourgeois artisans in Weber's study of the social psychology of religions reject the orgiastic elements of the religion of subordinate classes, while also avoiding the 'indifference' of upper-class religiosity, such as deism. While social classes may vary in terms of the nature of their adherence to religion, there exists, according to Weber, a dominant religious tradition which has the effect of uniting social classes around a common set of religious beliefs and practices. There is, incidentally, evidence that Weber may have adopted some aspects of Durkheim's sociology of religion in formulating this particular interpretation of the social functions of religion (Tiryakian, 1966; Seidman, 1977). The concept of theodicy is central to Weber's view of religion. Religion as a system of theodicies legitimates the powerful and compensates the dispossessed, thereby mitigating the full impact of contradictory class interest. Despite all the subtlety of Weber's analysis of religious meanings in the area of religion and social classes, Weber's position is *analytically* not far removed from the claim that 'religion is the opium of the masses'.

At the same time Weber does object to the notion of a simple economic determinism of religious belief by economic variables. He notes, for instance, that as one moves down the social scale there exists an increasing diversity of religious attitudes and this diversification 'proves that a uniform determinism of religion by economic forces never existed among the artisan classes' (Weber, 1965, p. 96). That this is a very poor argument against economic determinism as a theory in the sociology of religion is beside the point. What we can note is that Weber is arguing against *uniform* determinism rather than against determinism as such. Furthermore, in producing a simple dichotomy between the theodicies of the rich and of the poor, Weber ends by offering an obviously functionalist version of the social role of religion in a class society which is very similar to that provided by Marx and Engels. While these arguments are not in themselves conclusive, we can further strengthen our general position by examining Mannheim's sociology of knowledge as an additional illustration of our exegesis of the centrality of Marxist theories of knowledge within the sociological tradition.

Mannheim's relationship with theoretical Marxism is notoriously ambiguous. One central issue in his general sociology is that he wants to avoid the obviously self-destructive implication of Marxist relativism for objective social thought. Given Marx's apparent reduction of beliefs to interests, the development of the sociology of knowledge paradoxically threatened to dig its own grave. Most of Mannheim's efforts to avoid this relativising paradox prove to be unsatisfactory (Abercrombie, 1980). At one level, Mannheim attempts to protect the validity of sociological propositions by claiming that sociologists, as members of a free-floating intelligentsia, do not have a uniform set of vested interests of a political and economic kind which would otherwise vitiate the independent status of their knowledge. In addition, Mannheim weakens the force of the causal claims made by Marxists for the economic determination of beliefs by emphasising the merely relational connections between base and superstructure. These various approaches to a solution for the self-refuting paradox of the sociology of knowledge can and have been frequently attacked. The main point is that Mannheim's modifications of what he takes to be Marx's doctrine merely contribute to a conceptual muddle rather than solving it. Some aspects of the difficulty seem to rest on a confusion between causal statements and truth claims. Causal explanations of a set of beliefs in terms of the sociological characteristics of their bearers do not necessarily render those beliefs fallacious, because the question of the truth of a set of beliefs is logically distinct from the question of their causal origins and persistence.

Mannheim fails to break with Marxist sociology of knowledge in terms of epistemology; he also fudges the underlying issue of class interest as an explanation of social beliefs. Mannheim criticises Marxists for treating economic class as the only significant dimension of social relations and he proposes instead to treat a variety of social groups (generations, sexual categories, status groups) as significant in the existential determination of knowledge. As in the Weberian case, most of Mannheim's actual studies of systems of belief (such as conservativism) depend upon a Marxist category of social class rather than social group. In Mannheim's most famous study of beliefs, *Ideology and Utopia*, the explanation of these two systems of thought rests upon a dichotomous class model. The adherence of the dominant class to an ideological world-view has the effect of preventing that class from grasping facts which would otherwise 'undermine their sense of dominance'. The subordinate class by contrast adheres to a utopian outlook emphasising all the features of a society which might result in the collapse of the status quo. The chiliastic beliefs of Christianity are obvious examples of this utopian mentality. The official church as the spiritual agent of the dominant class 'made every effort to paralyse this situationally transcendent idea' (Mannheim, 1966, p. 116). Following Nietzsche's view of the connections between class resentment and religion, Mannheim refers to the resentment of the oppressed class as the main source of Christian ethics. Indeed, Christianity is 'primarily intelligible in terms of the resentment of oppressed strata' (Mannheim, 1966, p. 40). Whereas Weber sees religious theodicies in terms of upper-class legitimation and the compensation of subordinate classes, Mannheim treats Christianity as a religious system which provides an ideology for the dominant class and utopias for the oppressed class. However, in both cases Christianity provides in historical terms the dominant ideology of European societies in two senses. First, Christianity generated a theodicy for the rich and the poor in such a way that even opposition to the system of class relations was formulated in terms of the dominant religious ideology (Ossowski, 1963; Engels, 1966). Secondly, the ideology of the dominant class was normally able to contain heterodox, oppositional beliefs by virtue of the fact that the dominant class controlled the church.

Despite the diversity of beliefs, there is in Weberian and Mannheimian sociologies of knowledge the view that the dominant ideology incorporates the various social classes within a common way of life. Neither Weber nor Mannheim provides a convincing explanation of how alternative and oppositional beliefs (in Christianity, for example) are sociologically generated. Both theorists rely upon an *ad hoc* psychologism which explains religious beliefs 'primarily as an outcome of resentment'. Both Weber and Mannheim adhere – despite their numerous qualifications and objections to institutionalised Marxist thought – to a form of dominant ideology thesis which in essentials is compatible with the notion in the *German Ideology* that the ruling ideas of every age are necessarily those of the dominant social class.

The Sociology of Common Culture and Beliefs

Having established that Weber and Mannheim, despite their criticisms of vulgar Marxism, have not created an alternative non-Marxist theory of beliefs grounded in the idea of 'interests', we can now turn to the principal focus of this discussion of the relationship between theories of dominant ideology and theories of common culture. It is normally held that the central tradition in sociological theory for the analysis of culture starts with Durkheim's emphasis on the *conscience collective*, develops through the structural-functionalist theories of the cultural system in Talcott Parsons, Robert Merton and Kingsley Davis, and then re-emerges in the neo-Durkheimian commentary on the 'political rituals' of advanced societies. In order to locate Durkheim adequately within this historical treatment of the relationship between culture and social structure, it is important to start our discussion with a consideration of the common assumptions of nineteenth-century social philosophy.

It was a typical premise of the nineteenth-century French social philosophers that each historical epoch was characterised by a unique system of psychology and belief and that these systems could be studied from an evolutionary perspective. For example, Saint-Simon identifies three organic epochs and three stages of culture or thought (Markham, ed., 1964). In the classical period society had been based on slavery with a corresponding ideology of polytheism. After a critical epoch slavery was replaced by a system of feudalism in which a theological ideology was dominant. The feudal period was eventually replaced by an organic civilisation based on industrial production for which science or positivism was the characteristic mode of thought. This final epoch would not depend on political coercion but on the administration of society under the control of a new elite of scientists, industrialists and technicians. The traditional system of government by men was to be replaced by a system of government by principles (Kumar, 1978).

Saint-Simon's view has had a very extensive influence on both academic sociology and Marxism, but his ideas have been specifically coupled with the development of Comtean positivism. Comte's law of the three stages of mental and social life is clearly an elaboration of Saint-Simon's scheme. Thus, Comte distinguishes between a theological stage based on the political power of the military, a metaphysical stage in which rulership is exercised by churchmen and lawyers, and finally a positive epoch in which political control will be in the hands of industrial administrators. Comte, however, gives greater attention to the problem of social order in each epoch and develops an awareness of the role of social institutions in maintaining social stability. The harmony of the parts within the social whole depends on the subordination of egotistical motives to collective interests; this subordination depends in particular on the family, language and religion. In the first stage the family is the principal social unit, while in the metaphysical stage it is the state which plays this crucial integrative role. In modern society, Comte argues that social stability will come to depend on the development of a religion of humanity as the basis for the integration, not simply of families and tribes, but of the whole human race. The new age of altruistic co-operation will be under the scientific guidance of a new priesthood based on the principles of positivism. While positivism destroys the traditional religion which is founded on supernaturalist beliefs, positivism paradoxically demonstrates that society nevertheless requires as of necessity a *religio* which will create a social bond (Kolakowski, 1972, p. 80).

The way in which historians of sociological theory interpret Durkheim's theory of social integration depends in part on how they formulate Durkheim's relationship to Saint-Simon and Comte. Parsons, for example, claims that Comte is 'Durkheim's acknowledged master' and that every 'element in his thinking is rooted deeply in the problems immanent in the system of thought of which Comte was so eminent an exponent' (Parsons, 1937, p. 307). For Parsons, therefore, the key to Durkheim's sociology is located in the Comtean attempt to provide a positivistic basis for normative social control. However, this interpretation of Durkheim's account of social stability cannot be easily maintained. One objection is that Durkheim clearly acknowledged Saint-Simon rather than Comte as the founding father of sociology, despite Comte's early employment of the term 'sociology' in a letter to Valat in 1824 (Horkheimer and Adorno, 1973, p. 12). In his Bordeaux lectures on socialism of 1895–6, Durkheim by contrast admitted that 'it is to him [Saint-Simon] that one must, in full justice, award the honour currently given to Comte' of founding sociology, because in Saint-Simon 'we encounter the seeds already developed of all the ideas which have fed the thinking of our time' (Durkheim, 1962, pp. 142–3).

The impetus of *The Division of Labour in Society* was not only to criticise Herbert Spencer's account of the origins of social differentiation but also to counter Comte's view of its consequences. In his *Positive Philosophy* Comte argues that as the individual's activity is specialised, so individual interest is increased to the detriment of the solidarity of the group. By contrast, the main argument advanced by Durkheim is that the principal basis for social cohesion in an industrial society is the necessity for co-operation as an effect of the increasing division of labour. While it is quite clear that Durkheim wants to criticise utilitarian individualism for reducing social relations to individual interest, he also wants to criticise Comte's overstatement of the significance of moral integration in an advanced society. As Gouldner points out in his introductory essay to Durkheim's study of socialism, while Durkheim thinks that moral values are important for social stability, 'modern society no longer requires the *same degree* of moral consensus, nor does this consensus entail the same items of belief, necessary for earlier periods' (Gouldner in Durkheim, 1962, p. 14). The crucial problem for modern society is *not* value consensus but the absence of social linkage between the individual and the state. Durkheim regards Comte's emphasis on the family and religion as an inappropriate answer to this issue and looks instead towards the integrative role of corporate groups based on occupational differentiation. Gouldner argues, therefore, that Durkheim 'was under pressure to adjust Comteanism to Marxism. That there was somewhere a bridge between these two traditions was suggested by their possession of a common ancestor, Saint-Simon' (Gouldner in Durkheim, 1962, p. 29).

In this context it is interesting to recall Engels's observations on the relationship between Saint-Simon and Comte. In a letter to Tönnies, Engels observes that Comte manages to combine 'a series of brilliant thoughts' with a 'Philistine mode of outlook' (in Feuer, ed., 1969, p. 486). The explanation of this paradoxical combination is to be found in the fact that Comte 'took all his bright ideas from St. Simon, but mutilated them when grouping them in his own peculiar way' (in Feuer, ed., 1969, p. 487). Engels also goes on to observe that the Comtist groups in London have moved gradually towards the political right over the question of the working class. Engels's comments provide some additional support for Gouldner's view that Saint-Simon was a significant intellectual ancestor of Durkheim's sociology and Marx's political economy. Gouldner's exegetical essay does, however, refer specifically to Durkheim's first major publication (*De la division du travail social*, 1893) and to the lectures on socialism which were posthumously published by Marcel Mauss in 1928 under the title *Le Socialisme*. The question which we must address is: how far can Gouldner's specific interpretation be extended to Durkheim's sociology as a whole? This question is forced upon us because the conventional view of Durkheim, following Parsons's account of the inability of Durkheim's positivism to solve the problem of order, is that his early study of social differentiation was totally replaced by his subsequent interest in religious belief and ritual practice.

What is of particular importance for our view of ideology is the reappraisal of the abiding significance of *The Division of Labour* within Durkheim's sociology as a whole. Given the authority which has been enjoyed by Parsons's exegesis of Durkheim's sociology, most sociologists have treated *The Division of Labour* as peripheral on the assumption that it was totally superseded by the later writings on professional ethics, suicide and totemism. Anthony Giddens (1972, 1978) demonstrates by contrast that all of the subsequent analyses of religion, law, politics and urban civilisation are either discussed in or contained in *The Division of Labour in Society*. Where we would criticise Giddens's interpretation is over the issue of 'moral individualism' which, according to Giddens, replaced the collective beliefs of societies based on mechanical solidarity with the increasing division of labour. In our view Giddens retains a sort of Parsonian view of Durkheim by adhering to the conventional notion that the issue of normative social relationships was the key feature of Durkheim's sociology. We can illustrate this criticism by returning to Giddens's recent study of Durkheim (Giddens, 1978).

Giddens compares Durkheim unfavourably with Weber and with Marx, because in his studies of religious phenomena Durkheim did not develop any notion of the ideological functions of religion in legitimating social institutions and in serving class interests. But this comparison largely ignores the crucial fact that in both *The Elementary Forms* and *The Division of Labour* Durkheim wanted to study religion in pre-industrial, simple societies in which social classes did not exist, whereas Weber and Marx were principally concerned with the question of religion in the transition of societies to capitalist means of production. In this light, it is hardly surprising that Durkheim was not specifically concerned with the issue of ideology. Durkheim thought that modern societies would no longer require normative justification in the manner of traditional societies, because social solidarity would be generated by other factors, namely, the economic interdependence of individuals within a complex division of labour. More precisely, Durkheim argued that the *conscience collective* did exist in advanced societies (with organic solidarity) but that it 'became weaker and vaguer as the division of labour developed' and also that its 'average intensity and the average degree of determinateness' diminished (Durkheim, 1964a, pp. 285, 152). In terms of the content of the *conscience collective*, its religious, transcendental and collective aspects are replaced by secular, rational beliefs. While the 'domain of religion contracts more and more', the 'cult in behalf of personal dignity' and the religion of the individual are erected (Durkheim, 1964a, p. 172). Nevertheless, this development represents a definite shrinkage of collective beliefs and sentiments as society is secularised as an effect of the division of labour. On this issue there is much greater agreement between Durkheim, Weber and Marx than Giddens is willing to admit. Marx thought that in early capitalism, religion would no longer be dominant as men came entirely under the domination of the 'cash nexus' and Weber, in *The Protestant Ethic and Spirit of Capitalism* (1930) and the lecture on 'science as a calling' (Gerth and Mills, 1948), also noted that the religious would recede to the inner recesses of the personal.

There are at least two serious objections to this interpretation of Durkheim. The first concerns Durkheim's view of ceremonial activities in advanced societies which he presents at the conclusion to *The Elementary Forms*. Although Durkheim's study of Australian primitive religion is almost wholly concerned with elementary religious forms, Durkheim does in the conclusion of that study make some significant comments on the development of religion in modern society. He says in particular (1961, pp. 474–5):

There can be no society which does not feel the need of upholding and reaffirming at regular intervals the collective ideas which make its unity and its personality. Now this moral remaking cannot be achieved except by the means of reunions, assemblies and meetings where the individuals, being closely united to one another, reaffirm in common their common sentiments; hence come ceremonies which do not differ from regular religious ceremonies, either in their object, the results they produce, or the processes employed to attain their results.

It appears, therefore, that Durkheim rejects his previous argument in *The Division of Labour* that advanced societies would not require a common ideology. Following from this observation about the need for regular celebrations of common sentiments, numerous sociologists have written in a Durkheimian fashion about the importance of 'civic religions' in integrating modern secular societies (Bellah, 1964; Berger, 1969). However, having said that no society can exist without a common ceremonial, Durkheim immediately qualifies this assertion by admitting (1961, p. 475):

> If we find a little difficulty to-day in imagining what these feasts and ceremonies of the future could consist in, it is because we are going through a stage of transition and moral mediocrity. The great things of the past which filled our fathers with enthusiasm do not excite the same ardour in us, either because they have come into common usage to such an extent that we are unconscious of them, or else because they no longer answer to our actual aspirations; but as yet there is nothing to replace them.

The reason Durkheim found it difficult to imagine what a *conscience collective* would look like in an advanced industrial society had, in fact, already been spelt out in *The Division of Labour*. It is difficult to conceptualise such a collective symbolic phenomenon because the *conscience collective* of advanced societies *is* vague, indeterminate, lacking in intensity and in volume. The substitutes for religion which sociologists have discovered in football, coronations, independence day celebrations and civic flag-waving are indeed weak substitutes for the dense, dynamic, all-embracing *conscience collective*. Empirically, modern capitalist societies do not have, as we shall show, common cultures which embrace all classes and segments of society. In these terms, *The Division of Labour*, with its emphasis on the economic rather than normative ties between social units, is a far more accurate statement of the condition of modern capitalism than the hankering after mechanical solidarity which characterises certain passages of *The Elementary Forms*.

The second type of objection to this particular interpretation of Durkheim might be that it does not acknowledge the importance of

normative factors in Durkheim's treatment of occupational groupings and in his analysis of the moral nature of the state. The
advanced European societies in which the new system of organic
solidarity is emerging lack an adequate system of institutions connecting the individual with the state. Durkheim feels convinced
that the 'absence of corporative institutions thus creates in the
organisation of a society like ours a void whose importance it is
difficult to exaggerate' (Durkheim, 1964a, p. 183). Unless new corporate associations develop with a set of regulations for economic
exchanges, society will be subject to endemic *anomie*. These
occupational groupings are to be complemented by the emergence
of a democratic state which will act as a moral regulator of complex
societies. In simple societies the autocratic individual ruler embodies
the *conscience collective* of the whole community; in complex
societies Durkheim expects the state to increase in importance, but
at the same time its autocratic quality will diminish (Giddens, 1971).
Our previous arguments would still hold in relation to Durkheim's
normative view of politics and occupational associations.
Durkheim's view of economic norms was developed in *The
Division of Labour* and was not introduced subsequently as a cor-
rective to his early 'positivistic' formulation of social control.
Furthermore, Durkheim is not arguing that an over-arching, all-
embracing *conscience collective* is fundamentally necessary for
society, but merely that occupational groups are the best method
of controlling certain aspects of distribution within the division of
labour. Durkheim can still maintain that the *conscience collective*
will become weak, vague and less extensive while also claiming that
occupational norms are necessary if the anomic effects of rapid
economic changes are to be avoided.

It is absolutely clear, of course, that Durkheim diverges from
Marx by anticipating a capitalist society which can be perfectly
co-ordinated both by occupational group regulations and by co-
operative interdependence between workers in the division of
labour. Giddens is perfectly justified, therefore, in arguing that
Durkheim tends to conceive of conflict in terms of the individual
versus the whole rather than in terms of class struggle. However,
while Durkheim *anticipates* the emergence of harmonious industrial
relations, he is perfectly aware of the fact that existing capitalist
relations are essentially conflictual and disharmonious. In *The
Division of Labour*, he notes that industrial conflict is the inevitable
outcome of the social separation of owners and workers and that
these conflicts are especially evident in large factories rather than
in small-scale paternalist units. He is also aware that the working
class is incorporated into the new society by a combination of con-

sent and constraint. This incorporation which takes place because workers have no control over their situation necessarily breeds discontent: 'this tension in social relations is due, in part, to the fact that the working classes are not really satisfied with the conditions under which they live, but very often accept them only as constrained and forced, since they have not the means to change them' (Durkheim, 1964a, p. 356). This element of constraint in Durkheim's theory of social order has been generally ignored by sociologists, with the exception of Moorhouse (1973) who has employed aspects of Durkheim's view of the division of labour to produce an original interpretation of working-class incorporation.

Our argument has implied that Durkheim's studies of simple society, including the study of *Primitive Classification* (Durkheim and Mauss, 1963), cannot be employed to uncover Durkheim's explanation of social stability in advanced societies. By contrast, organic solidarity in an advanced society according to the *Division of Labour in Society* does not require a coherent common culture of the same intensity as societies characterised by mechanical solidarity. This interpretation could, of course, be seriously undermined by Durkheim's *Suicide* in which it appears that Durkheim emphasises the problem of anomie in a society where collective beliefs have been seriously weakened. Our thesis can be sustained by three observations on Durkheim's study of suicide. First, while the book is obviously and overtly *about* modern society, it is also in an important way a study *of* sociology. The theoretical focus of *Suicide* (1897) is not the increasing rate of suicides in France but that apparently individual choices to commit suicide can only be explained by social facts. In other words, the aim of Durkheim's study is to establish the validity of sociology as an autonomous discipline. Secondly, Durkheim's study of sociological explanations in the book on suicide is to be seen as a larger project to establish sociology as an objective analysis of morals. However, what Durkheim means by 'moral facts' in *Suicide* and in *The Rules of Sociological Method* (1895) is very different from Parsons's treatment of choice in the voluntaristic theory of action. For Durkheim, morality is about constraint. Thus, social facts consist 'of ways of acting, thinking, and feeling, external to the individual, and endowed with a power of coercion, by reason of which they control him' (Durkheim, 1964b, p. 3). Durkheim's sociology can be interpreted as the study of the mechanisms by which individual behaviour is coerced by the external social structure. In simple society the individual is coerced by religion, but the problem for Durkheim is to identify a comparable apparatus of restraint in modern society. In *Suicide*, Durkheim notes that 'religion has lost most of its power. And government, instead of regulating economic life, has become its tool and servant' (Durkheim, 1970, p. 255). While social differentiation and occupational groups may provide a method of social regulation, Durkheim recognises that France is a transitional society in which traditional forms of restraint based on a common culture have not been replaced by a new system of social regulation. Thirdly, we can show that *Suicide* is compatible with our interpretation of Durkheim by observing that economic changes in French society are an important part of Durkheim's explanatory model.

Of Durkheim's four types of suicide – egoistic, altruistic, anomic and fatalistic – two types may be disregarded on the grounds that they are the product of exceptional circumstances. Altruistic suicide occurs when there is little individuation and where the individual is absorbed by the social group. Most of Durkheim's examples are taken from sacrificial rites in simple societies and he comments that, apart from suicides in the army, 'as individual personality becomes increasingly free from the collective personality, such suicides could not be widespread' (Durkheim, 1970, p. 228). The same is true of fatalistic suicides among slaves resulting from excessive social regulation. It follows that egoistic and anomic suicides are the most typical suicides in a modern society where traditional systems of regulation and integration have either collapsed or declined. In this situation the suicidal drives of the individual are unleashed as the social checks controlling individual behaviour begin to crumble. The overall explanation of the disappearance of balance between personal individuation, social regulation and the suicidal tendency must be sought in Durkheim's account of social differentiation in *The Division of Labour in Society*. In the transition to organic solidarity, the secularisation and urbanisation of simple society undermines the system of regulation based on common culture, group personality and repressive law with the result that there are no longer any effective checks on the *courants suicidogenes* in society. The immediate cause of imbalance between individuation, suicidal drive and social regulation is, however, provided by rapid economic changes which result either in an unprecedented increase in private prosperity or in economic crises producing sudden impoverishment. If economic 'crises increase suicides, this is not because they cause poverty, since crises of prosperity have the same result; it is because they are crises, that is, disturbances of the collective order' (Durkheim, 1970, p. 246). Unlike wealth, human poverty is an effective restraint on aspiration.

According to Parsons's interpretation, *Suicide* represents an important analytical shift in Durkheim's account of social constraint because the explanation of suicide begins to move away from the positivistic assumptions of *The Division of Labour*. In our view, Durkheim's explanation of suicide requires the argument of *The Division of Labour* to establish the absence of a *conscience collective* or at least the diminution of its intensity and determinateness. However, it is unnecessary to overstate our case in order to criticise Parsonian sociology. We are not saying that Durkheim was not concerned with the issue of moral integration. Durkheim attempted to locate social stability in modern society at three levels: a system of economic ties arising out of social differentiation, a network of intermediary occupational associations linking the individual to the state and an emergent system of moral restraints generated by professional bodies. Durkheim also recognised that the working class in an industrial society would have to be 'constrained and forced' to accept its position in the social structure. There is little evidence in Durkheim's sociological studies to suggest that Durkheim thought that a modern society could possess an over-arching system of common values, norms and sentiments. There is little warrant for claiming that the *conscience collective* is Durkheim's 'master concept' (Parsons in Wolff, ed., 1964, p. 138) or that Durkheim provides the basis for a theory of social integration in terms of general values. It would be more precise to say that Durkheim developed a theory of social regulation in which the notions of moral restraint, social coercion and economic force played a key part.

Parsons's sociology is, therefore, a point of *departure* from, and not a summary of, the classical tradition of sociology from Saint-Simon to Durkheim and from Marx to Weber. We have already argued that in the sociology of religion, which Parsons identified as one of the major areas in which Weber apparently developed his concern with 'the problem of meaning', Weber's analysis of religious beliefs can be interpreted in terms of the role of religion within the social class structure. Religious theodicies legitimate the power of dominant classes and compensate for the deprivation of subordinate classes. Weber's sociology as a whole cannot, however, be conveniently divorced from the central interests of the Marxist tradition. It is important for our general approach to the dominant ideology thesis that, whereas Weber thought that routinised Calvinism was congruent with the conditions leading to the *origins* of capitalism, Weber did not think general religious values would play a part in the *maintenance* of capitalist relations. Indeed, the bureaucratic structures of rational capitalism would be antithetical to any religious ethos precisely because capitalism had driven a permanent wedge between the profane world of rational calculation and the world of charismatic inspiration. Whereas Weber had a view of future capitalism based on disenchantment in which 'material goods' possess 'an inexorable power over the lives of men' (Weber, 1930, p. 181), Parsons subordinates the non-normative (the economic substratum of interests) to the normative dimension of social relationships (Lockwood, 1956). A similar contrast exists between Durkheim and Parsons over the role of normative integration in advanced societies. Whereas Durkheim envisaged a society based on organic solidarity in which common values were not widely shared, not clearly articulated and not a requirement of social regulation, Parsons stipulates as a logical assertion that a society, at whatever level of social development, is unthinkable without the existence of a common, coherent set of values, norms and commitments. Parsonian sociology is, in other words, a common culture theory in a manner which was not true of Marx, Weber and Durkheim. The common point between these theorists is the notion that human beings are forced to behave in certain directions regardless of their own preferences and inclinations. For Marx, human agents are forced to enter into relations of production which are independent of their will, so that agents become the bearers of structural arrangements.

Much of Weber's sociology is taken up with the issue of what some contemporary sociologists have referred to as 'unanticipated consequences' of social interaction (Merton, 1957). Weber is concerned with how the logic of a social situation works against the beliefs and intentions of individuals. The logic of charismatic routinisation, the logic of patrimonial bureaucracy or the logic of the transformation of Calvinist salvationism are illustrations of this form of inquiry. In Durkheim, the central focus is on the regulation of individuals in relation to the social group, through culture in simple society and through social differentiation in advanced society. The constraints on individual behaviour which flow from the social structure and especially from the economic and political aspects of that structure, is thus a common theme to the explanation of social order in the sociology of Marx, Weber and Durkheim. By contrast, the explanation of social order in Parsons depends on the conjunction of shared values with psychological dispositions.

Parsons

The Hobbesian problem of order first emerged systematically in Parsons's *The Structure of Social Action*, although aspects of the problem were broached in earlier essays such as 'The place of ultimate values in sociological theory' (Parsons, 1935; Scott, 1963). Parsons's voluntaristic action theory is a twofold critical account of the logical difficulties which arise with rationalist and positivist theories of human action. If we accept the principle that the basic criterion of human action is the rational calculation of personal interest, then it is difficult to explain how society is possible because rational men will resort to force and fraud to realise their ends. If we attempt to establish a positivistic basis for the study of human action, then we will fail to take human values and human choice seriously because we will reduce the meaning of action to the biologically determined structure of human needs. The traditional approaches to the problem of social order in utilitarian philosophy, in political economy, or in Pareto's sociology, were inadequate because they had to resort to some simplistic notion of force or to postulate the existence of an identity of economic interests. In Parsons's view, force cannot provide the basis for any long-term social order and the notion of 'common economic interests' is actually incompatible with the rationalist individualism of utilitarianism from Hobbes to Spencer. The key to an adequate theory of order began to emerge in Durkheim's outline of the non-contractual element of the social contract and in Durkheim's study of ritual and religious belief on the one hand, and in Weber's definition of sociology as the interpretative understanding of the meaning of social action from the point of view of the social actor on the other hand. In Parsons's early sociology, therefore, an adequate theory of society had to recognise that actors select ends and means according to norms which are elements of a common system of values.

Although *The Structure of Social Action* explicitly develops a voluntaristic theory of action, the theory is not primarily an *interactionist* one. Values, norms and meaning do not emerge out of the process of social interaction; they are imposed on the unit act. The actor orients to the situation in terms of norms which already exist and which structure action. The meaning of action does not emerge from the ongoing processes of interaction but out of the values which must exist prior to, and independently of, the performance of unit acts. The nature of the structure of action in terms of values becomes much more obvious in Parsons's later work, especially in *The Social System* (1951). The cohesion of society (or of any social group or social unit) depends on the interpenetration of cultural patterns of general meaning, social institutions and need-dispositions at the personality level. The stability of the social system arises from the fact that the cultural patterns which are part of the general symbolic apparatus of society are also embedded in people's minds. The socialisation of the individual consists in the transfer of systems of interpretation and meaning from the cultural system to the social system of which the actor is a member. The internalisation process involves the transfer of values and expectations to the personality of the actor so that successful performance of social roles is both socially rewarding and psychologically gratifying. The individual is motivated to perform in a conformist or normative manner because conformist role performances are socially supported while at the same time the need-dispositions of the personality are satisfied and reinforced. The equilibrium of the social system depends on 'the processes of socialisation by which actors acquire the orientations necessary to the performance of their roles in the social system' (Parsons, 1951, p. 481). Parsons regards these propositions about the interdependence of culture, society and personality as constituting the 'most fundamental theorem of the theory of action' which states that 'the *structure* of systems of action *consists* in institutionalized (in social and cultural systems) and/or internalized (in personalities and organisms) patterns of cultural meaning' (Parsons in Black, ed., 1961, p. 342).

These integrated relationships between culture, society and personality are further elaborated in *Toward a General Theory of Action* (Parsons and Shils, 1951). System integration is defined in terms of the processes whereby value-orientation patterns are institutionalised at the social level via the mechanism of social roles with the effect of organising the behaviour of adult members of society. It is through the socialisation process that these value patterns are 'constitutive in establishment of the personality structure of the new adult from the plasticity of early childhood' (Parsons and Shils, 1951, p. 27). In this collection of papers, however, Parsons comes to rely very heavily on Tolman's 'purposive behaviourism'. The meaning of action is ultimately reduced to a simple behaviourist distinction between gratification and deprivation. In the interaction between ego and alter, there emerges a complementarity of expectations as each social actor seeks approval and gratification from the other – gratification being 'the primary functional need of personality' (Parsons and Shils, 1951, p. 180). The motivation of the social actor is thereby secured by virtue of the fact that socialisation provides the social actor with consistent and institutionalised values; furthermore, behaviour in terms of these common values brings gratification to ego via the socially supportive gestures of alter.

Although Parsons began to develop a lasting interest in Freudian psychoanalysis as an alternative to behavioural psychology, the basic theorem specifying the relationship between values, social relations and personality needs has never been abandoned. In its early formulation, however, the theorem had no elaborate view of the dynamic interconnections between culture, society and personality. The major addition to Parsons's sociology has been the development of the functional prerequisite paradigm of adaptation, goal attainment, integration and latency (AGIL) which first appeared in *Working Papers in the Theory of Action* (1953) in collaboration with Robert Bales and Edward Shils. The problem of order was subsequently conceptualised in terms of a process in which social systems reproduce themselves by systematically satisfying the prerequisites of their four subsystems. Adaptation and goal attainment refer to relations with the environment which is external to the system, while integration and latency problems refer to internal issues of the system itself. Thus, adaptation concerns the exchange between the system and the environment in terms of resources; goal attainment is the subsystem in which system goals are specified and resources mobilised to achieve these ends. Integration incorporates those processes designed to inhibit deviance and exercise social control. Finally, latency or pattern maintenance is concerned with generating motivation through the internalisation of culture patterns to the personality. The latency subsystem contributes stability to norms and commitments; the latency functions (tension management and pattern maintenance) 'differ from the integrative problem in the sense that they focus on the *unit* of the system, not the system itself' (Parsons and Smelser, 1956, p. 50). At the societal level, the AGIL paradigm corresponds to the economy, polity, culture and personality. The economic and political tasks involve the formulation of goals or ends and the allocation of resources to achieve those ends. Thus the most significant internal tasks of a social system are the creation of social solidarity (the integrative function) and the creation of appropriate motivation. Without successful solutions to these four system problems, equilibrium and integration cannot be maintained (Rocher, 1974).

Parsonian sociology has often been criticised for failing to provide an adequate account of power, violence and conflict; the failure to explain conflict is further connected with the absence of a satisfactory theory of social change (for example, Dahrendorf, 1958; Wright Mills, 1959; Gouldner, 1971). Parsons's attempts to answer or correct these criticisms by, for example, developing a functionalist theory of power and influence (Parsons, 1963a, 1963b) have only served to reinforce the belief that even a Parsonian explanation of power has to presuppose the existence of a value consensus (Giddens, 1968). While power flows from the possession of legitimacy founded on consensus, power deflation or the sudden loss of confidence is therefore 'deviance writ large' (Giddens, 1968, p. 266). Any attempt by Parsons to argue that his theory does not require complete value consensus, while at least making some concession to how actual societies are organised, can only serve to threaten the overall coherence of the original theory (Dahrendorf, 1958).

Another line of defence adopted by Parsons is to argue that he has never taken social order for granted; on the contrary, order *is* a problem. Thus Parsons (1970, p. 869) observes that his 'assumption throughout has been congruent with that of Hobbes in the sense that even such order as human society has enjoyed should be treated as problematical'. However, the *problematical* nature of 'the Hobbesian problem of order' plays a very weak and residual role in Parsons's sociology. To admit that order might be a precarious balance of consensus *and* forms of coercion (political force, economic coercion, moral restraint or habituation) would open the door to a dependence on the rationalist tradition of political economy from Hobbes to Marx. Parsons's defence is also weak, because the existence of order for Parsons is not based on careful analysis of historical evidence but is simply the premise on which his theory of social systems is built. In Parsonian sociology, if a collectivity exists, then it *must* possess an integrated system of values which are successfully internalised into the personalities of individuals-in-roles. In our study of dominant ideologies, we wish to show that a dominant ideology is not a *necessary* requirement of social order. Furthermore, at the level of societies or collectivities, general values do not enjoy the coherence and consistency required by Parsonian sociology. Part of the explanation of the absence of ideological incorporation (internalisation) is to be found in the weakness of the apparatus of transmission (socialisation) in pre-capitalist societies and in the fact that non-normative forms of coercion (to use Lockwood's terminology) have been historically more significant than normative forms of restraint.

Another indication of the unproblematic nature of 'the problem of order' is that Parsons can only explain a limited range of types of system disturbance or societal disorder. The other side of Parsonian order is not the resistance of workers to managerial strategies, the formation of oppositional ideologies, the emergence of class conflicts or revolutionary struggle; the other side of Parsonian theory of order is merely deviation from the all-pervasive system of dominant values. The dysfunctions of the social system are pinpointed by the emergence of deviant role-performance which is to be traced back to certain inadequacies in the socialisation process. There is a further limitation in this explanation in that the typical form of deviance is in fact intergenerational discontinuity. The most likely source of conflict in the social system is the inability of an adult generation to transmit its values to a new generation. These failures in the learning process whereby appropriate beliefs and performances are normally acquired result in various forms of passive and active deviation, but these deviations are still conceptualised as departures from or within a common system of values and norms.

One solution for Parsons would be to argue that any empirical society could contain more than one abstractly conceived social system. Conflict and change would be explained by the contradictory demands of the culture and institutions of the several social systems on the role performances of agents within the society. Values would thus be coherent within but not between social systems. This theoretical strategy would be analogous to certain contemporary Marxist formulations of the contradictory relationships between overlapping modes of production within a given social formation. Parsons has not, however, considered such a solution because his dominant mode of explanation of social change has been of structural changes within a social system in terms of their increasing social differentiation. Societies change as a result of their internal maturation of adaptive capacity towards their environments. In other words, Parsonian explanations of social change have been evolutionary rather than in terms of contradictory struggles between different systems.

Talcott Parsons has, therefore, been the most systematic exponent of a common culture theory in modern sociology. Starting from the problem of order, Parsons has attempted to explain social stability in terms of the intimate interdependence of cultural patterns, social institutionalisation and personality needs. In support of this theory, Parsons has claimed that previous theoretical perspectives on society which depend on either a rationalist/ empiricist or idealist epistemology have been inadequate. We have attempted to show that Parsons cannot legitimately claim a Weberian or Durkheimian ancestry for this sociology of moral consensus. We have also pointed to certain traditional criticisms of Parsonian sociology as an adequate theory of society. There are serious theoretical and empirical objections to the notion that all societies (social systems) require coherent value systems. While in our view most of the sociological and anthropological analyses of common values, shared symbolic universes and public systems of ritual practice properly apply to the understanding of pre-industrial society, Parsonian sociology requires that these perspectives also apply without major modification to advanced industrial society. Hence Parsons has been very reluctant to take Durkheim's rigid dichotomy between mechanical and organic solidarity seriously or literally. For example, while making some reservations about inter- and intra-collectivity integration, Parsons wants to claim that 'both types of solidarity (mechanical and organic) are characterized by common values and institutionalized norms' (Parsons, 1968, p. 461). One feature of Parsonian influence over modern sociological studies has been the tendency of researchers to seek out simple correspondences or analogies between the sacral beliefs and practices of simple societies and the profane beliefs and practices of modern societies.

Many of these theoretical problems arise particularly acutely in what we might term the 'neo-Durkheimian ritualist school' in both sociology and social anthropology. In contemporary sociology the view that modern capitalist societies require a powerful collection of rituals in order to sustain a core of common values was put most forcefully by Shils and Young (1953) in their article 'The meaning of the coronation' which became a focus of debate in functionalist sociology. In that essay it was argued that 'the coronation of Elizabeth II was the ceremonial occasion for the affirmation of the moral values by which the society lives. It was an act of national communion' (in Shils, 1975, p. 139). This 'national communion' was made possible by the fact that the British working class had by the 1950s been successfully assimilated into the moral order of the national society. A similar argument has been presented about the investiture of the Prince of Wales where the ceremony had the result of reaffirming the values associated with family solidarity and national pride (Blumler et al., 1971). While these studies concentrated on specific ceremonies, Bocock (1974) has attempted to demonstrate the ritual importance of a variety of social gatherings and public events for the social integration of modern societies.

The neo-Durkheimian analysis of value integration in late capitalism has been subject to a barrage of criticism. Birnbaum (1955) has criticised Shils and Young for providing no evidence for the supposed value consensus in Britain, for treating Britain as a gemeinschaft form of society and for underestimating the political opposition expressed by the class-conscious working class. Neo-Durkheimians have also been criticised for the conceptual and logical sloppiness of their analysis of 'consensus', 'ceremony' and 'integration'. Against Bocock, for example, Goody (1977) argues that the notion of a 'secular ritual' is so vague that it includes all standardised, regular activities of a non-technical character from coronations to croquet. Another criticism has been that in advanced

societies or societies undergoing rapid inclusion into capitalist relations rituals may actually heighten or create social conflicts and
intergroup tensions. In Mexico and the Caribbean the secular
rituals (cup match, carnival, Indian/Mestizo rituals, and so forth)
of these societies may generate intergroup conflicts and can be
regarded as rituals of confrontation (Geertz, 1959; Patterson, 1967;
Moore and Myerhoff (eds), 1977). The gist of these criticisms
(Lukes, 1977, p. 65) is that

> the neo-Durkheimian game can, no doubt, be played in reverse,
> to show how collective effervescences can serve to integrate and
> strengthen subordinate social groups, whether these are engaged
> in a struggle within the existing social order, or are aiming to
> challenge it, or at the extreme overthrow it . . . collective effer-
> vescences serve not to unite the community but to strengthen
> the dominant groups within it.

These objections are not, however, necessarily decisive. The anti-
Durkheimians claim that rituals and ceremonial events unite and
integrate social groups within a society, with the result that the
cohesion of the society as a whole is limited. In essence, this modification of neo-Durkheimian integration theory is not wholly
incompatible with a functionalist perspective. Shils, for example,
is perfectly aware of the paradoxical relationship between intra-
group and intergroup cohesion when he comments that the 'increase
in the integration of society occurs at the expense of the internal
integration of the parts of the society . . .' (1975, p. 80). The
important issue, therefore, is not the functional effects of ceremonial
practices, but the whole issue of whether there exists a shared
culture in advanced capitalist society or whether values are vague,
conflictual and contradictory. In our view, the great weight of the
empirical evidence goes against both common culture and dominant
ideology theories.

At the beginning of this chapter we started with the problem of the
relationship between Marxist accounts of dominant ideology and the
sociology of knowledge. This problem is subsidiary to the more
general issue of the existence or non-existence of social coherence
within societies. We have drawn some parallels between Marx's
analysis of class and ideology and the sociology of beliefs as
developed by Mannheim and Weber. We can also suggest a connection between Durkheim's view of organic solidarity and conventional Marxist notions about the centrality of economic constraint
in capitalism. By contrast, we have tried to show how it is that

Parsons's central emphasis on value consensus as the *sine qua non* of any society represents a break with the sociological tradition.

In our view, however, there is still a strong *analytical* parallel between functionalist approaches to culture and the problem in Marxism concerning the connection between the dominant ideology, the revolutionary ideology of the working class and the existence of alienation. That is, if the dominant class really does control the means of mental production, then how *do* deviant, oppositional and radical views emerge? If the apparatus of ideological control is as strong as some Marxists tend to suggest, how will change take place in capitalism? In the *Communist Manifesto* Marx and Engels did provide an elementary description of how the consciousness of workers would emerge out of the daily confrontation with capitalists by making a distinction between class-in-itself and class-for-itself. But this is a rudimentary starting point for a general theory of consciousness and, as we have seen, there are many reasons why this process of radicalisation has not taken place. The difficulties of Marx's account are most obvious, however, in connection with his theory of alienation. In Marx's earlier writing, the proletariat is described as a class which is broken, oppressed, alienated and robbed of humanity. The worker is physically, emotionally and mentally crushed by the despotism of factory life. How, therefore, will this class rise up against its capitalist oppressors to forge a new society out of the collapse of capitalism? In terms of the description of the working class presented in Engels's *The Condition of the Working Class in England in 1844* and in Marx's Paris Manuscripts, the possibility of the working class emancipating itself appears to be remote (Duncan, 1973). Although Marx also referred in *The Holy Family* to the working class as 'abased and *indignant* at its abasement', the theory of alienation in capitalist society would equally suggest that the working class more commonly responds to abasement by a mixture of reformist trade unionism, fatalism and escape into emotional religiosity.

There is, therefore, an ironic relation between Parsons's focus on common culture as a social requirement for stability and the conventional Marxist treatment of the dominant ideology. A number of writers have commented on this parallel. For example, what Parsons refers to as 'the dominant value system' of a society could be held to constitute its ruling ideology, and the 'hierarchy of values by which performances and qualities are ranked could be said to establish the hierarchy of roles that forms the basis of social class distinctions' (Morse, 1961, p. 148). A similar observation has been made by Giddens, in relation to consensus and coercion theories, when he notes that 'Marx always recognized the cohering effect of commonly held values and ideas (which, in the Marxist usage, are covered under the generic term "ideology"), and in fact built much of his theory upon such an assumption' (1968, p. 269). It is possible to render this parallel between 'common culture' and 'dominant ideology' in a much stronger form than in Giddens's formula. For Parsons, the common culture incorporates all social groups with the effect of excluding all forms of effective deviance from the crucial institutions and values of society. In modern societies, there exist a powerful apparatus and set of processes which ensure the distribution of these values and beliefs to all members of society. This common culture functions to distribute agents to their places (roles) within the various subsystems and simultaneously works to secure the motivation of agents to perform their social roles. The relationship between Parsonian common culture theory and conventional dominant ideology theses can also be illustrated by their common theoretical weakness.

Both perspectives on 'common culture' share similar problems of explanation and evidence. Parsonian theories of integration around central values have been notoriously incapable of presenting any truly convincing account of the emergence of deviant, oppositional values and of whole subcultures within society. The usual resort is to some inexplicable and temporary malfunctioning of the family system whereby internalisation of values is inadequately attained. The other problem for theories of cultural consensus is that most of the evidence points to the fact that values are not shared or that people adhere to contradictory values or that they have a merely pragmatic attachment to values. The debate that followed Merton's argument that working-class deviance was explained by attachment to the value of material success in a situation where legitimate means are lacking, was a good example of the difficulties encountered by the 'common culture thesis' in functionalist theories of criminality (Cohen, 1965; Downes 1966; Lemert, 1967; Taylor, 1971). The parallel problem for Marxism is that if the dominant class has a monopoly of cultural production, then how do forms of oppositional, alternative thought (such as Marxism) arise within the working class? It is quite common for Marxists to write as if the working class was a *tabula rasa* on which the dominant class inscribed its ruling ideas. For example, the ideological institutions are so powerful in Miliband's discussion of the 'process of legitimation' in *The State in Capitalist Society* (1969) that it is difficult to imagine how the system could ever be effectively opposed by the working class in terms of its own indigenous ideology. The second problem of 'the ruling ideas' model is that, in fact, the working class does not appear to be entirely and successfully incorporated at the ideological level. While the British working class is not part of the same ideological/cultural system as the dominant class, it has not produced an entirely radical or revolutionary alternative to the dominant ideology which has become part of a mass consciousness. Theoretical attempts to solve these ambiguities often appear to be *ad hoc* or to borrow from certain theoretical traditions which are themselves unsatisfactory. Lukács's employment of Weberian ideal types to distinguish between the actual beliefs of workers and the 'appropriate and rational reactions imputed [*zugerechnet*] to a particular typical position in the process of production' is one rather unfortunate illustration (Lukács, 1971, p. 51).

It is finally difficult to force a total separation between the sociological and Marxist approaches to common culture because it is possible to interpret *The Division of Labour* in such a way as to bring out a theory of economic constraint similar to that developed in *Capital*. In his study of the division of labour, Durkheim argued that the *conscience collective* which was fundamental to any society dominated by mechanical solidarity would not be fundamental to organic solidarity. Common sentiments would lose their intensity, volume and exactness; they would not disappear entirely, but they would be secondary to relations which were primarily economic rather than religious. A similar set of views was outlined by Marx and Engels. First, Marx argued that in most modes of production, extra-economic forms of constraint were required, as with religion in feudalism, while in capitalism economic constraint alone would suffice. Secondly, in his observations on cultural trends in British society, Engels presented a view of urbanisation and secularisation which was parallel to Durkheim's assumption that the sacred would diminish with social evolution. In Marx's theory of capitalism, the working class is subordinated because it is excluded from control of the means of production and it is held in this subordination because the sheer exigencies of survival in early capitalism make effective protest difficult, if not impossible. In Durkheim's theory, while constraint is recognised, much greater emphasis is given to the co-operative aspects of the social division of labour. There is a very important difference of perspective here, but what is equally important is that neither theory actually *requires* some notion of the normative incorporation of the working class in capitalism.

Durkheim provides a theory of how beliefs and practices are transmitted, by demonstrating the importance of public ceremonial, cultic rituals, totemic symbols and by certain socio-psychological mechanisms such as group effervescence. Durkheim was aware of the role of constraint in preventing the emergence of certain types of protest. He attempts to relate types of beliefs to changes in the total structure of society, notably in his account of the effects of the transition from mechanical to organic solidarity. What Durkheim does not develop is a theory of social class relations as consequences of changes in the economic organisation of society. He treats the problem of modern society simply as a question of the relationship between the social individual in relation to the community – hence he is predominantly interested in issues of altruism, moral individualism and utilitarian individualism.

In this chapter we have shown that there are common culture theories, aspects of which bear considerable similarities to the dominant ideology thesis, and secondly that there has been a tendency to present classical sociologists such as Durkheim as if they were common culture theorists. There are theoretical and substantive objections to both the dominant ideology and common culture theses. In the rest of the book we show that the evidence of feudal and capitalist societies does not support the claim that there are dominant ideologies or common cultures which have the effects attributed to them by the arguments presented in these two chapters. Neither the dominant ideology nor the common culture thesis provides a satisfactory account of social order. However, the argument here indicates that Durkheim can be interpreted in such a way as to show a degree of analytical overlap with Marx.

This area of overlap raises the possibility of an alternative conceptualisation of order. From Marx, Weber and Durkheim we derive the central importance of economic relations. Marx aptly refers to the 'dull compulsion of economic relations' in his description of capitalism (1970, Vol. 1, p. 737). We suggest that this operates at two levels. There is the control of the capitalist over the worker in production relations, because the worker has to eat to live. The owners of the productive means control workers who are separated from the tools of production and the control of the labour process. However, there is an additional constraint which emerges out of the economic interdependence between workers and capitalists in the exchange of labour power and wages: there is the interdependence between different economic units within the economy and there is the general social division of labour which Durkheim used as an explanation of social order, which together constitute system integration. There is, moreover, an additional meaning of 'constraint' which the idea of 'economic relations' does not convey, namely, the physical constraints of political force. We do not deny the *possibility* of ideological incorporation, but ideology generally plays a secondary, partial and insignificant role in social order. The ultimate irony, therefore, is that, while there was a measure of agreement between Marx and Durkheim as to the importance of non-normative constraint in industrial capitalism, there has also been a convergence between the Parsonian emphasis on common culture and the neo-Marxist fascination for the ideological superstructure.

Chapter 3

Feudalism

There has been since the middle of the nineteenth century a substantial degree of agreement between Marxist historians and sociologists that the Middle Ages under the feudal mode of production were dominated by religious institutions and religious beliefs, and furthermore that the emergence of the capitalist mode of production has everywhere resulted in a remarkable diminution of that social influence. In short, both Marxism and sociology have generally adhered to the thesis that capitalist industrialisation is normally accompanied by a process of secularisation. Of course, the nature of this adherence to a secularisation thesis has varied considerably. To some extent, Marxists inherited the Enlightenment tradition of Voltaire and the later Diderot in which the priests and their irrational beliefs manipulate the gullibility of the uneducated masses (Goldmann, 1973). Marx's famous comment that religion 'is the opium of the people [and] the abolition of religion as the *illusory* happiness of the people is required for their *real* happiness' was perfectly in line with the tradition of the French *philosophes*. Marx, however, had also been heavily influenced by the left Hegelian tradition of Strauss and Feuerbach. Marx's view of Christianity, therefore, cannot be treated separately from this theory of alienation; in capitalism, Christianity came to play a part in the general distortion of social relations which had its origins in commodity production. Thus Marx (Marx and Engels, n.d., p. 135) wrote

> The religious world is but the reflex of the real world. And for a society based upon the production of commodities, in which the producers in general enter into social relations with one another by treating their products as commodities and values, whereby they reduce their individual private labour to the standard of homogeneous human labour – for such a society, Christianity with its *cultus* of abstract man, more especially in bourgeois developments, Protestantism, Deism etc., is the most fitting form of religion.

To some extent, therefore, Marx appears to have moved from a relatively simple Machiavellian image of religion as an instrument of class domination to the notion that different forms of religious belief and practice correspond to different forms of economic production (MacIntyre, 1971). In the *Grundrisse,* for example, Marx pointed out that tribute was exacted in oriental despotisms for 'the exaltation of the unity, partly of the real despot, partly of the imagined clan-being, the god' (1973*a,* p. 473). While Marx thought that abstract Protestant individualism was the 'most fitting form of religion' for early capitalism, he expected the hold of Christianity to decrease as socialist criticism unmasked the pretensions of Christian belief and as the working class formed itself into a revolutionary force within capitalism. The interests of revolutionary working-class politics and the traditional Christian faith were diametrically opposed – 'the social principles of Christianity are sneaking and hypocritical whilst the proletariat is revolutionary' (Marx and Engels, n.d., p. 84). Engels was far more specific in providing a detailed account of the gradual but inevitable secularisation of British culture as a whole with the development of an urban capitalist society. As class relations became more sharply defined and overtly conflictual, the power of Christianity over the British working class would decline. Engels (1968, p. ix) did not provide much theoretical support for this sociological proposition, but he took secularisation as empirically self-evident:

> necessity will force the working men to abandon the remnants of a belief which, as they will more and more clearly perceive, serves only to make them weak and resigned to their fate, obedient and faithful to the vampire property holding class.

If Engels (1959, pp. 435 ff.) did provide a theoretical justification for this view of secularisation, then it was of the old rationalist variety that is to be discovered in *Anti-Dühring* in which religion is basically a philosophical misconception of nature.

In this sketch of Marx and Engels's treatment of religion we have presented their position as a coherent perspective, but in fact there are at least three separate arguments involved which are not necessarily consistent. The first argument is that religion is consciously manipulated by the dominant class to control the dominated class. The second is that religion is an aspect of human alienation in which religion is a 'reversed world consciousness'. The third argument is that religion (of particular forms) is only relevant (or dominant) in certain modes of production. It seems important to distinguish the second and third types of argument because, as they appear in *Capital,* they are contradictory. In the alienation argument, Marx suggested that Christianity, in its bourgeois Protestant form, was particularly well suited to capitalism. It follows that as alienation increases in capitalism, so the penetration and dominance of puritan Christianity increases. In the mode of production argument, Marx argued that Christianity would not be relevant or dominant under capitalism, because he identified Christianity with feudalism. Thus, one characteristic form of this argument (Marx and Engels, 1973b, p. 85) stated that when

the ancient world was in its last throes, the ancient religions were overcome by Christianity. When in the eighteenth century Christian ideas succumbed to the ideas of the Enlightenment, feudal society fought its death battle with the then revolutionary bourgeoisie.

The societies characterised by the dominance of the slave mode of production are ones in which 'ancient religions' were dominant. In similar fashion, Christianity was the dominant religion of the feudal period, but this dominance was destroyed by the rise of the bourgeois class which adhered to the revolutionary principles of the Enlightenment. This idea was expressed even more precisely in the famous footnote of *Capital* where Marx (1970, Vol. 1, pp. 85–6n) presented his sweeping historical generalisation:

that the mode of production of material life dominates the development of social, political and intellectual life generally . . . is very true for our own times, in which material interests preponderate, but not for the middle ages, in which Catholicism, nor for Athens and Rome, where politics reigned supreme. In the first place it strikes one as an odd thing for anyone to suppose that those well-worn phrases about the middle ages and the ancient world are unknown to anyone else. This much, however, is clear, that the middle ages could not live on Catholicism, nor the ancient world on politics. On the contrary, it is the economic conditions of the time that explain why here politics and there Catholicism played the chief part.

One problem then with Marx's account of the periodisation of religion is that we cannot believe both that Protestant Christianity is ideally fitted to capitalism and that religion is no longer relevant to capitalism which depends solely on economic coercion. We cannot have both religion as the principal example of capitalist alienation and religion as no longer reigning 'supreme'. One way out of this apparent inconsistency would be to argue that Catholicism was fitted for feudalism, while Protestantism was the ideal religion of the bourgeoisie in *early* capitalism (a Weberian rendering of Marx).

This argument, however, runs into difficulties since Marx also believed that it was the Enlightenment which was the principal bourgeois critique of feudalism, obscurantism and religion. Were the bourgeoisie simultaneously devout Protestants and atheist rationalists? Part of this problem rests on what precise meaning we will be able to attach to such phrases as 'the most fitting form of religion', 'remnants of a belief', 'succumbed to the ideas of the Enlightenment' and 'reigned supreme'. All these phrases are rather loose, colourful metaphors by which Marx in these passages hinted at the relationship between base and superstructure.

In recent Marxism, it has been writers like Althusser and Poulantzas who have attempted to provide a more precise meaning for this traditional problem of the base/superstructure relationship. It is not necessary to restate the various arguments which we have attempted to spell out in Chapter 1. What we are particularly concerned with in this section is the way in which Poulantzas has attempted to understand the role of religion in feudalism and its demise in capitalism. In *Political Power and Social Classes,* Poulantzas, following certain key quotations from Marx's *Capital,* argues that in pre-capitalist modes of production the direct producers are not completely separated from the means of production. While peasants in feudalism did not have a legal title to their land, they did enjoy possession of the means of production and labour conditions necessary for the production and reproduction of their own means of subsistence. Peasants had customary rights to common pasture, wood-gathering rights in forests and small plots of land within the village commune; they could, at least partially, support themselves in economic terms. This feudal situation is very different from that pertaining in capitalism where the wage labourer is forced to sell his labour power, because he does not have possession of any means of production. In capitalism, this economic situation of the labourer is sufficient to guarantee that he will surrender his labour power and no mechanism other than that of the market is required for the real subordination of the worker in early capitalism. In feudalism, the subordination of the peasant must rely on 'extra-economic factors', namely, ideological and political mechanisms.

Poulantzas on this basis interprets Marx's reference to ideology and politics reigning supreme in terms of the concepts of 'determinance' and 'dominance'. In the ancient world, the economic arrangements within those social formations determined the dominance of the political structure. In feudalism, the economic basis of the social formations determined that ideology (in particular, Catholicism) had the dominant role. In early capitalism, it is the economic structure which is both determinant and dominant, while in monopoly capitalism the political structure (the interventionist state) plays the dominant part within the social formation. This contrast enables Poulantzas to give a special twist to conventional interpretations of remarks by Engels which might suggest hesitation about the general validity of historical materialism. In the famous letter of 1890 to the editor of *Sozialistische Monatshefte*, Engels (Marx and Engels, n.d., pp. 274–5) observed that:

> According to the materialistic conception of history, the ultimately determining element in history is the production and reproduction of real life . . . The economic situation is the basis but the various elements of the superstructure . . . also exercise their influence upon the course of the historical struggles and in many cases preponderate in determining their *form*.

The economic structure is determinant 'in the last instance' in the sense that the general economic conditions of production and reproduction causally determine the role of politics and ideology in society. The economic is not chronologically operative 'in the last instance' but constantly determines the presence and role of other structures (since 'the middle ages could not live on Catholicism'). Because the economic is always determinant, the 'last instance never comes' in that it is important to think of these structures as 'ever-pre-given'.

Apart from their exegetical interest, these observations by Poulantzas do not take us very far in coming to terms with the precise role of ideology in feudalism. What, for example, does Poulantzas mean by 'dominance'? It may mean that it was important that members of the subordinate class (peasants) should be inculcated with a suitable set of beliefs in order to insure the extraction of a surplus in a situation where peasants retained access to the means of production, namely, the land. This sense of dominance unfortunately has many of the connotations of the 'ruling ideas' model according to which one class 'does' something to another class. The second sense in which Poulantzas could be interpreted treats 'dominance' in a functional perspective. To argue that religion (or the ideological structure) is dominant in feudalism would be to claim that it was functionally significant for the integration or maintenance of the system of economic relationships. This interpretation would, however, render Poulantzas's Marxism in a vague form because it would suffer from the general analytical problem of functionalism that it is difficult to isolate an institution which in *not* 'functionally significant'. The third possible meaning of 'dominance' would be that ideology was crucial for securing legal titles to land and hence for securing conditions of existence for the production process in the feudal mode of production. In their attempt to clarify the theory of the structures of the feudal mode of production, it is this third interpretation of the dominance of the ideological structure which Hindess and Hirst have tried to develop.

In *Pre-Capitalist Modes of Production,* Hindess and Hirst reject any notion that 'dominance' in feudalism refers to the subordination of *persons*. They argue (1975, p. 231) that 'dominance'

> provides the conditions of existence of exploitative relations of production, which in turn provide the *social* foundation for the political instance by creating the division between exploiters and exploited – a division internal to the system of production, and thereby creating the ruling class.

In the feudal mode, landlords have legal titles to land but peasants have an effective possession of land. The landlord class secures the economic exploitation of the peasantry in three ways: by controlling the size of the productive units which are allocated to tenants; by controlling the conditions of re-tenancy; and by controlling essential means of production such as pasture lands, water, drainage works and mills. The class conflicts of social formations characterised by the feudal mode were over these conditions of rent and tenancy whereby the landlord class sought to achieve the total subsumption of the peasantry to a condition of subordination. The ability of the landlord class to achieve this control over the peasantry depended on political conditions. This argument enables Hindess and Hirst (1975, p. 232) to establish a reformulation of the dominance/determination thesis:

> The separation of the producer from the means of production, the condition of exploitative relations of production, depends upon political/ideological conditions of existence. The feudal economy supposes the intervention of another instance in order to make the conditions of feudal exploitation possible.

In short, the conditions for the economic exploitation of the peasantry were political and ideological.

There are a number of difficulties with this attempt to reformulate the notion of the importance of 'extra-economic factors' in feudalism. There is, for example, a certain vagueness about ideology and its relationship to the political structure. Hindess and Hirst typically contract the two structures into one in the form 'political/ideological instance'. In practice, they have nothing to say about why ideology (or Catholicism in particular) should play any role at all in the control of units of rent or the landlord monopoly of mills. The separation of the ideological structure from political and economic conditions usually collapses in Althusserian Marxism, because ideology is treated as an aspect of the political state apparatus. The traditional metaphor of ideological superstructure and economic base has been translated into a thesis that political factors are 'conditions of existence' of the economic structure, so that *Pre-Capitalist Modes of Production* virtually ignores the specifically ideological features of the feudal mode of production. There are other issues to do with their conception of politics which are not strictly germane to our discussion of feudalism and ideology but which we can indicate briefly. Their argument comes down to claiming that the economic exploitation of the peasantry presupposes the existence of the state ('the political instance'). The state has two aspects, ideological and repressive, which are not separated in their argument. Since they do not provide a clear argument for the importance of the ideological state apparatus in feudalism, we must assume that the *political* control of the peasantry depends on the repressive apparatus. Are we to assume that the baronial control of drainage is an ideological practice? In our view this political emphasis is perfectly correct, but it is hardly original – it is, for example, central to Weber's analysis of domination (*herrschaftssoziologie*). The difference between Hindess and Hirst on feudalism and Weber on the monopoly of violence would be a question of 'structures' versus 'persons' – the claim that Weber reduces power to a question of interpersonal relationships.

Theories of the Great Divide

With the exception of writers like Goldman (1964) and Birnbaum (1971), the Marxist analysis of religion has not advanced much beyond the insubstantial commentary of Marx, Engels and Kautsky. If we want a more detailed picture of the role of religion in feudalism, we will have to turn to the research of social historians and sociologists. The majority of sociologists of religion hold to what we might call the 'theory of the great divide'. According to this view, before the explosion of population, urbanisation and industrialisation from 1780 onwards English society was Christian in that all social classes lived their lives through the dominant beliefs, symbols and rituals of the church. Modern society is secular because there no longer exists a common, over-arching set of beliefs and moral practices which is capable of providing a moral meaning for individuals within separate social classes. The alternative position which has been until recently the minority view might be called the 'incorrigibility thesis'. In this second position, the argument is that, since English society was never Christian, it could never be secularised. Another version of this argument is that, because 'religion' cannot be given any uniform, coherent meaning, it is impossible to identify any unitary secularisation process. Thus, whether modern Britain is secular depends on what you mean by 'secular', and since this cannot be adequately defined the question of secularity can have no precise meaning. Mediaeval society was incorrigible in the face of Christianisation. Obviously a range of variant forms of these arguments can be identified (Shiner, 1967; Luckmann, 1967; Herberg, 1962; Towler 1974), but these two positions will enable us to specify our own interpretation in precise terms.

Most nineteenth-century sociological perspectives were based upon a 'great divide' theory of history (Burrow, 1970). This characteristic world history was built into the principal dichotomies of ideal-type societies in this period. In British speculative anthropology and sociology Maine's historical jurisprudence was closely associated with the notion of a historical transition from status to contract, while Spencer's evolutionary sociology developed a comparison of 'military society' and 'industrial society'. In Germany, towards the end of the nineteenth century, Tönnies (1887) produced the famous sociological distinction between *gemeinschaft* and *gesellschaft* (Mitzman 1971). Durkheim's comparison of mechanical and organic solidarity was in fact simply one contribution to the long-established French debate (Hayward, 1959) over the problem of solidarity, individualism and the social division of labour. In these various typologies, social stability was identified with common adherence to religious values which were shattered by the onslaught of a new type of society based on rapid technical changes in production, concentrations of large populations around production units and the control of society by secular agencies. While these early sociological ideas contributed in various ways to the contemporary sociology of religion, it was Weber and Troeltsch who established the real foundation for the modern view of the secularisation process.

Although Weber was in principle hostile to any general evolutionary scheme of social change, his sociology does presuppose a 'great divide' because he thought that, while all pre-capitalist societies were founded on a system of authority of a charismatic or traditional variety, capitalist society was legal/rational in terms of law, politics and economic organisation. This historical rationalisation of the world was inextricably bound up with the secularisation of consciousness and values. It is possible to detect three aspects of Weber's theory of secularisation (Fenn, 1969). First, there was the general conception of a process of social disenchantment by which the numinous quality of reality would be replaced by the routine and commonplace. As the world became increasingly dominated by technical norms, the magical and spiritual dimension which gave life purpose and meaning would shrink. The paradox was that as the world became more rationally intelligible so it became less meaningful from a moral and religious standpoint. This paradox was closely connected with Weber's categorical separation of empirical fact and value judgement: 'The fate of an epoch which has eaten of the tree of knowledge is that it must know that we cannot learn the meaning of the world from the results of its analysis, be it ever so perfect' (Weber, 1949, p. 57). The second aspect of secularisation was the fragmentation of human culture into separate watertight compartments. Knowledge became bureaucratised into nice areas within which certain groups of scholars were officially regarded as experts. The single cultural universe of pre-capitalism was shattered by secularisation into a cluster of fragments which have no unified theme. The third aspect of rationalisation and secularisation was the emergence of unresolved value conflicts as the religious absolutes of previous epochs were finally destroyed. The problem of modern man was his inability to choose between alternative values in a society where no moral criteria have any real authority. For Weber, this problem meant the impossibility of authenticity in secular society.

These three themes (rational/technical culture, cultural pluralism and personal authenticity) continue to dominate sociological discussions of secularisation. They are, for example, particularly evident in the sociology of religion of Berger who has focused on the problems raised by pluralism. For Berger (1969), one of the key aspects of secularisation is the creation of psychological uncertainty of commitment of values in societies which are conflictual and pluralistic. Two prominent representatives of this primarily Weberian view of the paradoxical relationship between our ability to know and our capacity to believe are MacIntyre and Wilson. In MacIntyre's *Secularization and Moral Change* it is argued that prior to 1880 there was a moral unity based on a communal way of life. The moral unity was given symbolic expression by religious rituals and symbols, but this underlying moral coherence was eventually shattered by nineteenth-century urbanisation and industrialisation. The moral community was subsequently replaced by cultural pluralism based, not on community, but on social class.

The result was that, since there was no longer any authoritative communal backing for beliefs, the central issues of human life, birth, suffering, death and the hope for a future existence could no longer be properly raised, let alone adequately resolved. It is this loss of moral community which results in the decline of organised religion rather than the death of Christianity which produces moral uncertainty (MacIntyre, 1967; MacIntyre and Ricoeur, 1969).

A similar position has been argued by Wilson (1966). Secularisation takes place at the level of social structure, social culture and personality. Whereas the church was once the dominant institution within the social structure, industrialisation has produced a widespread specialisation and differentiation of social institutions. The church no longer has major public significance and has been relegated to areas of personal, domestic issues such as sexual norms, family life and antiquated *rites de passage*. In cultural terms, the authority of the clergy and theology is replaced by the authority of science and scientific experts. Theology is replaced even in traditional areas of human knowledge such as ethics where the methods and insights of social science increasingly gain ascendency. Secularisation does not mean the complete disappearance of organised religion, but it does mean that religion loses any real social or political significance. Thus, in modern Britain, while the major denominations undergo continual erosion, the younger generation exhibits some preference for the exotic, irrational cults of largely Oriental origin. These cults do not, however, have any real significance since they are predominantly ephemeral, marginal and a-cultural rather than counter-cultural. The very structure of life in industrial society reduces the space within which the divine might operate:

> The modern world is increasingly a rationally-constructed environment. Its technological basis, its electronic equipment, its computers, its laser beams, its pre-stressed concrete, and its mechanical apparatus dominate and organize an ever greater part of human activity. What place is there in this environment for the intervention of the supernatural? (Wilson, 1976, p. 7).

Opposition to the secularisation thesis has been dominated by Martin (1969, 1978). His objections to the conventional view of religious decline can be examined in three separate sections. First, the secularisation thesis is based on a myth that there once was a golden age of faith and in particular the thesis has to generate a utopian history of the mediaeval period as the high point of Christianity. Secondly, the thesis has an 'over-secularised concept of man' in modern society. In opposition to this perspective, Martin draws on a range of empirical research to stress the presence of supernatural, superstitious and irrational elements of belief and practice in modern industrial society (Abercrombie *et al.*, 1970). Sociologists have tended to exaggerate the decline or weakness of organised Christianity in secular society (Martin, 1967). Finally, Martin (1978) has drawn attention to major contrasts in the political importance of Christianity in different industrial societies, from pluralism in the United States, to dualism in Northern Ireland, to virtual monopoly in Italy. The secularisation process in these societies is clearly very different so that it is sociologically naive to equate a uniform process of religious decline with a uniform process of industrialisation.

Martin's criticism of the utopian image of mediaeval society as the great age of Christian dominance has recently drawn support from Goodridge (1975), who has attacked the secularisation thesis on the basis of evidence from the social history of mediaeval France and Italy. In the writing of social history, especially the religious history of mediaeval Europe, two dangers must be avoided. These are, first, the characterisation of a period in terms of the activities of elite groups and, secondly, the characterisation of an epoch through the behaviour of 'geographically localised groups'. To depict the mediaeval societies of Europe as 'religious' is to treat the religious behaviour of a small, urban, literate elite as typical of the whole society. It is also to accept a mythical history of pre-revolutionary France which was developed by Catholic romanticism against the secularising effects which the events of 1789 had in Europe as a whole. Recent historical research in France, Britain and Italy – by Marcilhacy, Thomas and Murray – presents a very different picture of poorly educated clergy, indifferent peasantry, the persistence of magical practices, superstition and periodic heretical uprisings. The conclusions of this religious sociology (rather than sociology of religion) have been most systematically enunciated by Le Bras (1963, p. 445):

> As much as it seems certain that the action of bishops and monks humanised the Barbarians, preserved the ancient culture, lifted the level of civilisation, so it seems also doubtful that Christianity was really known and lived by brutal and poorly educated societies.

The peasantry remained incorrigible (Martin, 1973). They were largely untouched by the civilising role of the church throughout the Middle Ages and they remained the main vehicle of magical, irrational practices up to the Counter-Reformation and the era of the Protestant evangelical movements of the nineteenth century when the peasantry as a class was transformed into urban wage labourers. Although we do not wish to accept the values which are an inevitable feature of the religious sociology of Le Bras and his followers, they have made a crucial contribution to our understanding of the fundamental *weakness* of the ideological apparatus of mediaeval Catholicism. It was precisely in the rural hinterlands where the vast majority of the population lived, outside the control and cultural influence of the great cities, that the church was at its weakest in terms of the quality of its priests, the regularity of sermons and the low level of ritual participation generally. The cultural dominance of the religion of the ruling class was limited by the weakness of the apparatus of ideological communication and transmission.

Feudal Culture

Having examined both Marxist and sociological versions of religion in feudal society and its inevitable secularisation under capitalism, we are now in a position to state our own argument concerning the notion of a 'dominant' or 'common culture' under feudal conditions. The secularisation thesis of Marxism and sociology is correct in arguing that Christianity was the dominant belief system and a central institution of feudal society, but it was dominant *only* in the sense of being influential among the ruling class. The incorrigibility thesis is also correct in arguing that the majority of the population (the subordinate class of peasantry) were not culturally incorporated by the dominant culture of orthodox, literate Catholicism, because the apparatus of education and cultural transmission was weak. What functions, then, *did* Catholicism fulfil in mediaeval society for the dominant class? There were two functions. First, Christianity integrated and unified the dominant class behind a common set of beliefs. In particular, the Christian view of monarch, chivalry and mercantile wealth minimised intra-class conflicts between various strata of the feudal ruling class. Secondly, the church's teaching on sexuality, monogamy and family duty gave some religious backing to the conservation of property within the system of noble families. The crucial feature here is that the moral/ confessional content of the dominant Christian belief/ritual system controlled women and guaranteed the role of the family as a system of contract by which land was accumulated. To argue that Christian ethics constituted the dominant ideology of the dominant feudal class is not to say that it was always and uniformly accepted by this class. We will in this chapter have to examine various aspects of deviance within this social class. For one thing, knights were themselves often illiterate, but they were far more systematically exposed (through the verbal instruction of the sermon) to the religious ideology of chivalry and honour. Furthermore, to argue the case for the dominance of Christianity is not to say that Christianity was in some way uniquely fitted for this role. What was important was that the dominant class should largely believe the same thing. Any system of belief which contained a strong sense of the importance of sexual norms and the family would have integrated the dominant class at this general level.

In presenting this argument we are criticising two common themes within Marxist treatment of ideology. Our thesis runs counter to the banal view of class struggle in the *Communist Manifesto,* where Marx and Engels quite incorrectly suggested that the 'revolutionary reconstitution of society at large' was in feudalism achieved as an outcome of the class struggle between 'lord and serf' and that the 'history of all hitherto existing society is the history of class struggles'. According to our thesis, what threatened feudalism as a system was not the conflict between lord and serf, which was admittedly a major feature of feudal society, but the conflicts within the ruling class. Provided the dominant class remained relatively united, the revolts of peasants against conditions of rent could be contained within existing socioeconomic arrangements. We also need to avoid the conspiratorial implications of some aspects of the claim in the *German Ideology* that the ruling ideas of each age have been the ideas of its ruling class. The lords were separated from the peasants by religion, language, culture and morality. The bridges between those two cultures and efforts by mendicant monks to cross those cultural bridges were few and far between. Peasants were universally despised in Ireland as *criadhairi* ('clayey ones') or *daoscar* ('dregs'), in English as 'clod-hopper' or 'cloddy', or in French as *paysan,* which carries the meaning of cultural rusticity outside the cultivated life of Paris; in Italy, the *popolani* were mere 'dogs'. Not only was the apparatus of transmission weak, but little effort was made to incorporate the peasantry systematically into the dominant culture precisely because *le paysan* lived outside cultured existence.

If the peasants were not controlled by the ideological apparatus of the church, then we need to provide some alternative explanation of how exactly the peasantry was contained by the dominant class. We must be careful, however, not to exaggerate the degree to which the dominant class could adequately control the peasantry.

The mediaeval period was one punctured by constant agrarian turmoil and disruption. These popular revolts under feudalism were closely connected with rapid changes in the demographic structure of society and hence in the land: labour ratio. In the century before the Black Death (1348-9) in England, landlords had a decisive advantage over the peasantry because they controlled the supply of land which was in scarcity. In the century after the Black Death, tenants appear to have extracted considerable advantages out of lords, given the scarcity of labour in relation to land. The period around 1378 and 1382 was a particularly good illustration of social conflicts relating to the precarious balance of people and land which periodically resulted in catastrophic famines (Mollat and Wolff, 1973). These popular revolutions of fourteenth-century Europe were, however, unusual in their dramatic intensity and significance. More characteristic of the Middle Ages were the constant disputes between individuals or between families rather than between social groups over customary rights and practices (Hilton, 1975).

Given these precautionary comments on social conflicts in feudal societies, what were the social mechanisms by which the peasantry was subordinated? The fact that the dominant class could not adequately impose its culture on the peasantry also works in reverse in terms of peasant consciousness. Given the general problem of communication in a society based on isolated rural communes, there was no coherent peasant class consciousness which could have mobilised the peasantry against the landlords as a class of oppressors. Material conditions ruled out the development of anything but a localised sense of identity and solidarity. However, even with a definite class consciousness, the peasantry was controlled by the landlord's hold over tenancy of land and by the landlord's monopoly of other means of production, such as mills and dikes. These features of economic control were themselves largely dependent on the superior military strength of the landlords as a class. Hunger, drudgery and disease did the rest. Our argument, then, is that the 'extra-economic' factors which Marxists claim were necessary in feudalism for the subordination of peasants had very little to do with the 'political/ideological instance' and a great deal to do with force, the threat of force and the dull compulsion of the economics of everyday life.

We are now in a position to present the historical evidence for the view that in feudalism the dominant ideology integrated the dominant class rather than controlled the subordinate class. In order to emphasise what might be termed the 'ideological gap' which existed between social classes in feudalism, we will consider three candidates for a 'dominant ideology' (religious beliefs and practices): namely, theodicy, theocratic kingship and the sacrament of penance. While these aspects of feudal culture look like suitable ideological items for the subordination of peasants, their real effect was the coherence of the dominant class. The next step in our presentation of evidence is to consider the sexual and moral norms of the dominant ideology relating to the conservation of family property. Our main focus here will be on the religious theory of chivalry, the concept of honour and the development of Courtly Love poetry.

Most conventional sociologies of religion contain the assumption that religion contributed to the ideological incorporation of subordinate classes by developing theodicies. It has become standard practice to quote the old adage about

> The rich man in his castle,
> The poor man at his gate –
> God made them high and lowly,
> And ordered their estate.

In technical terms, a 'theodicy' is a shorthand for the defence of God's justice and righteousness in the presence of sin (Hick, 1966). The term itself first occurred in a letter of Leibniz in 1697, but the problem of theodicy has exercised the minds of theologians from the foundation of Christianity. The great fountainhead of Christian theodicean thought was Augustine, who laid the basis for the Catholic analysis of divine purpose via the work of Aquinas. Augustine accepted the theology of the Adamic myth as a clear account of human original sin which he combined with the Platonic principle of plenitude to explain the harmonious fullness of the universe. This plenitude principle says that the universe is full, varied and complex. The existence of sin, especially metaphysical and natural evil, is part of that very complexity and variety (Bloomfield, 1952). Disaster, disease and death are examples of the plentifulness of the created universe. Theodicies, however, were not simply explanations of natural plenitude; they were also explanations of human and social variety and diversity. These aspects of Christian theodicy were woven into what Lovejoy (1936) regarded as one of the most important metaphors in the history of Western thought, namely, the 'great chain of being'.

This metaphor gives an account of the variety in nature and society as an illustration of the fundamental harmony of the universe by arguing that all grades of conscious life from insects to angels are linked to God by an infinite number of sections in a chain. The basic propositions of the great chain metaphor were that the universe is infinitely rich and plentiful, but each aspect of this complex reality is ordered hierarchically. Intelligent life is ranked closer to God than the inanimate world; the spiritual grades of angels are closer to God than man. There is, however, no break in the chain, so that nothing is excluded from God by virtue of the principle of complete continuity. The metaphor was also associated with the optimistic social philosophies of Leibniz, Locke and Pope because it showed that this world is the best of all possible worlds. In mediaeval philosophy, the Christian and the Platonic elements of the metaphor were often in a state of conflict precisely over the 'necessitarian optimism' of the plenitude principle. If God had literally created the best possible world to the exclusion of any alternative world, then God's creative will was limited by its own created objects. If God had not created the best possible world then the principle of plenitude had to be abandoned. This logical problem reached its climax in the heretical implications of Abelard's theology. Regardless of these internal problems of the doctrine, the great chain of being does appear to present an ideology which was perfectly suited to justifying the social grades within feudal society as an outcome of God's infinite justice and wisdom. Each class and every individual has a place in the scheme of things which has been ordained by God. The order of society depends upon each person accepting that place in society assigned to them by birth. The origin of all disorder was located in cosmic acts of disobedience by Satan and Adam who rebelled against their place in the universe by seeking after an equivalence with their Maker.

What evidence is there that such a doctrine was ever accepted by the European peasantry? It must be noted that the moral teaching of the church did not have the overtly conservative implications which sociologists like Berger have attached to religious theodicies. The sermons of the fourteenth century, and in particular those of John Ball, were full of severe condemnation of the egoism of the nobles, the gluttony of the clergy and the neglect of the poor. The research of Owst (1961) suggests that these sermons did have a definite effect on consciousness and that they inspired the social criticisms of the nobility and clergy which are present in Langland's *Piers Plowman* (1362) and Chaucer's *Canterbury Tales* (after 1387). Apart from the revolutionary implications of Ball's famous question – 'When Adam delved and Eve span, where was then the gentleman?' – the majority of these moralising sermons were critical of the moral behaviour of the dominant class, while teaching the poor the virtues of patience and acceptance of their place within the social order. As Mollat and Wolff (1973, p. 306) summarised this theological message, the sermon

> called upon men, whatever their station in life, to struggle against the vices peculiar to their social class. It discouraged them from seeking to rise in the hierarchy, which could be achieved only by great pride and avarice.

The sins of pride and avarice were two of the Seven Deadly Sins and were constantly attacked as causes of many lesser sins (Cuming and Baker, 1972).

The conservative social dimension of this moral critique was clearly illustrated in the popular preaching of the Dominican Humbert de Romans (1200–77). The Dominican Order had a special mission for training preachers to reach the uneducated rural poor and its handbooks for preachers (*De arte predicandi*) are a good guide to the state of religion in France and Italy in the thirteenth century. Humbert observed that the poor were covetous of the wealth of the dominant class and regarded them as 'the lucky ones' rather than rich because of their natural talents. While the church taught the virtue of asceticism, some poor 'blaspheme against God for having made them poor' (Murray, 1974, p. 308). If the typical sin of the poor was envy, Humbert criticised the rich for hard-heartedness in almsgiving and general neglect of charity towards the poor.

The moral sermons of the mendicant orders of the thirteenth and fourteenth centuries provide evidence that the friars did have a conception of the obligations of the various strata in society and that, although they were prepared to criticise the rich, their social message was conservative. Taking a more general perspective, however, the contact between church and peasantry was often minimal. The evidence is that the poor did not attend church regularly, did not hear the sermons, did not take the sacraments and were ignorant of the basic message of the Christian faith. Humbert himself complained that even when a crowd gathered to hear his sermons they kept up a constant distracting chatter. The great theodicy debate and the theory of the great chain of being were too literate and intellectualised to reach the poor.

There are many dimensions to the cultural separation which existed between the dominant and the subordinate classes in mediaeval Europe. In terms of language, the peasant spoke a vernacular language, while the church adhered to Latin and the court to French. The church did communicate with the poor through mimetic performances of Bible stories and through vernacular performances under the control of the craft guilds such as the Chester and York cycles. This popular tradition did not, however, become fully developed until after 1500 and this dramatic medium does not constitute a massive educational apparatus (Schlauch, 1967). Similar patterns of linguistic separation existed in Mediterranean France into the sixteenth century. In the eastern regions, the *langue d'oil* of the nobility was contrasted with the Romance dialects of the ordinary people. The Massif Central remained the haven of the *langue d'oc* dialect and culture into the seventeenth century. In France and England, the elite of the dominant class would often be fluent in several languages and court poets developed in the fifteenth century the 'macaronic poem' which required a special skill in the dove-tailing of several languages within the same poem (Davies, ed., 1963). It must be admitted that the church had at various times made definite efforts to close the gap between the two cultures. The Fourth Lateran Council brought in reforms which aimed at improving the standard of education among the clergy and the laity, emphasising at the same time the great importance of teaching in the vernacular. These efforts were less than successful. By the end of the dominance of feudalism in Europe, the effect of the invention of printing, the Reformation and Enlightenment, was to *increase* rather than to reduce this cultural separation of rich and poor (Burke, 1978).

This language barrier was reinforced by very high levels of illiteracy. The research of Le Roy Ladurie and, more generally, of the Annales school, into the peasants of Languedoc showed that nine out of ten rural proletarians were 'spiritual strangers to the civilisation of the written word' and were thereby strangers also to the religious revolution of the sixteenth century which involved a return to scriptural Christianity. The peasants of Languedoc 'were as allergic to culture as they were to the Reformation, and to the rudiments of lay learning as they were to the revival of sacred learning' (Ladurie, 1974, p. 162). The absence of the most basic literary skills – such as personal signatures – was the rule throughout mediaeval Europe, but this illiteracy was not a feature peculiar to the laity alone. The great reforms of Tridentine Catholicism were intended to establish as a universal pattern the existence of a resident, celibate and literate clergy who would win over for the first time the great pagan regions of Europe. These priests were in turn to generate a new literate laity familiar with the basic teaching of Christianity and faithful to its rituals. The historical inquiry of Le Roy Ladurie and Delumeau amounts to the assertion that Catholicism was the *minority* religion of Europe in the Middle Ages. While their work can be criticised, there is ample support for their view that the urban elite was a practising, orthodox Catholic social group, but the rural majority preserved their pre-Christian beliefs, festivals and practices. The urban dominant class had their priests; the rural poor of Languedoc, Brittany, Lancashire, Yorkshire and Norfolk had their sorcerers, witchcraft, pagan rites and folk culture.

In his monumental *Religion and the Decline of Magic,* Thomas (1971) has demonstrated a pervasive indifference and hostility to institutionalised Christianity in sixteenth and seventeenth-century England, combined with popular adherence to folk religiosity, witchcraft and demonology. The attempt by the Reformation to drive a clear wedge between the magical practice and the proper rituals of the church, between magical beliefs and Christian supernaturalism was, as the court verdicts and contemporary observation testified, a failure. So long as illness was regarded, at least potentially, as the consequence of some divine or supernatural causation, it was difficult to distinguish the Christian use of prayers to bring about a recovery of health and the use of Christian prayers by persons accused of witchcraft to restore the health of their neighbours. One reason for the eventual decline of formal accusations of witchcraft in courts of law and the repeal of the Witchcraft Act in 1736 was the growing scepticism of the intelligentsia of the dominant class as to the possibility of witchcraft, which made successful prosecutions in the courts difficult and then impossible (Trevor-Roper, 1967). A similar wave of witchcraft and demonic possession swept through France at the end of the sixteenth century. It was especially prevalent in the isolated, mountainous regions of Languedoc, the Rouergue, Pyrenees and the Jura. In the Rouergue around 1595 'sorcerers reigned unchecked in the region, thanks to the crass ignorance of the natives. These coarse, ungodly mountain folk were ignorant of the Bible, and because they lived in isolated farmsteads or hamlets far from any church, they did not go to Mass and were easy prey to every sort of demonic obsession' (Le Roy Ladurie, 1974, pp. 205–6). These observations support the principle that the witchcraft craze of the sixteenth century had a 'mountain origin', but in more general terms witchcraft was prevalent in all remote areas where the control of the church was weak and superficial. The Alps and Pyrenees were the centres of demonic possession, but areas such as Brittany were also infected by the witch-craze (Delumeau, ed, 1969). The importance of these witches' Sabbaths was that they represented an inversion of the culture of the dominant class. In the Black Mass in the region of Labourd in 1609, the Catholic Mass was celebrated in reverse by a priest who had his face to the ground while elevating a black Host. In Catalan witchcraft in the same period, Latin prayers were recited backwards, while in the Midi the Feast of Fools, Mass-bouffe and Mass-farce turned the church's sacred ritual into a public burlesque. In the absence of a real revolutionary strategy, the peasantry had to content themselves with a purely farcical portrayal of the idea that 'the first shall be last'.

These religious attempts to justify the social world through the theodicy of the great chain of being were at best only partially and spasmodically successful. Throughout the Middle Ages, despite numerous reforms of the ecclesiastical structure of Christianity, the majority of the population was cut off from the church by language, literacy, learning and liturgy. They stuck incorrigibly to their own folk, pre-Christian traditions and periodically inverted the symbolic world of the church in an orgy of satanic possession. Just as the apparatus for transmitting a general theodicy was underdeveloped, so the possibility of employing the theocratic theory of kingship and the sacrament of penance as a system of social control over the subordinate class was limited by the same social circumstances.

One important component of the 'extra-economic' structures of feudalism was the law. Writing about the legal apparatus of the feudal social system, Ullmann (1965, p. 19) observed that

> The dominant theme in the European Middle Ages was that supplied by Christian cosmology: it was the christocentric standpoint which impressed itself upon all classes of society, from the lowliest villein to the most powerful king or emperor. And it is this standpoint which explains the immersion of medieval governments and their laws in the Christian theme.

The system of mediaeval law was rooted in the social location of the king and in his contradictory role as simultaneously a theocratic and a feudal lord. The mediaeval conception of the origin of law was based on two antagonistic principles. In the first, the ascending principle, the king received his authority from the community and he was linked to his baronial peers by feudal relations of mutual obligation. According to this 'populist' view, the king was part of the community. In the alternative theory, the descending principle, the king was God's representative on earth and existed outside the control of the community as a consequence of kingly charisma. This descending principle had its ideological origins in the Christian theology of sacramental authority, the theory of papal authority, and in the sacral nature of Germanic kingship. The descending principle of kingly authority was a sort of anti-feudal view of kingship since it denied that the king had feudal obligations *vis-à-vis* his feudal peers (the barons). Similarly, no contractual obligations existed between king and community. In the theocratic, descending conception of kingship the relationship between king and community was one of obedience rather than loyalty and fidelity. In the theocratic perspective, power rested in the office of kingship rather than in the person so that the king could not be held responsible for failing to adhere to feudal contracts – 'the king can do no wrong'.

Mediaeval kings thus contained within their royal personages a legal contradiction. As feudal landlords, they had contractual relationships with their barons and the king was simply one among many. As a sacred person, however, the king had no enforceable obligations in respect of his peers. Indeed, the king had no peers. The political history of the Middle Ages can be interpreted as a struggle in which kings attempted to enforce the theocratic, descending principle and barons attempted to assert the feudal, ascending, contractual nature of kingship. In the period of the Angevin kings (1154–1215), for example, the theocratic definition of kingship was reinforced by the impact of Roman law which increased partly as a result of England's increased trade with Bologna, the centre of Roman law (P. Anderson, 1974). King John's government sought to realise the complete version of the Roman theocratic *imperium* with the doctrine 'what pleases the king has the force of law'. John's exactions and disseizins brought about strong opposition from the barons who, on the basis of their view of customary law (*leges Anglorum* and *lex terrae*), tried to force John to accept the ascending feudal definition of royal power. The result of these struggles was the settlement enshrined in Magna Carta, which placed a definite limit on the growth of state absolutism in England.

In the theocratic theory of kingship and in the conception of criminal jurisdiction as 'the king's peace', we appear to have a very clear illustration of the dominance of a religious perspective. But in what sense was the dominance of the law an example of the centrality of Christianity to European culture, as Ullman would have us believe? If the descending principle had been accepted fully by all strata in society, then presumably the legal apparatus of the state would have been greatly strengthened by the fact that the law was sacred. Ullman, however, suggested that if 'the less articulate strata of medieval society' had any view of the law at all, then they tended to adhere to the ascending 'populist' view of law-making. The real issue here is that the theory of kingship was not for popular consumption; it was largely the outcome of an ideological struggle within the dominant class over the issue of whether the king was unique or merely a landlord with baronial peers. Ullman himself admitted that this was the case: 'these populist manifestations on the lower and lowest levels of medieval society were of little concern to the kings, princes and popes; in themselves they were harmless and not influential' (1965, p. 24). These complex mediaeval systems of jurisprudence and constitutional theory were not, therefore, illustrations of a dominant ideology in the sense of uniting classes together under the control of the culture of the ruling class. They were fundamentally codes of behaviour for members of the dominant class in their relations with each other, not with the peasantry. Magna Carta was not a major advance in democracy, but a device for unifying the dominant class around a common legal document against the disturbing effects of arbitrary royal power.

It is, however, the sacrament of penance which above all promises to furnish us with an example of an 'ideological practice' which had the consequence of achieving the subordination of the peasantry to the ideological dominance of the landlords, via the agency of the confessors of the church at the village level. In the early church, confession by the laity was irregular, infrequent and private. Confession was normally offered once in a person's life and certain sins, fornication, homicide and idolatry, could not be absolved (Lea, 1896; Bieler, ed., 1963; Trinkaus and Obermann, eds, 1974; B. S. Turner, 1977*a*). By the eighth century, certain rules existed, such as the rule of Chrodegang of Metz, which ordered regular confession for monks and confession of the laity during Lent. The role of confession was radically changed by the Lateran Canon of 1216 which made confessions regular, obligatory and public, and also gave priests the sole authority to hear confessions. In order to aid priests in the work of confessing their laity, encyclopaedic *summas* of casuistry were published as systematic catalogues of sins and their punishments. Approximately twenty-five of these major works were published between 1216 and 1520 (when Luther burned the *Summa Angelica* at the gates of Wittenburgh) for the guidance of the intellectual elite of the church. These new regulations greatly increased the extent of ecclesiastical control over penance and they are to be seen against the background of the church's efforts to lift both the laity and clergy out of the illiterate, lax, quasi-Christianity of the thirteenth century. In conjunction with the thirteenth-century revolution in the sacrament of penance, there developed a system of indulgence. From the time of Cardinal Hugh of St Cher in 1230, it was held that as a result of Christ's atonement the church was a Treasury of Merit which could distribute this grace in aid of sinners. It was this system of indulgence which resulted ultimately in the commercialisation and malpractice celebrated in Chaucer's *Pardoner's Tale*.

It is evident that, whatever the religious theory asserted about the spiritually cathartic effects of a contrite confession, absolution and satisfaction, the confessional was intended to be a form of social control. Thus, Tentler observed that the point of these mediaeval *summas* 'was to represent law in the forum of penance and make conformity to the regulations of the hierarchy a strict matter of conscience' (1974, p. 117). Since Aquinas, *conscientia* has been treated as a private moral judge sitting within the 'Court of Conscience' of each individual and passing sentence over private actions. Much later, in Milton's *Paradise Lost* God declared to man: 'I will place within them as a guide/My umpire conscience' (Lewis, 1961). The church aimed at producing both an external, objective system of control in the sacrament of penance and an internal subjective mechanism in terms of the guilty conscience. Aubrey looked back to the period when the Catholic confessional operated as a time of moral stability. He wrote: 'Then were the consciences of the people kept in so great awe by confession that just dealing and virtue was habitual' (Thomas, 1971, p. 155). Most seventeenth-century Puritan reformers did, however, depend heavily on existing Catholic casuistry in the development of their own pastoral and moral theology (Wood, 1952).

These surveys of the 'compulsion to confession' and the role of guilt in social control are largely about the theoretical importance of the sacrament of penance, whereas in practice confession as a system of social control was not especially reliable and effective. Aubrey was paying service to the myth of the Middle Ages as an age of faith, while mediaeval bishops themselves constantly complained about the difficulty of getting the laity to regular confession. Roberto da Lecci thought that his parishioners who had not confessed for twenty years or more were a 'venomous synagogue of hell' (Lea, 1896, p. 250). Even if we assumed that parishioners made a regular confession, then most lay people would have made three or more confessions every year (unless they were dying) and these confessions would typically have been short and 'statistical' rather than drawn-out investigations of the inner self.

The effectiveness of confession as a system of social control was limited by the abuses and laxity which crept into the administration. The history of penance is one of decreasing severity, and the widespread availability of commercialised indulgence certainly meant that penance was not a particularly *punitive* means of control. The credibility of the system of indulgences, and thereby the whole sacrament of penance, must have been undermined by its commercialisation, at least in the eyes of the educated minority. The unedifying spectacle at the end of *The Pardoner's Tale* between 'sire Hoost' and the Pardoner:

Thou woldest make me kisse thyn olde breech,
And swere it were a relyk of a seint,
Though it were with thy fundement depeint!

is one fairly robust indication of the attitude of pilgrims to the
abuses which followed from the theory of the church as a Treasury
of Merit (Chaucer, 1935, p. 23). While the rural laity appears to have
been highly irregular in its attendance at confession, the full force
of ecclesiastical control over the dominant class was limited by the
ability of the dominant class to select its own confessors. It is, however, particularly difficult to interpret the effect of the confessional
on different social classes. The ability of the princes to select their
own confessors might have meant that the nobility was more exposed
to the influence of the church than was the case for the peasantry.
Similarly, the apparent laxity of Catholic teaching on sin (especially
in Scotist sacramental theology) could be said to have helped the
church come to terms with different and changing social circumstances. The problem of interpreting this ambiguous evidence was
revealed much later in the eighteenth century by the conflict between
Jansenists and Jesuits, when the latter were attacked for their apparent moral permissiveness. By contrast, moderates thought that any
attempt to use confessors as a moral police force would keep the
laity away from the church in droves. Radical secularists thought
that the confessional was influential and tended to corrupt the young
by exposing them to sins of which they would otherwise be innocent
(Groethuysen, 1968; Zeldin, ed., 1970). During the Middle Ages what
does appear clear is that attendance by the rural peasantry at confession was irregular and infrequent for the same reasons that the
peasantry absented itself from the Easter communion and other
festivals (Adam, 1964; Le Roy Ladurie, 1975). If any class was
exposed to the apparatus of the sacrament of penance, then it was
the dominant class itself. While the peasantry had a short, statistical
shrift, the women of the dominant class had their spiritual directors
and the princes their personal confessors.

Having argued that the Catholicism of the Middle Ages was not
the 'dominant ideology' under feudalism, we now have to consider
the effects of Catholic Christianity on the dominant class. Two issues
which turn out to be closely connected stand out in the teaching of
the mediaeval church. The first issue was the problem of coming to
terms with the rise of professional men of violence (knights) in the
aftermath of the Viking invasions in the second half of the ninth
century, the Carolingian dynastic wars and the confrontation with
Islam. The second issue was the moral behaviour required of knights
in particular and of the dominant class as a whole, finding its

religious expression in the notion of religious chivalry and its poetic expression through the medium of Courtly Love poetry. Feudal Europe can be said to have been divided into three classes – those who fought, those who prayed and those who tilled the land (Rosenwein and Little, 1974). The religious conception of chivalry attempted to establish some *modus vivendi* between the fractions of the dominant class (the secular and the ecclesial). In drawing a parallel between the asceticism of the monk and the asceticism of the warrior, the dominant ideology provided coherence for the dominant class. At the same time, the church's teaching on sexuality and family life attempted to curb the rape and pillage associated with warfare, but it also aimed to preserve the family structure as a system of contracts producing a stable mechanism for the transmission of feudal landed property.

Rape, plunder and warfare were initially incompatible with the ethos of brotherly love which characterised the creed of orthodox Christianity. Early mediaeval illustrations of tournaments, for example, depict the dead knights being carried off to hell by attendant devils (Barber, 1970). However, with the development of the Benedictine rule under Cluniac spirituality, the church came to terms with the existence of organised violence by accepting that wars were to be fought only by properly constituted authorities. The various penitential systems of Western Christianity elaborated the appropriate penances for killings which were the result of warfare conducted by anointed kings. In the tenth and eleventh centuries it was possible for knights to provide donations for the saying of prayers for their souls. St Odo's *Collationes* and *Vita Geraldi*, while condemning violence, were forced to accept the fact that the church had a peace-keeping function which could only be discharged by the use of force. Lay violence was justified if it was exercised against the enemies of church and community. Religious norms, under the title 'Truce and Peace of God', proscribed war on certain days and attempted to protect non-combatants (women, children, clergy and peasantry). These edicts outlined what might be termed the negative side of the culture of religious chivalry. The positive side sought to depict knighthood as a religious calling in the same way that sixteenth-century Protestantism turned entrepreneurship into a religiously legitimated vocation.

The spiritualisation of knighthood can be traced back to the sermons of Pope Urban II on the eve of the First Crusade who legitimised knighthood under the constraints of ecclesiastical regulation. Conceptions of religious chivalry were developed in the middle of the twelfth century by John of Salisbury, who stressed the importance of the 'soldier's oath' as a commitment to serve prince and community loyally. In condemning the unruly knights of his own day, he asked what was required of a duly ordained soldiery and answered (Dickinson, 1927, p. 119):

> To defend the church, to assail infidelity, to venerate the priesthood, to protect the poor from injuries, to pacify the province, to pour out their blood for their brothers (as the formula of their oath instructs them), and, if need be, to lay down their lives.

Only men who belong to this order of knighthood and keep the promises given in their oath are true knights. Writers like John of Salisbury and Stephen of Fougeres (*Livres des manières*) produced highly intellectualised versions of this theology of knighthood. These ideas of loyalty to church and state were popularised through the medium of the *chansons de geste*, such as the *Chanson de Roland, Chanson de Guillaume* and *Cantar de mio Cid*, which emerged out of the struggle with the Muslims in Europe (Arnold and Guillaume, 1931). In addition, the various handbooks for preachers suggested appropriate sermons for knights which would drive home the message of virtuous chivalry. A good illustration of this material is the handbook of Alan of Lille from the early thirteenth century (Lecoy de la Marche, 1886).

The ideology of religious chivalry was an attempt to weld together the ecclesiastical and secular branches of the dominant class. It was also designed to prevent knights from tearing their own society to shreds and to direct them outward against the enemies of the church. The church's teaching on welfare paid little attention to peasants, apart from recommending patience in the face of rape and destruction, and hope for a future salvation. But this was a very minor, insignificant aspect of the teaching which was specifically aimed at changing the behaviour of knights to make it conform to Christian norms. This teaching was not, however, entirely effective for the same reason that the church was in general an ineffectual system of ideological control in the Middle Ages. The church attempted to clothe the secular profession of war in a religious garb but constantly came up against an alternative code of honour, pride in arms and the desire for fame and power in this world. In the collection of *chansons de croisade* and in the lyrical poems of the troubadours, there is abundant evidence (part opposition, part penetration) of the religious and the secular conceptions of honour:

> To conquer glory by fine deeds and escape hell; what count or king could ask more? No more is there need to be tortured or shaved and lead a hard life in the most strict order if we can

revenge the shame which the Turks have done us. Is this not truly to conquer at once land and sky, reputation in the world and with God? (Jeanroy, 1934, Vol. 2, p. 208)

While some ideas of the clergy on chivalry, such as the prohibitions on attacking women, children, clergy and nuns, appear to have gained acceptance, other components of the church's teaching about homicide or about particular issues such as tournaments appear to have gained no support on the part of the class of knights. The impact of the church's teaching on chivalry in the early Middle Ages is probably best summarised in the study by Painter (1957, p. 91), who concluded his chapter on religious chivalry with this observation:

> it seems clear that the ideas of religious chivalry were current among the nobles of mediaeval France and may to some slight extent have modified their ethical conceptions. But it is certain that they never became so dominant in the feudal mind that the ideal of knighthood propounded by the church replaced the one developed by the knights themselves. The men of the thirteenth fourteenth and fifteenth centuries who were admired by their contemporaries as models of knighthood were not perfect knights according to the ecclesiastical ideas.

Painter's argument in relation to *this* aspect of mediaeval chivalric ideology need not be too damaging for our general thesis that the dominant ideology of feudalism provided coherence for the dominant class rather than subordination of the peasantry. At least religious chivalry provides a good illustration of a component of the dominant ideology which treated the peasantry as irrelevant and which was aimed at the ideological indoctrination of a particular group within the ruling class. To recognise that this 'indoctrination' was only partly successful is merely to point once more to the fact that the church was not a powerful ideological apparatus. In the feudal period it is easy (by comparison with advanced capitalism, as Durkheim recognised in *The Division of Labour in Society*) *to identify* the dominant ideology, as a pervasive, articulate set of beliefs and institutions. It is much less easy, by comparison with advanced capitalism where social research gives some rough indication of effectivity, to judge the success of these doctrines in controlling the agents of the ruling class. While Painter, Hilton and others appear to show that the church was not noticeably successful in controlling the behaviour of the nobility, it may be that religious ideas provided an important vehicle through which *changes* in dominant beliefs could be worked out (Hilton, 1966). For instance, when the dominance of the profession of knighthood began to decline with the slow development of urban markets, trade and merchants in the fourteenth century, the spirituality of the Benedictines gave way to the spirituality of the Franciscans. At the same time, the traditional preoccupation with the moral dilemmas of warfare changed to a new preoccupation with the problems of money, usury and trade. The religious symbolism of the Franciscan confessional corresponded nicely with the new world of commerce. Whereas Benedictine monks provided a religious teaching by which organised violence could be legitimated, the Franciscan friars were able to make these new forms of power based on commercial strength socially acceptable to the ruling class. This feature of mediaeval religious belief

> involved the Christianizing of an activity that had been seen as wholly exploitative and therefore morally unacceptable. In both (warfare and commerce) instances this activity was the occupation of the dominant class of a sector of society . . . Other sectors of society had not been aware of the moral problems of their age and the monks and friars joined with them in working out for the ruling classes an acceptable version of the previously objectionable activities. (Rosenwein and Little, 1974, pp. 31–2)

The dominant ideology can thus be seen as a response of the feudal intelligentsia within the church to the structural changes in society which were having effects on the moral consciousness of the dominant class as a whole.

One objection to this view is that our illustrations so far, theodicy, sacrament of penance and chivalry, are ideally suited to our thesis that it is the dominant class which is committed to the beliefs and practices of the dominant ideology. There must be some features of the life of the nobility over which the church appeared to have had no control. For example, knights were associated not only with honour as an ethos but also with Courtly Love which in its celebration of adultery appears to contradict flatly the whole Christian tradition. How can the celebration of adultery serve to integrate the dominant class behind a commitment to the family as a mechanism for the transmission of wealth? Our argument here is that Courtly Love recognised that sexual passion could only exist outside marriage precisely because holy wedlock *was* an economic contract between families.

Courtly Love poetry emerged towards the end of the eleventh century in Provence under the influence of minstrel tradition and the Arabic lyric poetry of Islamic Spain. The central themes of this new poetic idiom were humility, courtesy, adultery and the Religion of Love (Lewis, 1936). Whereas in the southern French tradition, platonic, unsatisfied, unrequited love between knight and ladies of noble birth was esteemed, in the northern tradition, under the influence of Ovid's *Ars amatoria* and Andrew the Chaplain's *De amore*, sexual intercourse came to be regarded as a necessary component of romantic, courtly love. In England an outstanding example of this genre is Chaucer's *Troilus and Criseyde,* which was written in the 1380s. Lewis, following the earlier scholarship of Jeanroy and Fauriel, suggested that one possible cause for the rise of the adultery theme in Courtly Love poetry was the existence of landless knights without a place in the territorial hierarchy and without an opportunity for marriage into a noble family. Their sexual and social frustrations were expressed in terms of service towards the baron's lady and in terms of unrequited love. Painter provides a more elementary thesis. Hungry minstrels in the duchy of Aquitaine found that love songs were more pleasing to noble ladies than conventional tales of warfare. These fashionable songs were adopted by William IX, Count of Poitou and Duke of Aquitaine as a method of embellishing his own tales of amorous adventures (Jeanroy, 1927).

In terms of thematic content, some aspects of the tradition represented a 'feudalisation of love', in that service of women was modelled on feudal service between the lord and his knights. The lover is the lady's man and he treats her in terms of *midons,* that is 'my lord'. His enemies are not husbands but rival lovers. In order to illustrate his humility and devotion towards his lady, the lover performs dangerous exploits such as Lancelot undertook in the service of his lady Guinevere. The elaborate, ritualistic courtesy towards ladies and devotion to their often whimsical commandments were the sexual counterparts of feudal service and courtesy. It was the adultery theme and the Religion of Love which appeared to challenge Christian mediaeval teaching on marriage and passion. For the church, sexual passion, even in marriage, was a sign of the Fall of Man and the only justification for sexual intercourse was the procreation of children. The church had been preoccupied throughout the Middle Ages with the sexual deviance of the various social classes in society. One of the key complaints of Humbert de Romans's sermons was the proclivity of all classes to lechery. He compared human sexuality unfavourably with the sexuality of animals. It was a common theme of Catholic moral teaching that sexual passion represented a loss of human rationality. In the Courtly Love tradition it was sexual love between men and women, regardless of their marital status, which actually developed and contributed to the virtue of the two partners. The romantic tradition argued that 'no knight can be brave unless he is in love; love gives the knight his courage' (Barber, 1970, p. 47). It was love for women which made cowards brave and fools wise. Love created the *preux* which was basic to the virtues of knighthood and thus was Lancelot strengthened by the sight of Guinevere. The implication of this theme was that a knight could hardly be a proper knight without infatuation for the wife of some great baron or king.

The obvious contrast between the Christian doctrine of *agape* as charity and the mediaeval *amour* as erotic, adulterous passion reached its final climax in the Religion of Love. Courtly Love poets produced a parody of Christianity in which Ovid's *Ars amatoria* became the gospel of the new Religion of Love, complete with its own cardinals and popes whose prayers were rendered up to Amor, the God of Love. Adultery and delight in sexual play were the orthodoxy of this Christian parody. In opposition to the Christian teaching about the irrelevance of this world, one theme of *Aucassin et Nicolette* is that it is better to enjoy the company of noble ladies in this world and risk eternal damnation, rather than to practise asceticism in the hope of a future heavenly paradise.

There are exceptions to this general theme that sexual happiness in marriage is impossible in the Courtly Love tradition of the Middle Ages. In von Eschenbach's celebrated *Parzival* (*c*.1198–1212), Parzival's romantic love for Condwiramurs is perfectly satisfied within a stable marriage relationship. The clergy and poets within the Christian tradition also tried to produce some sort of compromise or fusion between *agape* and *amour*. Dante's *La Vita Nuova* and *La Divina Commedia* presented a fusion of spiritual and sensual love which was centred on the personality of Beatrice. The problem of coming to terms with sexual love from the point of view of Christian theology was even better illustrated by Andrew the Chaplain's 'treatise' on love (Trojel, ed. 1892). This work is difficult to interpret. The Chaplain appears to speak through the words of several commentators in a series of dialogues between people of different social positions. Whereas Painter regarded the Chaplain's *De amore* as a frankly contradictory struggle between two alternative views of love, Lewis found in *De amore* a reconciliation between theology and Courtly Love poetry. The Chaplain admitted that everything that is good in this world depends on love, but, if we take his *in saeculo bonum* literally, then we recognise that love in this world, however good, is only temporary, superficial and restricted when it is contrasted with the true love of God.

The real nature of the Christian theory of love and the opposi-

tional nature of love poetry can, however, only be adequately understood in the context of customary practices of feudal marriage within
the dominant class. In the mediaeval period, at least from the late
twelfth century onwards, there was a radical conflict between the
lay aristocratic and the ecclesiastical models of marriage. The lay
model supported the existing social order by guaranteeing a line of
legitimate male heirs to protect the family's title to land. It provided
a supply of suitable daughters who could be used to create or to
preserve political alliances between feudal families. Marriage was
thus a treaty (*pactum conjugale*) between two feudal households.
The pact was too important to leave to individual choice, because
the future wealth of the household depended on the anticipated
motherhood of the new bride whose 'blood' was to produce a strong
line of male successors. In a system of inheritance by direct line
through male primogeniture, the high rate of infantile mortality
demanded great fecundity on the part of noble mothers if the
family's traditional claims to land were not to be undermined. This
central requirement of the marriage system gave rise to a number
of characteristic institutions and customs. There was, for example, a
strong tendency towards endogamy because marriage between
cousins provided a means for amalgamating properties which had
been separated by marriages in previous generations. Hence, the lay
model tended to oppose any narrow or rigorous definition of incest.
It was important that the wife receive only the seed of her legitimate
husband because any doubt over parentage would lead to disputes
over inheritance. The lay model regulated sexual impulses in the
interests of patrimony, subjugated women to protect property and
treated adultery as the worst sin against the household.

There was, therefore, some measure of agreement between the lay
and ecclesiastical model, since both recognised the dangers of
adultery and the absolute merit of female virtue. These agreements
were, however, minimal since the lay system did not require life-
long monogamy; indeed, it required a system of orderly repudiation
of wives. If a wife turned out to be barren, or gave birth only to
female offspring, or became too old to replace male children who
had died in infancy, then it was absolutely necessary for the husband
to take a new wife. Repudiation was in fact a very common feature
of mediaeval marriage within the dominant class. The church,
regarding marriage as an unfortunate but necessary protection
against carnal lust, strongly objected to remarriage and repudiation,
but

the resistance of the laity was quick to take advantage of a fissure
that had developed within the ecclesiastical system as a result of

the contradiction inherent in its insistence on both monogamy and exogamy. For while the Church proclaimed the indissoluble nature of marriage, it also decreed that any marriage in which the conjugal union was 'sullied' by fornication or incest be dissolved. (Duby, 1978, p. 21)

Since the lay model tended towards endogamous unions, there were numerous pretexts for repudiating an infertile wife on the grounds of an unwitting incestuous marriage. The crucial economic need for repudiation meant that landowning classes were forced to go to great lengths to prove the existence of incestuous alliances. The requirements of a sound matrimonial policy gave rise to numerous scandals involving false witnesses who were willing to testify to false genealogies. Eventually the church was forced to change its whole definition of degrees of incest in an attempt to control the more obvious abuses of the marriage system (Baldwin, 1970).

The lay marriage system also conflicted with the church's theology of conjugal love, in that it tended to institutionalise household concubinage. The optimal marriage strategy was to marry off all daughters to create political alliances and to marry only the eldest male offspring. This strategy had the effect of creating a pool of bachelors who could not marry because they had no title to family land. These 'youths' found a sexual outlet in the fantasy world of Courtly Love, in casual alliances with peasant women, in rape and in household concubines. The female offspring resulting from these unions 'formed a kind of pleasure reserve within the house itself' (Duby, 1978, p. 24), so that illegitimate sexuality was markedly endogamous in character. The behaviour of these 'youths' provided, at least in theory, a strong contrast to the eldest male who was expected to conserve his seed for the virgin brought to his bed by a marriage treaty. Despite the church's attempts to control customary marriage practices, mediaeval marriages between dominant landowning families remained primarily a domestic rite, the aim of which was not conformity to a divine scheme, but the concentration of feudal property and the consolidation of political relations.

The insistence on chastity and virtue for wives as a condition for the economic strength of the feudal family was also closely connected with the ideology of chivalry. Since noble birth was a crucial feature of knighthood, only true-born sons would be brave and worthy of their families. Knights who turned out to be cowards were regarded as being sons of unions between noble ladies and their varlets. Confusion of blood produced unreliable men. Laws relating to the seduction and rape of noble women were clear and severe, while an unwanted pregnancy would deprive a noble daughter of a part of the family inheritance. The need for chastity in wives, virginity in brides and fecundity in mothers was thus designed to secure the concentration of property in a line of male offspring who would also live up to the ideology of male chivalry.

The widespread existence of concubinage and organised court prostitution merely gave institutionalised recognition to the fact that noble men typically satisfied their sexual desires outside the marriage union, but these extramarital relationships did not threaten the fundamental importance of the family for feudal property. The Courtly Love tradition also in paradoxical fashion recognised that marriage was for procreation and the maintenance of property, whereas love was by definition an activity which took place outside the family. The economic bond between lord and lady was fully recognised by the romantic poets of the Courtly Love tradition. The 'platonic' aspect of the southern love tradition in which the knight's passion for his lord's lady was unrequited did not challenge this bond. Whether we regard the Ovidian emphasis of other romance poems as a direct challenge to the marriage contract will depend on what sort of interpretation is placed on the work of writers like Andrew the Chaplain and on the apparent reconciliation between Christianity and romantic love in Dante's work. It is important also to bear in mind the obvious fact that these heroic adventures of Sir Gawain, Lancelot and Chaucer's 'parfit gentil knyght' were fictional. While green knights, dragons, fairy queens and magical castles are elements of mediaeval myth, the Courtly Love poem probably does adequately reflect the attitude of knights that love was to be found outside marriage.

These literary commentaries on love are also important in providing further evidence of the gap between peasantry and nobility. Customary feudal law relating to marriage (in *Leges Alamannorum*), the church's teaching on monogamy and the Courtly Love tradition were systems of belief which were designed for, aimed at or served the dominant class. The subordinate class was held to be incapable of love. Andrew the Chaplain thought that the virtues which were necessary for courtly love would be unlikely to occur in persons of low origin. In one chapter, he commented on the situation of a noble who was unfortunate enough to feel sexual attraction for a peasant woman. According to Painter's précis (1957, p. 121),

If a man should desire a peasant woman so strongly that he could not resist the temptation, let him rape her on the spot. A courteous approach would be wasted on a woman who could not possibly feel love.

The argument that the troubadour's view of women resulted ultimately in a new attitude towards women, so that they were no longer
merely sex objects, must be prefaced by the observation that this
new attitude applied to women of a particular class (Chenu, 1969).
Courteous behaviour was, therefore, limited to noble ladies. For
example, in the chronicles of Froissart it was recalled that, as the
low-born English archers were raping low-born French peasants, two
knights, John Chandos and Reginald Basset, were busy rescuing two
noble girls 'pour la cause de gentilece'.

In the fourteenth century the feudal basis of knighthood began to
decline. The invention of gunpowder in 1313 and the growing
importance of infantry were important events in military history
which contributed to the gradual disappearance of the noble knight.
The last attempts to raise an army through the feudal levy of forty
days' service occurred in 1327 and 1385. The sale of noble titles
and emblems to groups outside the traditional military elite diluted
the traditional concept of the knight as a noble-born professional
man-at-arms. After the Hundred Years' War, the demilitarisation
of the English nobility gained momentum so that in Elizabeth's reign
only half the nobility had any military experience. This demilitarisation was in England associated with the movement of the landed
class towards commercial agriculture, especially the wool trade, with
the absence of a standing army and with the importance of England's
naval supremacy (B. Moore, 1968). The commercialisation of ground
rent and the development of capitalist agriculture in England put the
final touches to the 'obsolescence of the concept of honour' (Berger,
1970).

In the period from the tenth to the fourteenth century when the
knight had been a crucial stratum within the dominant class of
feudal Europe, the Catholic Church had attempted to come to terms
with organised violence, and with the sexual ethics of feudal love,
with only limited success. Catholicism had been a minority religion
within the dominant class. The illiterate peasantry had remained
largely incorrigible. There was a mediaeval 'dominant ideology'
which was a curious blend of Christianity and secular ideas of feudal
honour, but this ideology was aimed at the dominant class. Very
little sociological content can, therefore, be given to Marx's dictum
that in the Middle Ages Catholicism 'reigned supreme'. While the
notion of theodicy may have given the feudal class a sense of its
own social dominance, while the theocratic debate over kingship may
have provided it with a political theory and while the confessional
may have kept its daughters loyal to the family, Catholicism did not
provide a system of 'extra-economic coercion'.

The feudal mode of production did not require a powerful religious ideology aimed at the incorporation of the peasant class, although it did require a system of stable inheritance of land which would preserve and concentrate ownership within the great mediaeval families. Unigeniture had the important function of preventing the partition of the large estates into progressively smaller and increasingly uneconomic units of land. This requirement of unigeniture happened to take the typical form of primogeniture. The system of estate conservation maintained control over the land in the hands of the eldest son, while also, in the sixteenth and seventeenth centuries, encouraging younger sons, who had not received land other than the main inheritance, to seek out a calling in the church or in the ancient professions of law and medicine. Those societies which failed to adopt this system of estate conservation could not adequately reproduce their dominant relations of production. One influential book on the benefits of primogeniture was David Powell's translation (1584) from Welsh into English of H. Lloyd's *History of Cambria*. Powell argued that the existence of partible inheritance was a principal cause of the collapse of the Welsh nobility and of disputes between brothers: 'Partition is very good to plant and settle any nation in a large country not inhabited; but in a populous country already furnished with inhabitants it is the very decay of great families and (as I said before) the cause of strife and debate' (Thirsk, 1978, p. 188). The great landowning families of English feudalism saw primogeniture, therefore, as a crucial aspect of the reproduction of their class and as a source of political stability and control. Clearly, many landlords were unwilling often to adhere to a strict policy of entailment and primogeniture. However, those fathers who made large settlements on younger sons and daughters often found themselves forced into debt through mortgages raised on their estates.

These inheritance requirements of feudalism were aided by the very clear emphasis of Catholic morality on chastity and the sanctity of the marriage bond. Thus, we can say that a dominant religious ideology among the landowning feudal class had the consequence of helping the operation of the economic conditions of feudalism. It is necessary to state this relationship between the economic base of feudal society and its ideology in a weak formulation; the ideology 'helped' or 'assisted' the economic processes of feudalism. There were some aspects of Catholic family morality which actually stood in the way of feudal economic requirements, namely, the church's condemnation of the repudiation of barren wives. In general, however, Catholicism appears to have contributed to economic relations by supporting male dominance over women who were important for alliances, by confirming the importance of chaste sexuality in eldest sons and virginity in daughters, and by attempting to provide a code of ethics for wayward 'youths'. While this family morality contributed to the satisfaction of the economic interests of the dominant class, historical evidence on feudal societies does not allow us to claim that religion was a dominant ideology which had the consequence of successfully incorporating the peasantry.

Chapter 4

Early Capitalism

Dominant Classes and Dominant Ideology

What was the dominant ideology of early industrial capitalism in England? There have been distinct differences of opinion among modern commentators, notably between those who can find little obvious or coherent capitalist ideology in nineteenth-century England and those who point to an all-pervasive bourgeois ideology that permeated institutional and cultural life for most of the century.

Perry Anderson illustrates the former view in two papers published in the mid-1960s (1964, 1966). He starts from the analysis of class structure, arguing that the middle-class revolution in England was contaminated when the aristocracy transformed itself into a capitalist class whose interests were congruent with, rather than hostile to, those of the bourgeoisie. This contamination had two direct consequences for the dominant ideology. First, the bourgeoisie, when deprived of its historical role in overthrowing a feudal society, had no need to develop a coherent, justificatory ideology which would counter the symbolic universe of the aristocracy. Secondly, the dominant class, and particularly its political elite, continued to be dominated by landed and financial interests into the period of capitalist industrialism. This class was composed of the spiritual, and frequently even the genealogical, heirs of the traditional, pre-industrial aristocracy, and the dominant 'ideology' of this class comprised 'a miasma of commonplace prejudices and taboos', rather than anything that could properly be called a major ideology (P. Anderson, 1964, p. 40). Neither the aristocracy nor the bourgeoisie developed a systematic political philosophy on which a coherent ideology might be based, since the bourgeois utilitarianism of the early nineteenth century was no more than a 'sectional rationale of the workings of the economy' and mid-century liberalism was just an enfeebled version of this earlier doctrine (P. Anderson, 1964, p. 41). Traditionalism, which took the form of a veneration of dominant social institutions and deference in social relationships, combined with empiricism as the typical cast of mind to form a cultural ethos or hegemony of 'coagulated conservatism' (P. Anderson, 1964, p. 40) that was diffused, unarticulated, and based on aristocratic rather than bourgeois culture. Anderson differentiates aristocratic cultural hegemony from ideology, which he conceives narrowly as political philosophy that becomes hegemonic in society (1966, p. 17), and claims that, while the aristocratic culture played some part in limiting the scope of working-class challenges to the existing order, it did not extensively penetrate working-class consciousness.

This line of argument has provoked critical responses from both Marxist (Thompson, 1965) and non-Marxist historians (Tholfsen, 1976), who argue that early English industrial capitalism was accompanied by the growth of a coherent, bourgeois ideology which was both a political philosophy, to use Anderson's narrow conception of ideology, and, more broadly, an integrated and clearly definable culture that permeated political, economic and social life with a total system of beliefs. We agree with this second interpretation and in the following paragraphs identify the component elements of the dominant ideology. We start with philosophic radicalism, the ideology in embryonic form, then consider the mature ideological system of mid-Victorian society that has been so well documented by social historians (Briggs, 1959a; Best, 1971; Tholfsen, 1976), and finally look at the underlying philosophy of individualism that informs the ideology yet is both anterior to it and potentially subversive of the interests it justifies. We are chary, however, about attributing any great proselytising power to this ideology, such that it becomes assimilated by the new industrial working class, though the old aristocracy proves more receptive.

The rapid growth of industrial and landed capitalism, which constituted the economic expansion of late eighteenth- and early nineteenth-century Britain, soon came up against ideological barriers that stood in the way of the full development of a mature capitalist economy. The established ideological consciousness of traditionalism sanctioned social and political authority by reference to natural law. In part this provided legitimacy for the status quo, just by showing it to be an element of the natural order, but at the same time it emphasised the identity of natural rights that all men shared equally, despite differences of power and wealth, and the responsibility of superiors for the protection of subordinates' rights. Traditionalism therefore sanctioned the continuation of a web of regulatory and protective controls that prevented the rebuilding of the economy so as to incorporate capitalist rationality: it resisted the application of market principles to the labour force and to many product markets, the development of contractual relations of employment, and the withdrawal of the political authorities from economic affairs (Bendix, 1956, pp. 78–88; Hearn, 1978, pp. 70–83). Traditionalism harmed industrial capitalism by continuing restrictions on trading, on transactions in money and shares, on labour mobility and the creation of a surplus pool of labour (the consequence of the old Poor Laws), on free-market wage determination, and on the training and employment of craftsmen (Hearn, 1978, p. 80). Traditionalism imposed onerous financial burdens on the capitalist development of land, since the enclosure movement, which had created larger productive units, unencumbered by traditional peasant rights of grazing and cultivation and employing less labour, took place within the institutional framework of the old Poor Laws which obliged landowners to provide welfare for the poor. Population growth, at a time of declining demand for agricultural labour, and a series of poor harvests between 1790 and 1810 magnified the cost of poor relief. Finally, traditional restrictions on banking and shareholding severely inhibited the growth of capital markets and the development of financial capital, a sector of the economy that was dominated by the same landed interests that benefited from capitalist agriculture.

A new approach to political and social authority was required in consequence. This had to provide a philosophy of political and economic life that would break with natural law and the related theories of dependence, and the political supervision of the economy, while still justifying unequal power and wealth. As Bendix has pointed out, the rejection of social responsibility raised issues of legitimacy and social control that had to be solved if traditional ideological forms were to be rejected safely by the dominant class (Bendix, 1956, p. 78):

> How could the 'higher classes' deny their responsibility for the poor and at the same time justify their power and authority over them? How could the poor be taught self-dependence without developing in them a dangerous independence?

Philosophic radicalism, which was an amalgam of three related strands of ideological consciousness, Malthusian population theories, utilitarian jurisprudence and political philosophy, and the economic doctrines of classical political economy (Halévy, 1928), provided the necessary revision of the dominant ideology.

Malthus made a singular break with tradition when he transferred the responsibility of caring for the poor from society to the poor themselves, justifying the change on the grounds that poor people alone could save themselves from poverty, because any action by the wealthy would merely prolong the condition rather than ameliorate it. Malthusianism provided a 'scientific' basis for the denial of responsibility, establishing as a law of nature the simple fact that poverty in a world of finite resources could only be reduced by reducing pressure on these resources, that is by lowering the birth rate and thereby reducing the size of the population. This in turn could be achieved only by the sexual abstinence or moral restraint of the poor. The established subsistence provisions of the old Poor Laws succeeded only in aggravating the problem of poverty, by encouraging excess population growth, and their repeal would bring public policy into line with the laws of nature that scientific analysis had revealed.

The emphasis on the use of scientific method for the validation of ideas about society, and the substantive conclusion that individual responsibility should replace social obligation as the new basis of social thought, were echoed in utilitarianism and its related political economy. For Bentham in 1789, the basis of utilitarianism was a conception of morality in which egoism, the individualistic pursuit of self-interest, was supreme (Warnock, ed., 1962, pp. 33–4): man was a limitless desirer of utilities, with the right of unlimited appropriation of these, and such limitless desire was both rational and moral (Macpherson, 1967). Starting from this basic and *a priori* assumption, utilitarianism drew a number of logically and scientifically derived conclusions. Individual utility replaced obligation as the guiding principle of social organisation, with the consequence that Bentham could simply dismiss as wrong the old tradition of natural law with its ideas of responsibility and fundamental human rights (Warnock, ed., 1962, pp. 40–58), and erect in its place a new conception of law and government based on utility. Government had the right to infringe individual liberty only if it promoted relative utility, which was conceptualised as the general interest, social utility, or the happiness of the greatest number of individuals. The particular role of government was to promote the general interest in accordance with the criterion of social utility, by creating an artificial harmony where individual interests differed. The justification of legislation was that it maximised the utility of the greatest number of people.

From this emerged a distinction between public and private spheres of society. The public was the area where government had to act in order to reconcile divergent interests in accordance with the social or relative utility criterion. The private was an area where a natural harmony of interests prevailed, with the result that no artificial mechanism such as law was needed. The identification of social utility with the public sphere, and natural utility with the private, was transformed into the separation of society and economy. The former was ruled by the principle of social utility and belonged in the public sphere, whereas the latter was based on natural utility, the natural harmony and identity of interests, and belonged to that private sphere which was not amenable to human legislation and governmental intervention (Halévy, 1928, p. 508). There thus developed an intellectual division of labour within philosophic radicalism, between the utilitarians who focused on the artificial laws of social utility, and the political economists who studied the natural laws of economic exchange (Ricardo, 1891, p. 1) and the mechanical quality of an economy which was believed to work independently of human action.

Philosophic radicalism was therefore clearly founded on an individualistic hedonism that was manifest in the rejection of obligation for utility, maximisation of individual utilities and the glorification of continuous accumulation (Macpherson, 1967, pp. 206–9). It separated out the economy from other social institutions, placed it beyond political control and claimed that it worked according to natural laws. The purpose of state activity was to maintain social harmony in areas outside the economic system, but in as abstentionist a manner as was congruent with this purpose. In fact, Benthamites argued for the extension of administrative regulation, by both central and local government, in the 1830s and 1840s (Redlich, 1903; Finer, 1952). Considerations of social utility meant more state intervention in certain areas than had occurred before.

Philosophic radicalism was an ideology that justified the inviolability of property rights and the existing distribution of wealth. As Austin claimed in the 1830s, the protection of property rights maximised individual utility throughout the community, because it encouraged the right to accumulate capital to spend on productive investment, which in turn provided the bulk of people with employment and augmented the productive power of labour from which everyone benefited (Austin, 1832, in Warnock, ed., 1962, p. 325). The existing distribution of property was also appropriate because it promoted utility, in that the middle class was an intelligent and productive group that was free from the imprudent habits of the poor and the excesses of the unproductive rich (Halévy, 1928, p. 87).

The utilitarianism of the dominant ideology was never extended to the extremes of Godwin's formulation, that utility and the principle of the greatest happiness would best be realised by creating an egalitarian society and destroying existing economic and political inequality. This avenue of philosphical inquiry, which was implicit in the idea of general interest, relative and social utility, and greatest happiness, and which would have constituted a radical critique of the new capitalist society dominated by the alliance of bourgeoisie and aristocracy, was firmly rejected by the dominant ideology. Philosophic radicalism was the major strand in economic and political thought between 1820 and 1870 (Schumpeter, 1954, pt 4). But even when evolutionary theories and modified forms of liberalism replaced philosophic radicalism in the 1870s and 1880s, the central belief in individualism was reproduced in the new doctrines and continued to inform the dominant ideology, even if *laissez-faire* principles were to some extent eroded.

The religious revival of early capitalism and the growth of evangelism, which started with the nonconformist sects in the late eighteenth century and spread to the established church by 1880, provided a religious component to the dominant ideology. It has been usual to emphasise the distinctiveness of nonconformity, particularly of Methodism, in order to highlight the anti-establishment views of manufacturers who were opposed to the traditional order of pre-industrial England, a society dominated by the aristocracy and its established church (Gilbert, 1976, p. 205), or in order to show how manufacturers indoctrinated the working class (Thompson, 1963, pp. 350–75). There is no doubt that manufacturers in the first three decades of the nineteenth century found in Methodism a set of beliefs that suited their aspirations for greater social and political influence, but the significant religious unity of the evangelical revival in *all* Protestant churches, including the Church of England, has been obscured by the concentration on the social functions of Methodism *vis-à-vis* the aristocracy and the working class. The wider unity lay in two of its characteristic values: the emphasis on conversion, 'that central event in the religious development of the evangelical' (Tholfsen, 1976, p. 67), embodied in the moral transformation of the individual, and a new concern for the progressive sanctification of the individual by means of moral improvement. Together they created a moral climate of individualistic religiosity and self-improvement which was congruent with the secular values of philosophic radicalism. When one adds the moral approbation with which puritanism greeted material success, as evidence of a godly character, it is clear why, in an association to which Weber and Tawney long ago drew attention, Protestant and utilitarian beliefs develop in parallel (Thompson, 1963, p. 365).

If we turn to the religion of the early manufacturers, we can see how this added further elements which were associated primarily with the bourgeoisie rather than the dominant class as a whole. All nonconformist sects placed emphasis on the natural equality of men and their moral inadequacy before God, beliefs which in the late eighteenth and early nineteenth centuries were potentially destructive of the traditional social hierarchy (Gilbert, 1976, p. 83). Nonconformity, and Methodism in particular, contributed to the erosion of traditional social values which ascribed status purely in terms of inherited, landed wealth and family background, and which justified the position of the privileged in terms of the social responsibility and obligation of superiors towards their dependants. Of course, so far as dominant interests and the dominant ideology were concerned, nonconformity was double-edged. On the one hand, it helped to destroy traditionalism, reinforced the individualistic rejection of obligation and justified the rise into the dominant class of groups representing new economic interests. On the other, as we show below, its egalitarianism encouraged a democratic, collectivist and levelling consciousness among the working class that at one time posed a threat to the economic, social and political power of the dominant class (Hobsbawm, 1957; Thompson, 1963, pp. 390–4, and 1976a; Ward, 1972, pp. 80–95).

Wesleyan Methodism was especially adaptable to the interests of manufacturers, as Halévy (1949) and Thompson (1963, ch. 11) have shown, since it justified their own privileged position and provided motives for the obedience and hard work of their employees. The transformation of self-discipline into a sign of moral virtue and the emphasis on working for salvation by means of material activity on earth placed a moral value on the personal qualities and the activities necessary for commercial success and justified the manufacturers' prosperity as evidence of their godliness (Thompson, 1963, pp. 351–65). The self-made man was one who would be saved (Harrison, 1971, p. 9). The religious doctrine of good works and personal salvation became identified with methodical and reliable work habits where the working class was concerned, and provided the time and work discipline – an internalised motivation to work hard and in a disciplined manner – that was lacking in many early factory workers (Thompson, 1963, pp. 355–62). The moral opacity of Methodism regarding the human and social misery produced by early industrialism meant that religion would not be mobilised against industrial capitalism and, in this rather negative sense, provided additional support for the position of manufacturers. The secular values promoted by the Wesleyan clergy laid emphasis on deference to authority, respect for hierarchy within the church and society, and attitudes of submissiveness. Indeed, the ministry of the infamous Jabez Bunting saw Methodist leaders root out political and social radicals from the church and Sunday schools, and deliberately use the clergy in an attempt to indoctrinate congregations into support for the civil authorities and the established order (Ward, 1972, pp. 85–95). It is hardly surprising that Halévy should propound his celebrated doctrine, that the reason why England avoided a revolution in the first half of the nineteenth century was because Methodism had transformed the class interests of the dominant groups into a religious ideology that indoctrinated large sections of the working class into acquiescent acceptance of the social order. The Halévy thesis continues to influence the study of ideology and the working class (e.g. Thompson, 1963; R. Moore, 1974).

Mid-Victorian England had a less abrasive and more mellow ideology than had been evident between, say, 1810 and 1850. But the generalised dominant culture of Victorianism retained a firm basis in the philosophic radicalism and nonconformist, evangelical religiosity of the earlier period. Philosophic radicalism became mid-Victorian liberalism (Tholfsen, 1976, pp. 124–55), while Wesleyanism and other nonconformist faiths became routinised, losing some of their evangelising and missionary zeal and concentrating their attention more on organisational consolidation (Gilbert, 1976, p. 154). The Victorian modifications were partly matters of tone; the need for strident proselytising was greatly reduced once the aristocratic establishment accepted the bourgeoisie's claims to recognition in the Reform Bill of 1832 and the economic legislation of the 1830s and 1840s, and once the working class became more docile with the decline of Chartism in the 1840s. There was also a change towards a more complete ideological system, a culture that regulated a wider range of activities and beliefs. By simplifying a complex set of interrelated and mutually reinforcing cultural traits, and by freezing at one moment in time an evolving set of beliefs, we can identify four major elements in the culture of Victorianism: domesticity and family; respectability; improvement; conventional Christian morality.

The virtues of the family and domestic ties 'were sung more loudly than at any other period of English history', and there were as many treatises on domestic economy as there were on the more widely publicised political economy (Briggs, 1959a, p. 447). The family was regarded simultaneously as an institution sanctified by and embodying the Christian faith and as the basic building block of social stability, what Cooke Taylor called 'the unit upon which a constitutional government has been raised which is the admiration and envy of mankind' (quoted in Briggs, 1959a, p. 447). Conjugal duties, the laws of God and the peace of society were indissolubly linked in the minds of the Victorian dominant class. Indeed, much of the hostility that certain members of the landed aristocracy displayed towards the factory system in the first half of the century was determined by their fears for the traditional patterns of family life and social order. Lord Ashley tried to limit the hours of work in factories to ten per day in 1844 because he feared the 'moral mischief' that factories engendered, by which he meant the threat to social stability as much as the spiritual welfare of the operatives. He denounced the manufacturers:

> You are poisoning the very source of order and happiness and virtue . . . you are annulling, as it were, the institution of domestic life, decreed by Providence himself, [which is] the mainstay of social peace and virtue, and therein of national security. (*Parliamentary Debates,* ser. 3, LXXII, col. 1100)

'Respectability' was a value that embraced a cluster of attitudes and behaviour, including thrift, self-help and independence (Best, 1971, pp. 256–64). Respectability had a materialistic tone; the respectable man relied on his own resources to make provision for himself and his dependants by means of careful saving and the career advancement or success in business that followed from hard work and application. It was part of a bourgeois conception of a free, competitive and mobile society, in which hierarchy was based on achievement, which offered the individual a chance of prosperity (McLeod, 1974, pp. 13–15). In addition to this material element, respectability had a moral dimension. By leading an upright and Christian life, by striving for self-improvement and by presenting himself as a morally worthy person, an individual could achieve some degree of social status even if his material success was modest. In this second aspect, the doctrine of respectability had a levelling potential, since moral worth was independent of material prosperity. But in practice the prevailing interpretation held that manual work could not be respectable; however morally worthy, a manual worker would never be socially respectable (McLeod, 1974, p. 15).

'Improvement' was closely linked to respectability, a notion of the progressive intellectual and moral development of the individual (Tholfsen, 1976, pp. 61–72). It had a long tradition in the culture of the 'industrious classes', the bourgeoisie and artisans of the eighteenth and early nineteenth centuries. The emphasis on intellectual improvement was part of the tradition of secular individualistic rationalism which dated from the Enlightenment, while moral improvement was a part of the old Protestant tradition, to which evangelicalism had recently given new life by means of its emphasis on the progressive sanctification of the individual (Tholfsen, 1976, pp. 65–6).

The fourth trait was Christian morality, which was based largely on puritanism. Respectable people were expected to conduct their lives, at least in public, according to the ethical and moral standards of Christianity. More concretely, two specific areas of Christian morality took pride of place in the bourgeois Victorian mind. One significant area concerned familial values. These were concerned to sanctify family life, family cohesion and patriarchal authority, and to regulate sexuality. In the latter case, the Victorian moral virtues of chastity, the limitation of sexual relations to marriage and the limitation of intercourse even within marriage to the purpose of procreation were important components of personal and familial morality. Another significant cluster of beliefs elevated the discipline of character by self-denial and industry into moral virtues and condemned traditional working-class culture for promoting idleness and licentiousness. The puritan tradition favoured labour discipline and was hostile to nonproductive activity. Hence the attack on much of the old plebeian culture, particularly on leisure (Malcomson, 1973, pp. 158–9), and the emphasis on time-and-work discipline in place of traditional attitudes towards work.

Towards the end of this era a softer form of Christian morality emerged, when self-sacrificing philanthropy came to be regarded as a sign of true religious feeling (Stedman-Jones, 1971, p. 6). Although philanthropy ran counter to the principles of Malthusian population theory and the doctrines of self-help, it remained compatible with the broader spirit of *laissez-faire*. Philanthropy was a voluntary activity, a personal decision to care for the poor, and as such was quite different from the obligatory social responsibility thrust on the dominant class by the old Poor Laws. Moreover, the underlying assumptions made about the poor were quite compatible with Victorian values, since the poor were individually to blame for their own predicament. They were to be encouraged to act according to the respectable virtues so that they might raise themselves from the state of poverty, and malingerers were to be distinguished from the deserving poor when charity was dispensed (Stedman-Jones, 1971).

Beneath the various components of the dominant ideology lay the fundamental value of individualism. During the early capitalist period a hedonistic theory of social action was clearly the organising principle of philosophic radicalism and mid-Victorian liberalism. Even in the later period of capitalist development, the doctrines that replaced philosophic radicalism after 1870 still retained an individualistic framework of assumptions. In economics, the

Ricardian system was ousted by the Marshallian paradigm and hedonistic man was replaced by an economic man who had an 'ethical obligation' to pursue capitalist economic rationality (Parsons, 1937, p. 164). In social philosophy, utilitarianism gave way to varieties of evolutionism based on atomistic individualism, such as that of Spencer. Indeed, individualism had had a long history in English bourgeois thought, both secular and religious. One effect of the Enlightenment on secular culture had been to foster a conception of man as a rational individual who was 'held in thrall by institutions and customs that violated the principles established by reason' (Tholfsen, 1976, p. 72). Ignorance and authoritarian government went together, and both could be over-thrown by the diffusion of knowledge and education; once ignorance was overcome, men could build a free and egalitarian society based on reason. There was thus a profound commitment to individual intellectual improvement, to the development of man's capacity for reason, which then formed the basis of a radical critique of traditional society and the inspiration of a new order. As Weber and Tawney have clearly shown, the religious legacy of the Protestant Reformation also promoted individualism, notably via the belief in personal salvation that, in the Calvinistic or puritan form, was to be justified by the individual's conduct of his practical affairs, and in the Lutheran form had to be earned in practical activity. Some historians claim that the syndrome of beliefs associated with individualism has an even more ancient ancestry, stretching back to the mediaeval period. For example, Goldman's *The Philosophy of the Enlightenment* connects the beliefs concerned with contract, individualism, free will, universalism and equality with the rise of commercial markets as early as the thirteenth century (Goldman, 1973, pp. 18 ff.). Similarly, Chenu (1969) traces the rise of the individual, subjective conscience and the transformation of morality from objective laws to subjective intention from the growth of urban markets in the thirteenth century. Whatever is the case, the elements of bourgeois individualism are clearly in evidence in England during the seventeenth and early eighteenth centuries, and pre-date the major expansion of capitalist industrialism.

It is appropriate now to ask two related questions: did the dominant class believe the dominant ideology, and what functions did the ideology perform?

The ideological components that we have outlined were initially the beliefs of an *ascending* rather than a dominant class, and were primarily oriented towards the traditional aristocratic dominant class. Gramsci notes that such ideologies are particularly powerful, and English bourgeois thought of the early and middle nineteenth century certainly formed an impressively wide-ranging, systematic and coherent set of beliefs. These justified the material interests of industrial capitalism, and the social and political aspirations of a bourgeoisie that meant to become a part of the dominant class. As the ideology of an ascending class, bourgeois thought was intended (and the intention was quite conscious and explicit in Bentham's jurisprudence) to destroy the traditional assumptions of the landed aristocracy about the appropriate nature of society and economy. We entirely disagree with Anderson, that the English bourgeoisie failed to perform one of the historical roles assigned to it by Marxist theory, which is to formulate an ideology that destroys traditionalism.

The destruction of the traditional ideology, however, involved no parallel destruction of the traditional dominant class, which was based on landed wealth. There was a harmony of material interests between bourgeoisie and aristocracy in nineteenth-century England that contrasts sharply with the contradiction that was so apparent elsewhere in Europe (B. Moore, 1968, pp. 29–39). This relatively low level of antagonism was manifest in that peculiar synthesis of bourgeois and aristocratic culture that was so characteristic of the dominant class from the mid-nineteenth to mid-twentieth century. The bourgeoisie became gentrified, aping the lifestyles and social mannerisms of the old landed aristocracy, and buying themselves and their heirs into the ranks of the landed interest, so that the dominant class remained, in Anderson's language, the 'sociological' heirs of the pre-industrial aristocracy. However, the *reciprocal embourgoisement* of the aristocracy is important too, since the landed groups seem to have accepted most of the economic thought and some of the political and social beliefs that made up the dominant bourgeois ideology.

There is a lack of direct evidence of aristocratic beliefs, in comparison to the volume of information on bourgeois thought, but the permeation of bourgeois ideology into the old aristocracy may be inferred in other ways. It can be shown that the new justification of capitalism as an economic system, the destruction of traditional constraints and some of the social beliefs of utilitarianism found favour within the old ruling class, while the claims of the bourgeoisie to enter into the dominant class were accepted. We have already shown that the husk of traditionalism was a significant and costly constraint on the aristocracy itself; those who were engaged in the capitalist development of the land or who saw an opportunity to invest surplus agriculture capital in industrial and commercial ventures had a commitment to capitalism that created a similarity of material interest with the bourgeoisie. On this basis, it is a plausible argument that large sections of the aristocracy were at least receptive to the new ideology of capitalism. Thompson and Moore suggest that, despite the continued hold of the aristocracy on the levers of political power after the middle class was enfranchised in 1832, which was manifest in the aristocratic domination of governments and Parliaments over at least the next forty years, landed politicians steadily pursued bourgeois policies that gave concrete expression to bourgeois ideology (Thompson, 1965; B. Moore, 1968, pp. 29–39). This can be seen most vividly in the spate of social and economic legislation which was enacted in the sixteen years after the first Reform Act. An aristocratic government and Parliament passed a new Poor Law that was modelled on the population doctrines of Malthus and the *laissez-faire* beliefs of the political economists. It followed the political economists by introducing free trade into previously protected areas and abolishing the minimum price levels of corn. It reformed the laws regarding banking and joint-stock companies in a move to create the capital markets necessary for the continued expansion of capitalism. This government introduced a Public Health Act whose impetus was the utilitarian notion of the general interest and the need artificially to reconcile divergent egoisms, and whose provisions incorporated some of Bentham's ideas about local government (Redlich, 1903; Finer, 1952).

The harmony of interests grew as an increasingly symbiotic relationship between the two sections of the dominant class developed. In the second half of the nineteenth century bourgeois and landed capitals began to merge as the result of a process of horizontal imbrication and as social mobility into aristocratic society took place on a growing scale. (P. Anderson, 1964). There were occasionally significant divisions between the two groups which represented the different segments of capital in the first half of the century. For example, the repeal of the Corn Laws and the passage of the Factory Acts represented defeats for the aristocracy and bourgeoisie respectively, although even these defeats were of greater symbolic than material significance (D. Moore, 1965). After 1850, this division of interest had the character more of a party political myth than of a description of a fundamental antagonism.

Religion certainly had a firm basis in both the industrial and landed sections of the dominant class. Religious participation was clearly linked to social class position, with evidence of high participation rates among the upper classes that declined as one descended the social hierarchy (Inglis, 1963, pp. 322–4). The nature of this religious belief is obviously difficult to gauge, but it seems to have been sincerely held in many cases and participation in organised religion appears to have been more than an unthinking social convention (McLeod, 1974, pp. 205–8). The morality which underpinned many of the elements of the dominant ideology appears to have been based on real religious belief.

The familial component of Christian morality seems to have contained an important material meaning for the functioning of industrial capitalism, particularly before the reform of the banking and company laws opened the way to the expansion of capital markets. There is evidence that early manufacturers relied on the wealth of close relatives for the continued accumulation of capital and investment in plant, and that factories were often jointly owned as tenancies in common, which reinforced the natural cohesion of the family by legal means. Assets had to be preserved against division with each generation, and 'at the very core of the traditional family was this life and death struggle for wealth' (Foster, 1974, p. 180). It seems that familial ideology played its part in preserving units of capital.

We have emphasised the importance of bourgeois ideology for the destruction of traditionalism and the creation of a climate of opinion favourable to capitalist industrialism, which initially justified the economic and social interests of an ascending class and then came to provide the existing dominant class with a justification which allowed it to pursue its own emerging material interests. It needs to be made clear that the bourgeois ideology may never have been absorbed in its entirety by the landed class, and that a restricted and weakened form of 'gentry paternalism' continued in the countryside, as the consequence of that particular character of landed property which Marx aptly described when he said that 'landed property . . . is capital [which is] still afflicted with local and political prejudices' (Marx, in Struik, ed., 1973, p. 126). This description has recently been elaborated, so as to show how traditionalism continued to maintain some hold on values and relationships that were not centrally concerned with the functioning of the economy and the agricultural unit of production (Johnson, 1976, p. 32):

For the estate had a much more than economical value, more than could be cashed on the market. It carried a stock of status, the 'deference' or anyway the voting power of tenantry and an enormous stock of cultural capital and of leisure. These assets derived from the internal character of landed capital. Through his intermediary, the tenant farmer, the owner of ground rent won both money and time – cash and leisure for all the old gentry political functions: conspicuous consumption, ideological show (Edward Thompson's 'theatre'), amateur justice, all kinds of patronage and, of course, politics at the centre.

The continuation of the landed tradition of *noblesse oblige* can be found among 'radical' Tories such as Oastler and in the novels of Disraeli. But the commitment of the landed interest as a whole was not great, since the culture was never allowed to stand in the way of economic and social policies based on the bourgeois ideology.

Subordinate Classes and the Dominant Ideology

Did the working class of early capitalism hold the dominant ideology? The nineteenth-century bourgeoisie was concerned to indoctrinate the working-class with a set of beliefs that would render it more docile, lead it to accept the new economic and social order and provide effective work motivation. The dominant ideology was expected to justify capitalism in the minds of the new working class as well as the old aristocracy. Many modern historians and sociologists start from the premise that the bourgeoisie did succeed in establishing its own ideology as the value system of the working class at some point during the nineteenth century. One position suggests that the working class, notably the leading strata which made up the labour aristocracy, absorbed the dominant culture virtually intact as the consequence of a process of em-bourgeoisement (Perkin, 1969). A somewhat less extreme view of this process of incorporation is more common, namely, that the cultural hegemony of the dominant class in fact established the basic presuppositions of all belief systems and set the boundaries within which working-class thought had some limited autonomy, rather than determining the precise content of working-class culture (Gray, 1976; Hearn, 1978.) Others have concentrated on just one concrete element of the dominant ideology rather than its totality as a hegemonic culture, such as the bourgeois religion of Methodism (Halévy, 1944; Thompson, 1963; R. Moore, 1974).

The nature and periodisation of developments in working-class consciousness in the course of the nineteenth century vary from historian to historian. Halévy (1949) suggested that bourgeois religion had a stabilising effect throughout the first half of the nineteenth century, and was the main reason why the social antagonisms of the first five decades failed to provoke a coherent class consciousness and revolutionary response. The interpretations of early nineteenth-century working-class unrest, particularly of

Chartism, which were current prior to Thompson's re-evaluation of this period in the mid-1960s suggested that popular movements could be explained in terms of long-established radical traditions among the artisans and the spontaneous response of the poor to economic depression (Cole, 1941), or in terms of the problems that people experienced in the transition to an urban and industrial life (Smelser, 1959). Recent historiography has resurrected the first five decades as the period when the working class developed a radical and unincorporated class consciousness, following Thompson's seminal work *The Making of the English Working Class* (1963). Thompson himself described a working-class consciousness that was pulled in two directions between 1790 and the 1830s. On the one hand he showed the development of an autonomous culture which was resistant to bourgeois hegemony and which produced a radical class consciousness. On the other, he revived Halévy's argument about the restraining hand of Methodism, which contaminated working-class consciousness at least until the 1830s and acted as a conservative force. Others have voiced fewer reservations about contamination from Methodism or other sources in this period (Hearn, 1978). Historians who accept the recent interpretations of the making of the working class now identify the major issue facing historical analysis as the explanation of mid-Victorian stability. One popular line of argument is that there was a major ideological caesura within working-class thought in the 1840s and 1850s, which led to the supremacy of bourgeois cultural forms within the working class and thus to ideological incorporation (Gray, 1976; Tholfsen, 1976; Hearn, 1978). Historians with a view of the whole century note the re-emergence of unincorporated thought with the emergence of labourist and socialist ideas after 1880 (Gray, 1976).

Any attempt to describe and discuss working-class culture in the nineteenth century comes up against a major problem. We do not know, nor can we know, how the mass of the working class in early British capitalism behaved or in what its culture consisted. Harrison has commented (1974, p. 220) that

> A chronic shortage of primary materials hampers all studies of the common people. They simply did not leave the quantities of literary evidence that the letter-writing classes bequeathed to posterity; and their oral traditions have so far proved weak or silent . . .

There is evidence from literate members of the working class and from the working-class institutions which kept written records, but this is relevant to the labour aristocracy rather than to the working class as a whole. Thus our analysis is of necessity primarily concerned with the labour aristocracy, but we can infer the beliefs of the wider working class from the evidence of its collective behaviour.

Our argument is that direct indoctrination into the dominant ideology and the somewhat less direct absorption of dominant values via cultural hegemony were never as successful as some have held. We make two claims in substantiation of this position. There was less agreement with, and more opposition to, dominant bourgeois society among the labour aristocracy than is compatible with incorporation and where some agreement existed this was due to the independent evolution of working-class culture rather than acculturation. We further suggest that the working class in the mid-Victorian era had a distinct, autonomous culture which was corporate rather than hegemonic, by which we mean that it was non-assertive and inward-looking, but scarcely penetrated by bourgeois culture (P. Anderson, 1964). This culture evolved in a continuous rather than discontinuous fashion, and it is as important to focus on these continuities as it is to look for apparently abrupt shifts.

Throughout the period 1790–1850, which includes those crucial decades which Thompson has dubbed 'the making of the English working class', there was a clear historical legacy of radical, rationalist thought, the origins of which ultimately stretched back to the Enlightenment (Thompson, 1963, pp. 711–79; Tholfsen, 1976, pp. 25–72). This tradition had a significant effect on the objectives, analysis and strategy of nineteenth-century radicalism. Both working-class radicalism and bourgeois liberalism shared a common core, at least until Tom Paine's ideas made inroads into working-class thought after the Napoleonic wars. The belief in man as a rational and progressive creature lay behind the emphasis that both working-class and middle-class radicals typically placed on the objective of improving the individual and society, an improvement that would take the form of man's emancipation from ignorance and superstition, once a new social order that promoted individual development and was itself based on reason had been created (Tholfsen, 1976, pp. 29–31). The radical tradition analysed society's ills in political terms and suggested political strategies for their solution. The origin of social ills lay in the parasitic and self-serving aristocratic cabal which governed the country, and there was a long history of conflict between the 'industrious classes' and the 'old corruption' which would be solved by an extension of the franchise so as to create a more representative government.

The popularisation of Paine's ideas after 1815 began the bifurcation of the radical tradition into a bourgeois liberalism, that was concerned to defend the sectional interests of the bourgeoisie, and a powerful, working-class, radical movement. Paine's commitment to a popular sovereignty and an egalitarian political system turned working-class radicalism into something that far outstripped middle-class meliorism. His ideas made possible

> A sustained assault on the ideological and political structure of the established order: a confident rationalism that insisted on putting received ideas and practices to the test of reason, a total lack of reverence for traditional authority, a deep commitment to popular sovereignty, a truculent egalitarianism, and an eagerness for swift renovation based on universal principles. (Tholfsen, 1976, p. 33).

Paine extended the traditional radical concern with political inequality to consider the broader forms of economic and social inequality, but assumed that a properly designed political system would remedy these other ills. The political realm remained the arena in which working-class objectives were frustrated and which, once conquered, would enable the working class to realise its other aspirations.

There were two distinct types of radicalism by 1832, both of which had emerged from a common rationalist core (Thompson, 1963, p. 727). There was an interaction within working-class radicalism between the rationalist strand and other elements of working-class culture, which produced a distinctive working-class consciousness. Working-class rationalism, unlike the highly individualistic variants which formed one basis of the bourgeois ideology, was joined to a strong collectivist tradition. As Thompson has shown, the early working class inherited communal values and institutions which played a significant part in the growth of a collectivist and corporate class identity in the second quarter of the nineteenth century (1963, pp. 418–27). 'Improvement' became a corporate attribute involving the collective improvement of the working class and the progressive realisation of its intellectual abilities. The communality of the working class coexisted with values of a more individualistic hue, which were still compatible with collectivism. The eighteenth-century artisan values of self-discipline and self-help, joined with a sense of community purpose, formed the culture of the 'respectable' working class which spread widely through the labour aristocracy during the industrial revolution. A belief in the progressive intellectual and political emancipation of the working class, a tradition of working-class mutuality and collective self-help, and an emphasis on the personal virtues of self-discipline and self-help combined to form an autonomous culture by 1830 that was not permeated by bourgeois ideology.

Tholfsen (1976) has suggested that the radical tradition which the middle and working class had once shared is what explains the shift from a working class that for five decades was engaged in one form or another of social protest and class organisation to a class that was quiescent and incorporated after 1850. He argues that the workers' own beliefs predisposed them to accept the bourgeois interpretation of the shared inheritance. In other words, bourgeois cultural hegemony was successful because workers already had, as part of their own culture, beliefs which could subtly be altered so as to incorporate the working class. We dispute this interpretation below, and suggest that working-class culture and ideology remained largely unpermeated even after 1850.

New concepts were added to old-style working-class radicalism in the 1820s and 1830s. Political demands remained, but they were set within a new appreciation of the social and economic context of capitalist industrialism. The language of class entered the common discourse of artisans and other literate workers, as indeed it did within the ranks of the dominant classes (Briggs, 1960; Hollis, 1970). The working-class press formulated an image of class opposition and an embryonic interpretation of society's ills in class terms, and raised the social and political consciousness of its readers to a higher level (Hollis, 1970 *passim*). Radical capitalist economists provided new ideological weapons which de-mystified political economy, when they developed the labour theory of value and the notion of exploitation. By demonstrating that manufacturers were just middlemen, and that capital had 'no just claim to any share of the labourer's produce, and what it actually receives is the cause of the poverty of the labourer' (Hodgskin, quoted in Tholfsen, 1976, p. 56), they created concepts which might have enabled the working class to understand its predicament.

The climax of this emerging class consciousness was to be found in Owenism and Chartism, between the mid-1820s and the early 1840s. The Owenite co-operative movement, which had spawned over 500 local co-operative societies by 1832, 'took the ideas and principles of eighteenth century radicalism and turned them against a society that narrowly restricted the values that it professed to esteem' (Tholfsen, 1976, p. 53). Owenism denounced a bourgeois society that was based on the principle of competitive individualism, and promoted the labour theory of value. Owenite co-operation was thus more than an economic movement concerned with a more equitable distribution of goods. The tradition of rationalist philosophy combined with the new anti-capitalist economics in the belief that the working man was 'a rational and moral agent . . . whose exertions produce all the wealth of the world . . .' (King, 1828, quoted in Hollis, 1970, p. 216). The working man must be allowed to develop his intellectual and moral powers in a new society which contained no repressive elements. But the absence of any *political* dimension to Owenism, in particular its failure to consider class power and the role of the state in maintaining private property rights and capitalism, meant that the movement was naive and ultimately utopian in its belief that co-operative socialism would simply grow up alongside capitalism; Owenism was strong on objectives but weak on means (Thompson, 1963, pp. 805–6).

Chartism was perhaps a more significant movement, in terms of both its practical impact and its role in heightening working-class consciousness, in so far as one can make broad generalisations about such a decentralised and locally based phenomenon. The old radical beliefs in the objective of emancipation and improvement, and in the efficacy of political means for the transformation of society, reappear once more. The political demand now is for swingeing reform of the political system, rather than the limited extension of the franchise which middle-class liberals had advocated, and this was expressed in a set of ideas which encompassed the destruction of both the political and economic power of the dominant class by the sovereign working class (Tholfsen, 1976, p. 85). This was a radically egalitarian movement which was intent on destroying class power, in order to abolish the economic and social ills which capitalist industrialisation had created. But it was also essentially a reformist rather than a revolutionary movement, which chose to work via the established political institutions. Some Chartists turned to acts of a more violent nature after the petitioning of Parliament in 1842 failed to persuade MPs to legislate for the sovereignty of the people. Large numbers of both rank-and-file supporters and the intellectual (often artisan) leaders gave up the movement when it became obvious that the Six Points would not be won by the strategy of political reformism and that Chartism could do nothing to improve the condition of the working class (Briggs, ed., 1959b, pp. 29–98). The movement failed to create a coherent social theory, or even a common stock of ideas, which would canalise the wide diversity of grievances which made up Chartism (Briggs, 1965, pp. ix–xii). It failed also to provide any guide to the realisation of the Six Points once Parliament had rejected the petition. The achievement of Chartism was to forge a sense of class identity out of the disparate working-class movements of the 1830s, to give expression to the hostility which the working class had felt for the bourgeoisie and to suggest that class conflict was the basis of social divisions, and to show how political economy obscured the true workings of the economy (Briggs, ed., 1959*b*, pp. 29–98 and 288–303). Chartism, indeed, can be viewed as an attempt by working-class radicals to promote a hegemonic ideology over society as a whole, despite the shortcomings of specific programmatic proposals and the lack of clearly articulated theory (Nairn, 1964).

Chartism's institutional structure was also impressive. The range of different working-class groups was wide, and embraced the artisan elite, the new working class of the factory production system and the older working class of the domestic production system. The geographical spread of Chartism and the co-ordination of agitation over wide areas were novel, and in effect it was the first national mass protest movement. It was impressive in purely numerical terms, as when 50,000 people assembled at Kersal Moor in 1838 in one of the largest public demonstrations ever seen in the nineteenth century.

The subsequent rapid decline of Chartism in the mid-1840s and the coming of mid-Victorian stability undoubtedly marked a change in the collective behaviour of the working class and a softening of the way in which working-class beliefs were expressed. But it is more difficult to prove that there was a fundamental shift of working-class ideology during this period, let alone that there was anything approaching ideological incorporation. In the first place, one must avoid that exaggeration of the unity and sophistication of working-class ideology in the 1830s and 1840s which those who claim to show how different were the 1850s, 1860s and the 1870s often promote. The only developed and coherent set of beliefs was a series of political demands based on traditional working-class radicalism. There was indeed a groundswell of new ideas and forms of consciousness, the unity of which can be seen in hindsight but which was never more than implicit at the time. Moreover, even the claim that there is such a unity underpinning the social movements of the 1830s and 1840s must be hedged with important qualifications. Chartism's many local variations make it difficult to identify general characteristics with certainty. The working-class ideologues of the period were literate men who were perhaps untypical of the rest of the working class. The working class was itself internally stratified into segments which enjoyed widely different material interests and social conditions, and were receptive in different degrees to Chartism. It remains uncertain how far the mass of the proletariat absorbed the new forms of consciousness, although evidence of Lancashire Chartism suggests that many people participated in the mass agitation of 1838 and 1842 as a response to hunger and severe economic distress rather than for any other reason. There were undoubtedly strong feelings of hostility towards the dominant class, but there was little rationalisation of these feelings or coherent analysis which would suggest that the new ideas had made a great impact on the mass of Chartist supporters (Briggs, ed., 1959b, pp. 41–55). Any analysis of Owenism and Chartism must therefore conclude that a variety of new concepts for the analysis of capitalism became *available* during the 1830s and 1840s, which taken together marked an advance in working-class ideology. But the evidence does not show how far these ideas were disseminated beyond the radical leadership, and there are grounds for wondering just how deeply the new radicalism did become rooted within the mass of the working class.

In the second place, there is evidence of continuity of beliefs and culture into the mid-Victorian era. In the short term, the collapse of Chartism meant merely a change of direction for many of its leaders rather than a withdrawal from the working-class movement. They became activists again in the more concrete though limited causes which had been swept up into Chartism after 1837, causes such as the Ten Hours campaign, the trade union movement, the anti-Poor Law agitation, and the anti-Corn Law campaign (Briggs, ed., 1959b, pp. 55–64). In the longer term, analysis of working-class consciousness and culture suggests that the elements found before 1850 continued as part of an autonomous culture right through the period, though their practical expression took less aggressive forms than before.

Working-class consciousness in the mid-nineteenth century continued the autonomous traditions of working-class radicalism, and in particular it remained collectivist and impervious to bourgeois individualism. Where the culture of the working class displayed some similarity to that of the bourgeoisie, this was more the result of a distinct pattern of historical development and a reaction to the objective position of the class than the outcome of acculturation. Moreover, these cultural similarities are more apparent than real. These arguments can be supported by a discussion of the extent to which the working class was influenced by those dominant, mid-Victorian characteristics of domesticity and family, respectability and improvement, and religiosity, and by the individualistic ethos which underpinned bourgeois society.

Familial values can be dealt with briefly. Contemporary observers of the early and middle years of the nineteenth century frequently commented on what they saw as the breakdown of the working-class family, both extended and nuclear, as the result of employment in factories and migration from the countryside to the towns (for example, Kay-Shuttleworth, 1832). This picture of family disruption during the early industrial revolution was until quite recently echoed by historians, especially by Smelser (1959), who also noted the re-emergence of stable family life after the mid-century. However, new research on working-class family life in Lancashire (M. Anderson, 1971, 1976) shows clearly that industrialisation and urbanisation did not have the commonly cited disintegrative effects on either the extended or nuclear families, and that traditional family patterns were carried from the countryside to the towns. Similarly, evidence of female employment demonstrates the strength of domestic and familial values among working-class mothers who gave up factory work in order to care for their families (Hewitt, 1959). The existence of structural differentiation is characteristic of working-class family life after the 1830s, but this was no new development, since the same differentiation within families was found in the countryside prior to industrialisation (M. Anderson, 1976). In short, there is nothing to suggest that working-class familial values represent anything other than the autonomous working-class tradition, uninfluenced by outside propaganda.

Many historians place considerable emphasis on the working class absorbing certain other elements of the dominant ideology, notably the cluster of values associated with respectability and improvement. In particular, the labour aristocracy is thought to have experienced a process of embourgeoisement after 1850, which led it to adopt these bourgeois values. The internalisation of the dominant ideology by the labour aristocracy is given as a major reason for mid-Victorian stability (Perkin, 1969, pp. 340–407); Tholfsen, 1976, pp. 197–229). This interpretation has considerable popularity as an explanation of the behaviour of the labour aristocracy and, by extension, of the wider working class, in terms of ideological incorporation. There are a number of arguments which suggest that it is not a plausible interpretation, however. In the first place, we have already shown how the values of self-help, independence, respectability and improvement, and the institutions which embodied them, had their origins in traditional artisan culture. Secondly, the meanings attached to these beliefs within the working class remained very different from those of the bourgeoisie, and one cannot simply assume that the same terminological labels describe the same cultural contents. As Crossick (1976) and Gray (1976) have shown in two case studies of the labour aristocracy, apparently bourgeois beliefs had distinctive, corporate and class meanings for the proletariat, as the collective self-help and communal improvement of the working class, as the independence of workers from degrading dependence on credit or charity, and as the respectability of a class that was imbued with class pride and demanded corporate recognition.

Corporate, class values were embodied in the institutions which the labour aristocracy dominated. Trade unionism became the main vehicle of collective self-help, because it was quite obvious that working-class individuals could do nothing to improve their lot on their own, nor would they ever be accepted as equals by the dominant classes, contrary to the bourgeois rhetoric of a free, competitive and mobile society with a social hierarchy based on individual achievement (McLeod, 1974, pp. 13–15). Indeed, trade unionism illustrates very clearly the antipathy between bourgeois and proletarian versions of self-help doctrines, and trade unions themselves were deeply loathed within the middle class (Crossick, 1976; Gray, 1976). The whole range of working-class institutions, which in addition to trade unions included friendly societies, savings banks, co-operatives, building societies and various institutes for intellectual improvement, shows the depth and vitality of working-class culture, its autonomy and its essentially communal and egalitarian character. Even those more obviously individualistic values, such as thrift and personal self-help, which formed part of the definition of the respectable working man received concrete expression by means of the individual's participation in institutions which celebrated the communal spirit of working men.

The objective circumstances of the working class in the mid-nineteenth century, and the very different position of the bourgeoisie, provide a further reason why the labour aristocracy gave such different meanings to what superficially appear as dominant values. The prosperity of the Victorian economy at this time created an environment in which labour aristocrats could markedly improve their living standards, provided that they were individually prudent (for example, by saving for house-purchase), and collectively used their strength to improve rewards at work, via unions, and their position as consumers via co-operatives. But any individual's life-style was also insecure, since illness, advancing age and the periodic contractions of business activity might leave him without work. Here, too, individual prudence and collective self-help were necessary in order to provide for such contingencies (Crossick, 1976; Gray, 1976, pp. 121–30).

Working-class consciousness also contained markedly oppositional elements. The sense of class solidarity which the labour aristocracy shared was linked with an awareness of conflict even during the social stability of the three mid-Victorian decades: 'the engagement of the labour aristocracy in class conflict must be kept firmly in view' (Gray, 1976, p. 145). The economic and social positions of the labour aristocracy were not freely granted by the bourgeoisie but had to be fought for, primarily by means of trade union activity

(Gray, 1976). The language of the labour theory of value, exploitation and class conflict was retained, even in those institutions whose
practical activity was no longer directed towards the overthrow of
capitalism and class society. The co-operative movement did work
to improve the lot of the working man within the existing system,
as the proponents of embourgeoisement claim, but still kept a clear
and publicly articulated conception of the opposition between the
interests of labour and capital (Tholfsen, 1976, p. 162). The shift
which undoubtedly occurred within working-class culture after 1850
was less than the proponents of ideological incorporation are willing
to allow. Working-class ideology lost its active edge, that outward-
looking element of Chartism and Owenism which sought to translate
ideology into actions which would change society. Instead, it became
a more inward-looking and hermetic culture (P. Anderson, 1964), a
class consciousness that provided no stimulus to action on the scale
of the 1830s and early 1840s, whose practical expression was found
in the creation of distinct working-class institutions and a localised
struggle against some of the effects of capitalism on workers as producers and consumers. The labour aristocracy of mid-Victorian
Britain was not successfully suborned in the manner in which
theories of ideological incorporation would have us believe, but
always defended its interests and institutions against the bourgeoisie.
After 1880, indeed, the labour aristocracy provided much of the
leadership, radical-labourist and socialist, of the new working-
class movements in industry and politics. It was in the vanguard
of the various waves of radical action which marked the period
between the 1880s and the early 1920s (Hinton, 1973; Gray,
1976).

   Our analysis of the culture of the labour aristocracy is at odds
with several conventional interpretations which, although they differ
widely in many respects, place emphasis on various forms of ideological indoctrination or manipulation (Hobsbawm, 1964; Perkin,
1969; Foster, 1974; Crossick, 1976; Gray, 1976; Tholfsen, 1976). The
three authors whose evidence we cite in support of our interpretation – namely, Crossick, Gray and Tholfsen – are in fact representative of the conventional approach to working-class beliefs and
institutions. However, the evidence and analysis which they present
point more towards a conceptualisation of working-class beliefs as
autonomous, largely unpermeated and covertly oppositional than
to their own conclusions. Historians themselves are divided about
the interpretation and significance of the labour aristocracy. In two
recent papers, Musson (1976) and Moorhouse (1978) point to the
analytical ambiguities and the problems of evidence which beset
existing theories of labour aristocratic incorporation, and the con-

sequences of this for the subordination of the working class generally.

The Halévy tradition of historical analysis assigns a key role to the bourgeois religion of Methodism for the pacification of the working class, an analysis which Halévy (1949) and Thompson (1963 and 1976a) clearly limit to the period 1790–1830 but which R. Moore (1974) extends into the second half of the nineteenth century. As was the case when respectability and improvement were closely examined, so too we find that religiosity is a poor indicator of ideological hegemony after 1830, and possibly before. In the first place, the statistical evidence which is available for organised religion provides evidence of very little working-class religiosity in the nineteenth century. Only a tiny proportion of the total English population participated in the organised religion of any faith. The membership of all the Methodist sects combined was in the range of 3·6 to 4·4 per cent of the total population throughout the nineteenth century; the density of Easter Day communicants of the Church of England was in the range of 7·2 to 8·9 per cent; and the density of those attending Roman Catholic masses was in the region of 4 per cent as the result of Irish immigration after 1850 (Gilbert, 1976, pp. 28–46). Public religious observance and church membership were indeed (statistically) deviant forms of behaviour in the nineteenth century. The great bulk of the working class were members of no church and attended no religious ceremonies (Gilbert, 1976, pp. 59–68), particularly in large towns where Protestant churches had negligible support (Inglis, 1963, pp. 1–2; McLeod, 1976, pp. 281–3). Data on the participation of different working-class groups are available for the first four decades of the nineteenth century, though not after 1837, which indicate that artisans and other higher strata of the working class were somewhat more likely to participate in organised religious life, mainly in Methodism, than the mass of workers (McLeod, 1974, p. 283; Gilbert, 1976, pp. 59–68).

Secondly, the nature of religious beliefs may well have differed between the classes. The evidence is incomplete. One recent analysis of religion in rural England in the mid-nineteenth century, where religiosity was stronger than in the towns, indicates that, among those members of the rural working class who were religious, *popular* religiosity was based only in part on Christian beliefs and owed much to paganism (Obelkevich 1976). Obelkevich shows that the structure and content of popular religious belief differed from what was promulgated in either the Anglican Church or the Methodist Chapel, and was based heavily on traditional superstition and magic. In particular, God had less reality than the devil, Jesus had hardly any place at all, and nature was saturated with magical forces. Thompson's description of popular Methodism among factory operatives and even, indeed, his description of Wesley's own dogmas, suggests that old superstitions and Christianity were also quite possibly linked in the urban working class (1963, pp. 362–8, 405–12).

Thirdly, there is evidence that Methodism was not particularly successful as a form of indoctrination which produced a politically pacified working class, and that the secular values of the religious leaders were often as poorly absorbed as their religious doctrines. The views of the Wesleyan Methodist ministry and its leading lay members, which supported the existing order and reflected the dominant ideology, tell us little of the beliefs of the rank-and-file membership even in the Wesleyan Church, let alone in the many other varieties of Methodism. Historians differ in the emphasis which they place on indoctrination and stabilisation prior to the 1830s. Hobsbawm (1957) notes that non-Wesleyan Methodists were closely connected with politically active, radical working-class movements, including trade unions, and expressed a variety of proletarian values. He regards Methodism as complementary to, and supportive of, political action (Hobsbawm, 1959, p. 130). Thompson claims to disagree with Hobsbawm, but he too notes how the non-Wesleyan sects, rather than the Wesleyan Methodists, did display confrontationist, class-conscious, proletarian values in the early nineteenth century, and how later even many Wesleyans became radicals (1963, pp. 390–4; 1976a).

Both Thompson (1963) and Ward (1972) comment on the fissiparious tendencies of Wesleyanism prior to the 1830s. The emphasis that Methodism placed on two values, the equality of all before God and the community of believers within the church, resonated with the democratic-egalitarian and communal-collectivist values of the working class. These aspects of Methodist belief and popular culture were in permanent tension with the actual organisation of the Wesleyan church, which became increasingly centralised, hierarchical and inegalitarian, and with the values of the clergy and leading lay figures who represented bourgeois culture. This tension resulted in the secession of sects which were less ambiguously proletarian than Wesleyanism, and in the great social division *within* Wesleyanism, between working-class members who tried to democratise the church and use it to broadcast radical social doctrines, and the bourgeois laity who allied with the ministry to support the existing order (Ward, 1972, *passim*). After 1830 Wesleyanism became a more middle-class religion as it lost the commitment of many working-class members (McLeod, 1974, pp. 281–2; Ward, 1972, p. 92), and the tension between the two cultures was resolved in this way. In the 1830s and early 1840s, non-Wesleyan Methodism and Chartism proved to be highly compatible, and 'Chartist activity appeared in most areas where working-class commitment to Methodism was strong' (Hearn, 1978, p. 207). This compatibility was due both to the similarity of the working-class values in the two movements and to the impact of non-Wesleyan organisational techniques – which provided for democratic, participative involvement on a decentralised yet co-ordinated basis – on the structure of the political movement (Hearn, 1978, p. 205).

There is no doubt that working-class activity changed after 1850, and that capitalist economic organisation and class society were no longer opposed in the manner of the first five decades of the century. At the same time, working-class ideology lost its outward-looking character. We have argued against the view that quiescence was the result of ideological indoctrination and bourgeois hegemony, because there is no evidence of any major and discontinuous shift in working-class culture within the decade and a half which followed the effective collapse of Chartism. On *a priori* grounds, such a shift seems unlikely in such a short period of time, given what we know about the stability of values in a wide variety of cultures and given the inadequacy of the agencies of ideological transmission in early capitalist England which we discuss below. The evidence itself also suggests that change was only gradual, and that any apparent discontinuity results from an exaggeration of the sophistication and extent of class consciousness before 1850 and an underestimation of such consciousness after this date. An important fact has been lost sight of in the discussion of ideological hegemony. Workers may accept the economic order of capitalism and its class-based social organisation at a factual level, as an enduring system. This factual acceptance need not involve any signs of normative acceptance or indoctrination. Habituation and a realistic appreciation of the strength of the existing order do not add up to any form of commitment, nor even to a decline in workers' awareness of alternative and more desirable systems. There are several alternative explanations of the stability of the three mid-Victorian decades which do not rely on ideology and which support our case.

The simplest is that after five decades of continued agitation the working class had achieved nothing except to exhaust and demoralise itself as the result of this unavailing struggle (P. Anderson, 1964). In this context, it is worth pointing to the resistance of the dominant classes and the operation of the state's apparatus of repression. Repression included the routine imprisonment, deportation or execution of agitators. During the 1830s and 1840s, police forces were created for the first time, the army was used to maintain internal order, and the effectiveness of the army against insurgency was increased by the new network of railways, all of which demonstrated the growing strength of the state's potential for coercive control (Mather, 1959). Government and judiciary were not afraid to use the state's capacity for violence, and this capability itself became more effective as the century progressed.

A second explanation is the success of reformism during the mid-Victorian era. In the new age of prosperity, trade union action and other forms of collective self-help were associated with higher real wages and improved material conditions of life, for the labour aristocracy at least. Working within the system was a realistic strategy which delivered the goods. This strategy implied no endorsement of capitalism. It was the natural response of a proletariat which had found itself unable to combat capitalism but which still needed somehow to escape from the grinding poverty which was otherwise its lot. Since support for Chartism had tended to follow the trade cycle, popular agitation being most pronounced during recession and closely linked with hunger and economic distress, the improved economic climate of the mid-Victorian period was probably also responsible for weakening one of the sources of active popular support for radical causes. In the political sphere, the extension of the franchise to the upper strata of the working class in 1867 and the growth of citizenship rights suggested that some progress was possible, and provided some reinforcement of the traditional, radical-artisan belief that society might move toward the realisation of the values of independence and self-reliance in self-government as the result of reasoned and constitutional action (Crossick, 1976). Economic and political developments suggested that the existing order might be improved as the result of working-class pressure and piecemeal reform. This in turn relates to a point made previously, that the radical, rationalistic tradition of working-class elites inclined them towards political action, and towards action of a non-insurrectionary character. The absence of a revolutionary-socialist ideology in Britain until the end of the nineteenth century meant that there was no real challenge to this tradition which would provide the cultural impetus that was necessary for more extreme forms of action.

Thirdly, the working class was internally divided into strata whose sectional interests overcame any identity of interests which they might share by virtue of their common class position. This was accompanied by cultural differences between the various groups which heightened the significance of the stratification. In this respect, the Marxist-inspired analysis of the labour aristocracy is correct, since it emphasises the wide gulf between the leading stratum and the rest of the working class. In terms of their material prosperity (Hobsbawm, 1964; Musson, 1976), the quality of their working life

(Hinton, 1973; Foster, 1974), and the beliefs and institutions which comprised their culture (Crossick, 1976; Gray, 1976; Tholfsen, 1976), labour aristocrats differed from the rest of their class. This isolation from the mass of the working class extended into the area of social relationships and the tendency for aristocrats to live their lives apart from the rest (Crossick, 1976; Gray, 1976, *passim*). Internal stratification, when carried to the degree found in the mid-nineteenth century, obviously impedes class-based activity and may, as in Britain, lead workers to be concerned with internal rather than external class relations. The decline of internal differences at the end of the century, when the market, work and social conditions of the various strata began to converge, opened the way to a more united class movement. The significance of internal stratification was its effect on class coherence, not that it led to the embourgeoisement of the labour aristocracy.

The machinery of ideological transmission was hardly well developed or effective before the late nineteenth century, which partly explains why the impact of the dominant ideology was so limited. There was no mass education, no mass media and very limited adult literacy. There were low rates of social interaction between bourgeoisie and proletariat outside the workplace, since both classes lived in geographical and social isolation in the major towns at least (Stedman-Jones, 1971, p. 247; Crossick, 1976; Gray, 1976). All that was left was personal contact at the place of work, religion and Sunday schools, and the possibility of bourgeous influence on working-class institutions.

Historians do not know a great deal about work relations of this period, but we can make a few tentative suggestions on the basis of information which may indirectly suggest what went on. As is well known, the management of labour and the production process in a number of nineteenth-century English industries relied heavily on subcontracting and indirect employment (Bendix, 1956, pp. 53–6; Hobsbawm, 1964, pp. 299–300), which suggests little contact between the mass of employees and the factory-owner. Certain key workers, foremen and craftsmen, who acted as intermediaries between the owner and the labour force, may have been in regular contact with a source of bourgeois ideology, but it is difficult to see how the mass of rank-and-file workers had much contact in these industries. In his study of managerial ideology, Bendix (1956, p. 203) suggests that owners had little need to worry about the indoctrination of labour once workers were dependent for their livelihood on industrial work, because the discipline of unemployment and payment by results provided all the compulsion that any owner would ever require. During the transition to industrial capitalism, some concern for the ideological apparatus within the factory was evident and was related to what owners saw as the problems of instilling time-and-work discipline into the labour force, but the dull compulsion of economic relations soon provided the discipline and reduced the need for any process of indoctrination.

We have already seen how ineffective organised religion was as an agency for transmitting beliefs. Sunday schools, however, look more likely to have had some major effect. By the 1820s, almost every English working-class child outside London was attending Sunday school for some time at least, and the census of 1851 showed that half of the 5–15 age group were enrolled in the movement (Laqueur, 1976, pp. 42–61). This would appear to support Thompson's view that these schools played an important part in the process of indoctrination into bourgeois values (1963, p. 375). The conclusions that Laqueur reaches in his study of the Sunday school movement, however, do not point in this direction (1976, *passim*). His claim is that the schools grew out of the demand, from within the working class, for basic education and the transmission to children of the values of the respectable working class (industry, thrift, self-discipline and improvement). While businessmen and the clergy founded many schools, as is well known, there were also many which were founded by working men themselves, which is less well recognised. Even within the schools that were of middle-class foundation, it was not uncommon for instruction to rely on working-class teachers and to be financed out of collections from the parents. Thus, suggests Laqueur, we should see all these schools as genuinely popular institutions that promoted working-class culture. Because the schools were run independently of the churches and committees with which they were associated, it would be mistaken to read off the content of the teaching and the values received by students from the motives of social control and indoctrination of the founders. Laqueur's thesis may be unorthodox, but other historians of mid-nineteenth-century religion have endorsed his analysis, at least with regard to nonconformist foundations. It is possible that the Anglican ones (which accounted for about 40 per cent of enrolments) may fit less easily into this analysis (McLeod, 1978). The well-known difficulties which the Wesleyans experienced with teachers who disseminated radical political propaganda in the 1820s can be understood more easily if the independence of Sunday schools is accepted. Both the Wesleyan and Anglican clergies had prohibited the teaching of writing to children in the 1820s, which they identified with the aims of the political radicals and the religious undenominationalists, for fear that writing might promote political and religious subversion

(Ward, 1972, pp. 95–6). Once again, we find evidence of the autonomy and distinctiveness of working-class culture in the mid-
century decades, the difficulty of identifying the true nature of this
culture by reference to the dominant values and institutions which it
superficially resembles, and the frailty of the attempted indoctrination.

Lastly, there is the possibility that members of the bourgeoisie
had access to other working-class institutions which enabled them to
promulgate the dominant ideology. Here we come up against a
shortage of evidence and contradictions within the evidence that is
available. Detailed investigations of the organised life of the working
class, and of the labour-aristocratic institutions which dominated this,
have shown in the case of South-East London and Oldham that
there was a real divorce between the working class and the local
bourgeoisie, that the institutions were genuinely independent, and
that the only discernible tendency was for the separation of the
classes to grow (Foster, 1974, pp. 212–3; Crossick, 1976). A similarly
detailed study of Edinburgh shows, on the contrary, that the local
bourgeoisie acted as urban leaders, were the patrons of local co-
operative societies, mechanics institutes and educational associations,
and provided speakers to enlighten the labour aristocracy on subjects
such as political economy (Gray, 1976, p. 136). Such widely varying
local conditions, and the paucity of the existing information, make it
impossible to know what was the typical pattern, if indeed there was
a typical pattern. There is certainly little evidence one way or the
other that the bourgeoisie attempted to disseminate dominant values
via working-class institutions.

Hearn (1978) has recently advanced a variation of the 'hegemony
thesis' which is based on the critical theory of the Frankfurt school,
notably on Marcuse and Habermas, rather than on the Marxism of
Gramsci and his followers. His claim is that pre-industrial English
culture was 'two-dimensional' in that there were systems of instrumental and symbolic action, and that the former was subject to the
latter. Specifically, the economy was regulated by traditional cultural
standards which expressed underlying social obligations and relationships. During the process of capitalist industrialisation, Hearn
claims that traditional culture and consciousness were suppressed,
along with the capacity for critical transcendence which they sustained. They were replaced by a technical rationality and instrumental, purposive action, which freed the economic system from
cultural constraints and allowed it to provide its own legitimation,
which in turn buttressed the private interests which controlled the
productive forces. From the viewpoint of working-class culture, what

took place was the destruction of ideas, objectives and aspirations which were potentially in opposition to the new socioeconomic system, which were replaced by others that were supportive. Concretely, there was a shift away from natural law and the belief in traditional social obligation, and an assault on traditional attitudes towards work and leisure which were inimicable to industrialism. The outcome of this process, which had its greatest impact between the mid-1830s and early 1850s, was to create a working class that accepted capitalist industrialism as the natural order of things, and that, because it was severed from its old culture, had no basis which would permit it even to imagine alternatives to the existing system.

This variant is no more satisfactory than the others. Hearn is misinformed when he says that the potentiality of critical transcendance was driven from the English working class, which the spread of varieties of socialist belief later in the century clearly shows. The working class created new ideas in the 1830s and 1840s which were not part of its traditional culture, and which socialist thought later extended and made more systematic. Nor was traditional working-class culture destroyed. We have emphasised the continuity of one strand of working-class culture in order to refute those who treat the values of the 'respectable' working class as indoctrination. There was in addition a different strand, which we touched upon in the discussion of religiosity: namely, the culture of drink, gambling, fornication, idleness, thriftlessness and superstition, which made up the 'rough' working class. Both elements were to be found in pre-industrial England, and both survived the transition to industrialism. Hearn's argument, which concerns the second strand, is that the old patterns of working-class culture, with their strong leisure and play components, were inimicable to efficient capitalism, because they stood in the way of productive efficiency as well as providing a source of oppositional values. Extending the sort of argument which Thompson popularised in his discussions of time-and-work discipline, Hearn concludes that capitalism needed to destroy this traditional culture and was successful in its task. Thompson (1976a) himself, however, argues for the *continuity* of precisely these cultural elements, and asserts that the old plebeian culture was confronted by the new rationality but was only partially changed. He adds, moreover, the cautionary admonition that neither historians nor sociologists in fact know *what* the old plebeian culture was really like, since so few have examined it with any care. There is simply not enough reliable evidence of pre-industrial culture to substantiate arguments based on its presumed transformation.

Chapter 5

Late Capitalism

To reduce the argument so far to a set of basic propositions, we can make three main points. In feudalism and early capitalism there are indeed identifiable dominant ideologies. These are held by the members of dominant social classes but not by those in subordinate classes. One reason why lower classes do not hold these ideologies is the weakness of the mechanisms of transmission. We shall show that this state of affairs is rather different from that which obtains in late capitalism, where the dominant ideology is much less well defined, is made up of a number of disparate elements and contains several internal inconsistencies. In late capitalism there is some ideological incorporation of the working class, though less than has recently been believed, and the mechanisms of transmission are well developed and partly effective.

Dominant Classes and the Dominant Ideology

One significant difference between early and late capitalism is that the functioning of the modern capitalist economy no longer depends on the existence of a class which retains capital within the family structure. As is well known, there have been major changes in the structure and ownership of the British economy since the war, which have included the increased concentration of industrial and commercial activity into the hands of large corporations, with the result that Britain now has one of the most concentrated economies in the capitalist world (Aaronovitch and Sawyer, 1975, pp. 59–154; Hannah and Kay, 1977, pp. 1–9). The control of enormous sections of industrial and commercial capital lies in the hands of a comparatively few giant corporations. The capital invested in these corporations is rarely owned by families in the manner of nineteenth-century capitalism, but increasingly the equity of large corporations is vested in the hands of financial institutions such as pension funds and insurance companies, other corporations and the state. More than half of all the shares now traded on the stock exchange are bought by institutions rather than by individuals (Erritt and Alexander, 1977). Equally, firms requiring short- or medium-term capital will raise this directly from the banks or from private sources or by the issue of more equity shareholdings. Three developments clearly show how the structure of the economy has moved away from the private, family-centred economy of the classic, early capitalist system. There is, first, the growth of 'monopoly' capitalism, in the sense of the extreme concentration of control over, and to a lesser extent the ownership of, industrial and commercial capital in the hands of a few corporations. Secondly, there has been a parallel development of 'finance' capitalism, by which we mean the central role of financial institutions in the equity and loans markets. Lastly, the activity of the state as both a 'monopoly' and 'financial' capitalist has become more pronounced.

There is thus an obvious and growing separation between the ownership and the control of capital, as economists and earlier generations of sociologists have correctly emphasised. We take the point that this separation is not absolute. There are indeed family firms, firms with large minority shareholdings owned by individuals or single families, senior executives and company directors with direct financial stakes in their firms, as has often been pointed out by those who dislike the conclusions which many early commentators drew from the tendency of ownership and control to become separated (Aaronovitch and Sawyer, 1975, pp. 157–94). We also agree that the managerial capitalism which results from this separation is unlikely to differ greatly from traditional capitalism on matters such as the importance of profit-making as the goal of managerial behaviour (Giddens, 1973, pp. 167–173), or the ways in which managers control their subordinates. The advocates of the 'managerial revolution' were wrong to place their faith in a great change of managerial style, because the logic of the economic system has the same force whoever runs a firm. These revisions of earlier discussions of ownership and control are correct, but they do not touch on what we regard as important, namely, that there has been a significant weakening of the association between ownership and control between early and late capitalism. A large section of the dominant class is relatively propertyless; the traditional ideology of property has been attenuated, because it is no longer so necessary for the functioning of the mode of production nor for the material interests of a significant dominant group. At the same time new elements have been added which reflect the changing structure of the economy and the composition of the dominant class.

Of what does the dominant ideology consist in late capitalism? Many sociologists are quite sure that there is an ideology, which they refer to under a variety of titles such as 'bourgeois ideology', 'ideological hegemony' or 'core assumptions', and imply that this is coherent and definable. The content, however, remains remarkably elusive in all existing texts, not because it is so self-evident that it need not be spelled out, which is implicit in much discussion, but because it really is difficult to define precisely.

The first thing to be clear about is that the evidence concerning the beliefs which dominant groups hold and disseminate is not satisfactory. There is a noticeable failure in existing research to study directly the values, beliefs and social consciousness of the groups which make up the dominant class. Whereas sociologists have long been concerned with the problem of why the British working class has been docile, an issue which is widely accepted as important in theoretical and empirical sociology and which underlies the discussion of ideology, they have neglected the equally important subject of dominant class consciousness. Consequently, the evidence of dominant ideologies is collected indirectly and at second hand. Content analysis of the proclamations made by what are taken to be 'ruling-class' institutions, such as the Conservative Party and business organisations, of the biases of government and the law, both of which comprise part of the dominant institutional order which is held to embody the ideology of the ruling class, and of the bias of the mass media, is one common strategy. In the case of the mass media, the assumption is made that these media do disseminate a coherent set of values which derive from a dominant ideology, or even that dominant groups directly control what is published or broadcast via their ownership of the press and com- mercial television. The elucidation of specific instances of bias, such as television coverage of industrial relations which is hostile towards industrial militancy and the activities of shop stewards (Glasgow University Media Group, 1976), is used as evidence for a more generalised bias which reflects the dominant ideology. The ideology either appears as a set of concrete items which apply in specific circumstances rather than as a more all-embracing set of values, or merely as a generalised conservative bias which supports the status quo against challenge. This latter claim is so vague and trivial that the concept of ideology loses any utility.

In the literature, much of the specification of ideology rests on *a priori* reasoning in addition to indirect evidence. A common theme is that the dominant ideology functions to make legitimate in the eyes of subordinates the system of social inequality and the privileges of dominant groups. Thus the content of the dominant ideology to some extent varies according to the judgements which different observers make about its material basis. One line of analysis holds that private property is the fundamental basis of class division, and that ideology has to justify the ownership and rights of property, the profits of ownership and the unhindered operation of the allocative mechanisms that preserve the wealth of the property, namely, market forces (Moorhouse and Chamberlain, 1974; Westergaard and Resler, 1975). This is a fairly traditional account of a capitalist ruling class and its justificatory belief system, which is unconcerned with changes in the capitalist economy or the composition of the privileged. A different approach takes the occupational structure and its associated inequalities of income as the 'backbone of the class structure, and indeed of the entire reward system of modern Western society' (Parkin, 1972, p. 18), rather than private property. The justification of income inequality by reference to the economic laws of supply and demand and the functional importance of different occupations, thus becomes the central characteristic of ideology. Parkin nevertheless still sees an important role for the ideology of private property. This assumes some change in the structure of the economy, from traditional capitalism to the modern form where ownership and control are less closely linked and management is relatively propertyless.

There are problems of defining the dominant ideology and supporting this definition with solid evidence which are inevitable in the present state of knowledge. What we propose to do here is to follow the current practice of mixing second-order and occasionally impressionistic evidence with *a priori* reasoning, so as to arrive at a construct which appears plausible. We review the elements of the ideology, following existing literature, examine the consistency of these elements with each other, and see how they are located by reference to the interests of various dominant groups.

We assume that all forms of capitalist economy have beliefs which justify accumulation: ideologies of accumulation attempt to provide socially sanctioned values which make legitimate the appropriation as profit of the value created by collective labour, since profit is the basis of accumulation and therefore of the reproduction of the economic system. What is less certain is that all forms of capitalism require ideologies of private property in the fashion of early capitalism, since reproduction now largely occurs in the hands of the state and corporate bodies. Westergaard and Resler assert that the 'core assumptions' of the modern British value system are 'property, profits and market' (1975, p. 17), a sentiment that is echoed by other recent commentators on ideology. But evidence suggests that not all of the traditional notions about property still command support among those institutions which are commonly believed to represent the interests of the dominant class.

We suggest that the rights of property can be divided into three categories. The first is the right to *own* private property, which is something that political parties, the media and government, the agencies which institutionalise or transmit ideology, do not challenge. The second is the right to *transfer* property via inheritance, which the government has restricted for more than three-quarters of a century; though death duties, of course, were a limited and not particularly effective means of restriction. The third is the right of property-owners alone to decide how to use or dispose of their property. This right has been progressively curtailed by government for years and, indeed, the changing conception of property rights in British law was discussed in sociological journals nearly three decades ago (Friedman, 1950). Certain notable examples can be found in postwar history. For example, changes in the law regulating landlord and tenant relationships, intended to provide tenants with security of tenure and rents that are unrelated to market forces, severely curtail the property rights of *rentier* capital. Changes in employment law which give employees their own 'property' rights effectively reduce the rights of industrial capital. Again there have been restrictions on the movement of personal capital outside the United Kingdom, and both outside and within the United Kingdom in the case of industrial capital. These examples are illustrative of the impact of an interventionist, statist philosophy on the conduct of government, and the consequential tendency to restrict a range of what were previously regarded as inviolable property rights.

Such a restriction of private property rights is indirect evidence of the dominant ideology. Yet the advocates of the dominant ideology thesis commonly assume that government, political parties and other agencies of the state apparatus provide the institutional embodiment of bourgeois ideology. The Gramscian tradition suggests that ideological hegemony is achieved because bourgeois ideology has permeated all the major social institutions, of which the state is one of the most significant: 'Sociologically, the state could be defined as an institutional complex which is the political embodiment of the values and interests of the dominant class' (Parkin, 1972, p. 27). If this is indeed the case, then the actions of government suggest that some private property rights no longer have the same force in the dominant ideology that they once did.

Most restrictions on property over the last three-quarters of a century have, of course, been introduced by Labour or Liberal governments, and it may be argued that such governments do not represent the interests of dominant groups. If this were the case, then government activity against property rights should be interpreted as the mobilisation of deviant and radical values opposed to the dominant interests. This in turn would suggest that ideological hegemony is of only the most limited effectiveness, and also that the political realm has considerable independence from the economic base and the control of dominant groups. Against this view, it has been suggested frequently that the modern labour movement does in fact promote dominant interests, partly because the force of the dominant ideology is so powerful that it permeates even a nominally socialist movement, and partly because, for reasons connected with the inevitably oligarchic tendencies of democratic organisations, the social origins of labour leaders, and the fact that leading Labour Party and trade union representatives rub shoulders with the dominant class, senior members of the labour movement 'conspire' with the dominant groups to reduce the threat of damage to their interests (Hindess, 1971, pp. 34–46, 142–6; Parkin, 1972, ch. 4).

More convincing and less contentious evidence of a shift in the institutional representation of the ideology, therefore, can be found in the activities and pronouncements of bodies which more straight-forwardly represent dominant interests, such as the Conservative Party and the Confederation of British Industry. In this context, it is noticeable that postwar Conservative governments have largely tolerated the restrictions on property which they have inherited from Labour administrations and have so far displayed a definite commitment to the principles of welfare rights and state interventionism (Gamble, 1974), which differs only in degree from that of Labour. The adherence of the Conservative Party to a diminution of property rights has probably been motivated to a greater extent than that of the Labour Party by an interest in improving profitability and capital accumulation. The welfare consensus within the party can be seen in part as a tactical response to the class antagonism of the pre-war period, a compromise of some material interests for the preservation of the social stability which capitalism requires (Gamble, 1974, pp. 209–10). The state's economic policies such as those designed to enforce competition by, for example, the abolition of manufacturers' rights to determine the retail prices of their goods, have been intended to make British capitalism more dynamic.

The same failure of institutions which represent dominant interests to support the rights of property-holders can be found in the recent debate over 'industrial democracy'. British company law at present recognises only ownership rights; company directors are obliged to consider the interests of shareholders and of no one else. Yet both the Conservative Party and the CBI recognise the need to change company law in order to dilute the rights of owners with those of employees, and to make directors accountable to employee as well as shareholder interests. Discussion has centred not on the property rights of investors, but on the rights of management. The Bullock

Report on industrial democracy proposed dividing the board of directors into two equal-sized groups of employee representatives (normally shop stewards) and shareholder representatives (normally top management), with a third group of individuals chosen jointly (the '2x plus y' proposal). But business opposition to these proposals has concentrated on the consequences, for profitability and accumulation, of the dilution of managerial control, rather than on the consequences for the dilution of shareholder power, notably in the campaign mounted by the CBI which has been a most forceful opponent of the report (Elliott, 1978, pp. 244–59).

This all suggests that the dominant groups whose voices are transmitted through institutions such as the Conservative Party and the CBI, and perhaps through all governments regardless of their political persuasions, are indeed concerned with profit and the reproduction of capital, but somewhat less with the full range of property rights. There is certainly an ideology of accumulation which permeates all the institutions of modern capitalist society, but its content differs from that of early, competitive capitalism. Along with the partial decline of property rights there have been significant changes in attitudes towards the state which, in contrast to traditional *laissez-faire* doctrines, is now given a new role in the process of capital accumulation. The state is now expected to create profitability, and the postwar history of both major political parties shows how their leaders are equally committed to protecting the interests of capital, particularly the interests of the large-scale corporations and financial institutions which make up 'monopoly' and 'finance' capital (Gamble, 1974; Panitch, 1976). In part this is achieved by an 'arm's length' relationship between government and business, whereby macroeconomic planning creates the appropriate economic environment for business activity and welfare policy creates an appropriate social infrastructure which business would otherwise have to provide itself. But postwar governments have, in addition, used more direct means to maintain accumulation processes, which in effect suspend the operation of the market as the major allocative mechanism and replace it with state direction. These means include grants, subsidies and investments in the private sector, the taking into public ownership of ailing firms whose collapse would have significant repercussions elsewhere, and the fixing of artificially low prices for the products of nationalised industries. The 'capitalist state' is an essential and integral part of the reproduction process of modern capitalism, and its role is firmly fixed in the political philosophies which guide government, administration and political parties.

The other elements that are customarily assigned to the dominant ideology can be dealt with more briefly, since they do not involve the same complexity as the property element of the ideology of accumulation. What we might call the managerial ideology is perhaps the element which has been the most extensively discussed in modern sociology. The justification of social stratification as income inequality which is determined by the principles of supply and demand in the market and the functional importance of differing occupations has a central place in the justificatory beliefs of dominant groups and permeates the entire moral order (Parkin, 1972, p. 27). By emphasising the importance of individual mobility and achievement, in particular the opportunity for anyone with the ability and the motivation to rise through the occupational and income hierarchy, the ideology makes inequality appear to be the result of natural law, while income differentials appear as fair and just (Hyman and Brough, 1975, pp. 199–207). We use the label 'managerial' to indicate that this ideology is concerned to justify, not the ownership and rights of property, but the economic privilege and social power which the relatively propertyless managerial stratum that controls modern industry wields. As is well known, this ideology conceals a reality where privilege is often inherited and where the qualities that are rewarded are to a large extent determined by those with power, that is, market principles and functional imperatives are allowed to work only within a socially defined framework of what qualities are to be rewarded, which systematically favours the privileged rather than others (Parkin, 1972, p. 27).

The managerial ideology is also concerned with privilege and power in the enterprise as well as the wider structure of social stratification. Since the rights which derive from property ownership, even if they are still effective, no longer reside with those who run industry, then traditional property ideologies can provide no moral basis for managerial power. Recognition of the growing separation of ownership and control in the years preceding and immediately following the last war provided the impetus for a novel definition of the goals and functions of management. The advocacy of a 'managerial revolution' became popular in academic circles with the work of Berle, Burnham and Marriot. It then spread widely outside academic circles as a conceptualisation which justified and exalted management even among political groups which were implacably opposed to the old-style bosses and sometimes to capitalism *per se*. For example, the Labour Party widely adopted this perspective in the early postwar era, that managers were different and socially responsible (Panitch, 1976). Managerial ideology promoted the notion of 'managerial professionalism' as the corollary of the 'managerial revolution'. This initially emphasised two features, professional expertise and professional ethics which included a service orientation. The first emphasised the technical competence of management, which was based on an established body of knowledge, while the second suggested that managers would consider the interests of all the parties involved in the firm and not only the interests of capital represented by shareholders (Child, 1969, pp. 218–21).

The second element was subsequently dropped, leaving the justification of managerial power to depend on managers' presumed technical competence (Child, 1969, p. 232). This is the counterpart of functional explanations of social stratification, which justifies management by reference to meritocratic success rather than ascriptive factors such as ownership or inherited position. The CBI has taken a managerialist rather than an ownership line in its opposition to the Bullock proposals, emphasising that the competence of senior managers will be made less effective if diluted by employees who do not have this technical competence, who delay decision-making, and who lack the detached objectivity of management (Elliott, 1978, p. 243).

Finally, the managerial ideology disseminates an image of the firm as a community based on shared interests. In its crudest form, the image which has been promoted has been of a unitary community in which conflict, if it occurs at all, is pathological. In its more sophisticated versions, the community ideology recognises divergent interests within the firm, a pluralism of groups, but still denies that there is any fundamental conflict between managers and managed, or capital and labour (Fox, 1973). The reality behind the ideology is of course different, and managers rarely run their firms according to the community principles that they espouse. They appeal to their subordinates in the language of high trust, which suggests that managers trust low-level employees to work well and exercise their discretion so as to promote the interests of the firm, but then they structure work in ways which deprive subordinates of autonomy and discretion, because they do not *in fact* believe that the identity of interests within the firm is sufficient for workers to be trusted in any concrete manner (Fox, 1974).

The ideology of state neutrality and state welfare occupies an important place in the political culture of Britain and other pluralistic societies. The polity is characterised as a liberal democracy which ensures equal citizenship rights for all, despite economic inequality (Marshall, 1950), and so prevents the emergence of a ruling class which superimposes political subordination on economic subordination. The state is thought to inhabit neutral ground in liberal democracy, even-handedly balancing the interests of a plurality of competing institutions and groups, being biased only to the extent that it attempts to redress the deleterious effects of economic inequality by mobilising public resources for welfare purposes. The state is presented in a way which suggests that it is in no sense captured by one group or class, nor that it favours capital at the cost of other interests. In other words, the 'capitalist state' is presented in a manner which denies the central role of the state in the accumulation and reproduction of capital and further denies the fact that, in the process, the state systematically promotes the interests of those who own or control capital (Offe, 1975).

The final element of dominant ideology mentioned in the literature concerns culture as ideology. Whereas the three elements so far designated (the ideologies of accumulation, managerialism, state neutrality and welfare) are discrete phenomena which can be specified in terms of their content and their boundaries, and can thus be studied empirically, culture as ideology is a more diffuse notion which can be specified only in broad generalities and which is difficult to verify in the same way as other elements. Anderson (1964), as we saw in the previous chapter, has identified modern, bourgeois culture as empiricist and traditionalist and as a continuation of the ideology of the old agrarian dominant class. These cultural traits are held to inhibit speculation and philosophical modes of inquiry which would penetrate the true nature of class society, and to create respect for hierarchy and deference to authority. They are thought to dominate all cultural forms within society, to deprive the working class of the possibility of an autonomous world-view and an independent culture, and so to incorporate the working class into capitalist society. We have argued against Anderson's view that the early capitalist bourgeoisie did assimilate traditional dominant-class culture and have established that the bourgeoisie in fact had its own culture. Nevertheless, the two cultures are not incompatible, particularly with regard to empiricism which can be found in both, and the bourgeoisie would no doubt be content to promote within subordinate cultures the characteristics of deference to authority and the inability to reason critically, in addition to the more typical elements of bourgeois ideology. Of these latter elements, the one that is most widely regarded as definitive of bourgeois culture, as colouring bourgeois consciousness in all its activities, is individualism. This characteristic emphasis runs through the cluster of social beliefs which we have just labelled as the managerial ideology. It is to be found in the typical literary and artistic artefacts of this class. It also justifies the bourgeois emphasis on a particular view of consumption rights;

namely, the organisation of consumption on market principles which provide for individual choice (as in the individual's right to choose how to educate his or her children).

One region of early capitalist, bourgeois ideology is noticeably missing from this list, namely, traditional morality. That area of belief which concerned religion, sexual and personal morality, and the sanctity and social significance of the family, has collapsed in modern bourgeois culture. At the level of institutional practices, legislative reform of the old laws regarding homosexuality, divorce and abortion, and changes in the Anglican position on contraception, divorce and re-marriage, suggest that neither the state nor the church resists this collapse and that both provide the means for it to accelerate. At the level of personal belief and class culture, there is now moral pluralism; the individual is free to 'do his own thing' and to shop at the supermarket of moral choice (Berger, 1969), rather than to follow a prescribed morality. This collapse of traditional morality became possible with the decline of the family's function within the economy. The growth of joint-stock, corporate capitalism marked the end of an economic system which depended on the accumulation and transmission of capital within the family, and destroyed the material basis which gave point to a morality based on familial values and the regulation of sexual activity. The 'pluralisation of life-worlds' (Berger, Berger and Kellner, 1974) within bourgeois culture signals the end of this class's economic function within the late capitalist mode of production, an argument which we develop more fully in Chapter 6.

Several observations need to be made about these elements of ideology. The most obvious is that the dominant ideology is not internally consistent. Indeed, some of the elements are mutually contradictory. The welfare consensus conflicts with the belief that the wage hierarchy ought to be determined by market principles or by functional importance, since welfare programmes in effect raise the pay of those at the bottom of the scale above its true market and functional worth, and are intended to do so. The notion that the state should be neutral between vested interests and social classes in liberal democracy is in conflict with the belief that state activity should promote the interests of capital accumulation, so benefiting the groups which represent capital, and with the fact that the state is not neutral.

The second observation is that there is a range of different material interests within the dominant class which includes those of senior managers and directors of large corporations and financial institutions, owner-managers of small firms outside the large-scale sector of the economy and *rentiers* and other landowners who derive their wealth from property. These different 'fractions' of capital can be expected to respond in different ways to the different ideological elements. Managers of large corporations in the 'monopoly' sector of the economy have long supported the welfare compromise, which creates social stability and socialises the costs of providing a high-quality labour force. Interventionist economic planning maintains the environment necessary for large-scale companies, particularly those with high-technology, capital-intensive operations (Galbraith, 1967; Kidron, 1970). Other interest groups have resisted the growth of state interference in the social and economic arenas. In the early 1960s, for example, there was a notable clash within the Conservative Party between large- and small-scale industrialists over the policy of encouraging industrial rationalisation and concentration, in order to create larger and more efficient units, and of increasing the forces of competition in the market place, a policy that ran counter to the interests of small-scale capital (Harris, 1972, pp. 235–40). Large corporations in the 1970s have accepted and implemented legislation which adds to the rights and increases the power of individual employees and trade unions, in part because their traditions of 'enlightened' employment policies and the presence of powerful trade union organisations mean that many legislative reforms merely codify existing practices. Small firms tend to oppose new legislation because it interferes with managerial prerogative and is expensive (Rogally, 1977).

We earlier emphasised how beliefs about property rights appear to have changed, judging by the institutional embodiment of the dominant ideology. But it seems plausible to suggest that many of those who own significant amounts of private property are more likely than those who do not to hold traditional notions about the unimpeded inheritance and transfer of property, and about owners' rights to use or dispose of their property as they wish. We would expect to find landowners, both *rentiers* and farmers, in this category, along with the owners of small or medium-sized firms. Since successful managers have sufficient surplus income to create capital during their working lives, and indeed a number do create modest personal wealth in this way as they grow older (Diamond Report, 1976), one might also assume that some managers come to accept parts of the property ideology. If so, this would coexist uneasily with the managerial ideology of meritocratic achievement, particularly when inherited property creates social advantages for children and grandchildren. There is of course a tension between achievement ideologies and a belief in the rights of the wealthy to buy privilege for themselves or to pass on wealth and privilege to their heirs, which has often been commented upon (R. Turner, 1953–4). The final inconsistency is that some parts of the ideology do not gain support even from those who disseminate them. Nichols (1969, pp. 167–207) has noted that a sample of businessmen were hardly concerned with social responsibility though they paid the notion lip-service, while Fox (1974) has demonstrated that managers routinely operate on the basis of low-trust principles while employing the rhetoric of high trust.

These comments show that the dominant ideology lacks internal consistency, with the result that many of its constituent elements are contradictory. They further suggest that not all of the dominant groups believe in all of the elements. Thus we have a dominant ideology that is neither coherent nor subscribed to by all its supposed proponents. It no longer has that central core of Protestantism and utilitarianism which made early capitalist ideology such a coherent and widely held set of beliefs.

Subordinates and the Dominant Ideology

Do subordinate groups believe the dominant ideology? Here we come to an area where there is more factual information available, since one section of the subordinate population, the manual working class, has been investigated in some depth. There are difficulties in measuring attitudes and beliefs by means of interview schedules, which is the research technique most commonly used to identify the nature of working-class consciousness, but the data which result from interview surveys and from ethnographies based on other techniques such as direct and participant observation are broadly in agreement. They show that large numbers of subordinates are relatively disaffected from the existing social order and certain parts of its normative system. The failure of subordinates to accept all of the dominant ideology forms common ground between the various contributors to the discussion of working-class consciousness, but what remains a matter for debate is just how much of the ideology is rejected and what practical consequences, if any, this rejection may have.

It is worth noting at the outset that certain theoretical preconceptions have had a great influence on the interpretation of the evidence. The first is the acceptance of a particular version of the Marxist problematic, that anything less than a radical class consciousness – which involves an understanding of the structure of class society, collective solidarity with others in the same class and opposition to those in the dominant class, and a clearly-conceived alternative social order for which to strive (Mann, 1973) – represents an undeveloped consciousness and an accommodation to (even acceptance of) the dominant ideology. The second, which usually goes with the first, assumes that the rejection of dominant ideologies and the material order which underpins them will take political forms. The social divisiveness which inequality creates is assumed to have consequences ultimately for public order and to give rise to *incivisme* (Goldthorpe, 1974). Both these preconceptions demand what seem to be unreasonably stringent conditions for the rejection of the dominant ideology. The first seems to be unaware that the possession of a coherent, well-formed and clearly articulated philosophy is a rarity even in the dominant class, and is probably found only among certain intellectual groups. Rejection of the dominant ideology may well be partial, involving the penetration of the ideological character of some rather than all the elements, and the formulation of alternatives may be partial too. The dismissal of workers' consciousness as accommodative because it lacks coherence and totality, and because it is not based on radical, socialistic values (Parkin, 1972), understates the extent of the rejection that occurs. On the other hand, the failure of subordinates to develop an all-embracing alternative, which leads some authors to label consciousness as inconsistent (Mann, 1970), ignores the consistency that is found within limited areas of workers' oppositional consciousness, particularly if one recognises that people often express abstract ideas in a somewhat inarticulate manner. The second preconception simply misidentifies the location where the dominant ideology breaks down. There is a clear rejection of parts of the ideology in the *economic* rather than the political realm, and the dominant ideology fails to deliver the goods with regard to the social integration and control of industry (Goldthorpe, 1974).

A currently popular line of argument is that working-class disaffection is manifest in, and limited to, various forms of dualistic consciousness which simultaneously endorse and reject different parts of the dominant ideology. Recent attempts by Mann (1970), Parkin (1972), Westergaard (1970) and Nichols and Armstrong (1976) to explain a variety of interview data suggest that workers will often agree with dominant elements, especially when these are couched as abstract principles or refer to general situations, which is normally the case in interview surveys using standardised questionnaires, but will then accept deviant values when they themselves are directly involved or when these are expressed in concrete terms which correspond to everyday reality. Subordinate

individuals display modes of social consciousness in which beliefs
are incoherent and barely articulated (Westergaard, 1970; Nichols
and Armstrong, 1976, p. 128), and what beliefs there are seem to
be inconsistent with each other since they embrace both deviant
and dominant values (Mann, 1970). The working class widely
endorses vague, populist slogans which divide society into rich
and poor, but at the same time accepts conservative political values
which justify the existing institutions of government and master
symbols which evoke traditionalism and indoctrinate workers to
accept the status quo, for example, in the appeal of nation above
class (Mann, 1970; Nichols and Armstrong, 1976, pp. 145-6).
Mann later indicates that certain aspects of dualism result from
subordinates' own, non-distorted, perceptions of reality, though
other aspects are the products of ideological distortion, since
elements of the dominant ideology (such as its emphasis on the
need for industrial harmony and teamwork between the two sides
of industry in order to protect subordinates' economic interests)
are factually correct within the existing economic order (1973, p.
68). In addition, Mann emphasises that subordinates neither require
nor possess any well-developed value system which represents the
internalisation of the dominant ideology. The *actuality* of obedience
and satisfactory role-performance is all that dominant groups
require of subordinates, not the internalisation of an ideology.
Subordinates typically accept the existing order on a pragmatic
basis that involves little normative involvement and accounts for
the incoherence of their value systems (1970). Mann therefore
offers three distinct explanations for subordinates' acceptance
of the social order: ideological indoctrination, particularly at the
level of political values and master symbols; the non-distorted
appraisal of self-interest, which leads to realistic agreement with
certain dominant values; pragmatic apathy, a state in which subordinates are not concerned with either dominant or deviant values.

Parkin provides a less complex conceptualisation of dual
consciousness and its limits, which rests more firmly on the
hegemony of the dominant ideology (1972, pp. 79-102). The
dominant value system originates among those with power and
advantage and is embodied in the major institutional order. This
value system endorses inequality, while its institutional expression
means that it permeates the consciousness of subordinate groups
and creates a moral framework which promotes acceptance of the
existing structure of material rewards and social honour. Subordinates accept this dominant value system but add to it their own
subordinate values, which modify but do not destroy the system,
presenting a 'negotiated' version which leaves the essentials intact.

The subordinate values are those of local working-class communities, and all local communities tend to produce the same values on account of the similarity of working-class conditions, which include conflict with those in authority, an 'us' versus 'them' model of society, and an emphasis on the distinctiveness of working-class life. These are 'accommodative' values which reconcile people to inequality and low status.

Parkin clearly believes that deviant values provide only the most limited countervailing force to the dominant ideology, a perspective which Mann shares in those parts of his argument which rely on ideological indoctrination. The empirical evidence for this interpretation is less clear-cut, however. Mann (1970) surveys the evidence collected in the 1950s and 1960s in America and Britain which, in the British case, does not lend much weight to conclusions about the successful internalisation of dominant values. The British data show how large numbers of working-class subordinates do not clearly endorse the fairness and legitimacy of the opportunity structure, do not accept the conventional political values that government is responsive to democratic pressure and even-handed in its treatment of different groups, and reject the bourgeois value of individualism. The data on master symbols such as nationhood are American rather than British. Among middle-class subordinates, however, dominant values are more universally accepted. These data are partial and ambiguous, and permit a variety of interpretations without suggesting one which is obviously correct. On balance, the interpretation of the data as demonstrating incoherence and pragmatism, that is, that people do not have much in the way of beliefs, probably does least violation to these facts. Other evidence which is presented below, however, suggests a more strongly held and radical set of values in one area of the dominant ideology, and a more extensive rejection in a second area, than Parkin and Mann would appear to believe.

The obvious problem with dualism is *where* to place the emphasis. On the one hand there is the view that people are primarily indoctrinated, but have some freedom to develop their own non-conforming values. On the other is the view that acknowledges that ideology permeates working-class thought, but maintains that deviant values can be more radical and more widely held than Parkin seems to believe, more coherent in some areas than Mann and Westergaard would suggest, and mark the existence of a working-class culture that is independent of bourgeois culture (Moorhouse and Chamberlain, 1974; Swingewood 1977). On balance, we favour a view that gives working-class culture more autonomy than ideological hegemonists would grant it, while recognising some permeation in particular areas, that does not expect to find a totally consistent and clearly articulated value system among subordinates when this is absent among dominant groups (though we note that parts of the working-class value system *are* coherent and articulate), and that recognises the force of pragmatism.

The ideology of accumulation is not internalised in all its aspects, and it is in this area of the dominant ideology that recent research shows some subordinates to have the most coherently deviant values. A survey carried out in the early 1970s into the attitudes of working-class tenants in London toward private property (mainly the ownership of housing) demonstrates how subordinates decisively reject the traditional property ideology (Moorhouse and Chamberlain, 1974). Not surprisingly, tenants rejected the rights of owners to use or dispose of their property as they saw fit, which is an encroachment on property rights endorsed by government. Large numbers also approved of squatting in empty houses, occupying factories which have threatened to make workers redundant and usurping from the owners of firms their rights to run their businesses as they like, a more radical attack on property rights that is not endorsed by the dominant institutions. Remarkably, these tenants also attacked private property as an institution, in the sense that they denied the right to *own* property in certain circumstances (for example, the right to own more than one house). The official ideology disseminated by the major institutions has relinquished certain property rights which are essential neither for the functioning of the mode of production nor for the material interests of certain dominant groups, as we suggested in the previous section, even though other groups within the upper class may still need and believe the full-scale ideology of property. But the dominant ideology has never questioned this one fundamental right of property ownership.

Moorhouse and Chamberlain's research shows how many people attacked the principle of accumulation itself and not only its manifestation in certain forms of private property. People argued against profit as the criterion and dynamic of economic activity, which is to deny the ideology of accumulation which maintains reproduction. In place of accumulation, and it is here that we find evidence of a fairly coherent and explicit alternative model of social organisation which goes beyond the simple rejection of dominant ideology, it was proposed that human need should be the *raison d'être* of economic activity. This alternative value system is incomplete and formulated at a low level of abstraction but, nevertheless, it demonstrates that radical and non-accommodative values which have a degree of coherence and consistency are found in opposition to particular elements of the dominant ideology. We cannot be sure how far this evidence is representative of subordinates more generally, since studies of working-class consciousness have been surprisingly unconcerned with how people perceive the economic structure and how far they accept this element of the ideology, and have concentrated instead on images of society which deal with social class and power. We just do not have information in a form which would allow us definitely to resolve the issue. However, other pieces of evidence suggest, indirectly, that the existing principles of accumulation probably do *not* command much support (even if they are not rejected). Many workers clearly question the basis on which surpluses are distributed between labour and capital, wanting more to go, as wages, to labour, and this is true even of workers who are not particularly radical in other respects (e.g. Goldthorpe, Lockwood *et al.*, 1968*a*, p. 89). Wage bargaining between labour and management embodies, on the labour side, ideas about what is a just wage which give no room to managerial arguments about profitability and ability to pay, or about the market principles of supply and demand which ought to determine the level of wages, but which depend instead on 'social' rather than 'economic' criteria, for example, need, skill and customary differentials. This is why, to the despair of the mass media of communication, trade unionists ignore those appeals for wage restraint which appear to be matters of common sense if one accepts the ideology of accumulation. This discussion must remain speculative in the absence of firmer evidence, but there are plausible grounds for doubting whether the working class really accepts this element of the ideology.

The occupational structure and its associated inequality of rewards is challenged less fundamentally than property rights or, perhaps, the principle of accumulation. To be sure, some people reject the occupational criteria on which reward is based and feel, for instance, that physical effort and danger should count for more than non-manual skills, education and 'responsibility' (Young and Willmott, 1956). But these are minority views and large numbers of people agree at least on the significance of education, training and skill as criteria of economic worth and social honour (Hill, 1976, p. 183; Coxon and Jones, 1979, pp. 129–40), which in turn implies some endorsement of the meritocratic version of inequality. Though this endorsement may be largely normative (i.e. an agreement that inequality *ought* to be meritocratic) rather than evaluative, since significant numbers believe that the achievement structure does *not* in reality work as it should do (Veness, 1962, p. 144; McKenzie and Silver, 1968, p. 140), which suggests that people can both endorse the ideology and penetrate the reality. Information on attitudes toward the reward structure suggests that most people feel this to be 'fair', that they accept the existing hierarchy of incomes as normal and natural (Hyman and Brough, 1975, pp 199–207). Low-level subordinates typically adopt as comparative reference groups other occupations with a similar position in the hierarchy to their own rather than make comparisons with those who are significantly higher, and it is claimed that inequalities have little salience (Hyman and Brough, 1975, pp. 39–45).

Interpretation of this sort of evidence is not entirely clear-cut, however, since people who happily endorse the existing *structure* of incomes as fair, and there is a broad consensus on this, often do not accept the *level* of higher incomes (Behrend *et al.*, 1970, pp. 6–7). Indeed, low-level subordinates do not appear to know what people above them in fact earn, and when some higher salaries are made public, as during pay negotiations in the public sector, resentment can be strong (Clegg, 1971, p. 9). Nor does acceptance of the structure imply acceptance of market principles and functional importance in fixing pay levels, since attitudes to these reflect notions such as need, in the case of the low paid who are thought to deserve more than the market will bear, or social worth, in the case of junior doctors and nurses who contribute more, presumably, than their functional importance or market strength would provide (Behrend *et al.*, 1967, ch. 6). Behrend's research, moreover, shows popular support for restricting the pay rises of politicians, civil servants, company directors and managers, and those with high incomes in general, while raising those of the low paid and socially worthy (1967, ch. 6). Broad endorsement of dominant values about inequality of income therefore conceals disagreement on a number of issues concerning fairness and allocative mechanisms.

Those aspects of the managerial ideology which deal with the structure of inequality within industry are more decisively rejected, however. Commonality of interests may be accepted, in the sense that workers and managers as a matter of fact have to co-operate under the present system if any goods are to be produced. But the inherent conflict of interests that exists between labour and management is visible to most workers. Indeed the relationship between men and management is based on power rather than authority, on low trust, on anomie and normative conflict (Fox, 1974; Goldthorpe, 1974). The rejection of managerial ideology sometimes may extend even to the rejection of the special technical competence claimed for managerial jobs (Hill, 1976, pp. 114, 150), or to a denial that managers have this quality if it is in fact required. British industrial relations since the war have been marked by high strike rates, by encroachments on managerial prerogative which restrict managers' rights to manage, and by aggressive wage-bargaining which poses serious threats to profitability and accumulation (Donovan Report, 1968). The conduct of industrial relations reflects value dissensus, the rejection of hierarchy and submissiveness, an appreciation of the virtues of collectivism in place of bourgeois individualism and the naked conflict of material interests. This marks the major failure of the dominant ideology to perform its stabilising function and is the one area where rejection of the ideology has direct consequences for social order. The lack of any moral framework to economic life means that the divisive impact of social inequality is not curbed by the creation of normative consensus, and the concrete, day-to-day activity of subordinates reflects a state of affairs in which social integration has partly collapsed.

The evidence that subordinates support the ideology of liberal democracy is hardly convincing. Between half and three-quarters of working-class respondents to surveys endorse statements which suggest that big business has too much power in society, that there is one law for the rich and another for the poor. (Goldthorpe, Lockwood *et al.*, 1968*b*, pp. 25–7; McKenzie and Silver, 1968, p. 128; Hill, 1976, pp. 187–90), and that the upper class is hostile to working-class interests (McKenzie and Silver, 1968, p. 135). All of this suggests that the majority of workers does not endorse dominant beliefs about the distribution of power and the interests of dominant groups. Information about social imagery shows that a proletarian model of society is widely held, but with varying degrees of intensity, within the class (Roberts *et al.*, 1977, pp. 37–65). This model is based on a belief in the class-ridden nature of British society and the antagonism of class interests. This evidence provides valuable insights into people's perceptions of social structure and power, but unfortunately it does not tell us anything directly about other issues such as citizenship rights in the political system, political pluralism and state neutrality. Surprisingly few sociologists have been centrally concerned with issues relating to the political structure and its institutions, just as few have dealt with the economic structure, and so what information is available is limited and partial.

On the issue of political efficacy, whether or not people feel that government is responsible to pressure from below, large numbers of subordinates do not feel any strong sense of efficacy. More than a half of McKenzie and Silver's sample and more than two-fifths of Nordlinger's did not believe that they could have any influence on government. On the issue of even-handedness, only one-third of the people interviewed in a recent study reported that they were definitely convinced that the British political system 'works for the interest of most of the people most of the time' (Robinson and Bell, 1978), and two-thirds of the people questioned in a 1960s study thought that big business and the upper class controlled government (Nordlinger, 1967, pp. 105, 109). Mann (1970) has suggested that data like these represent simple-minded and populist responses to slogans about political power, which coexist with more conservative political values. The basis of this assertion is not obvious, however, and there is evidence to the contrary. In the first place, these views of the political order fit coherently and logically with the proletarian model of society, and with the statements about social power and class interest. In the second, support for some of the master symbols of the political system is not at all strong: McKenzie and Silver found that only two-fifths of their sample wanted to retain the House of Lords and about a half wanted to retain the monarchy (1968, pp. 145–52).

However, the evidence must remain less than conclusive for several reasons. Taking the evidence as it stands, there is consistently a slight majority of working-class subordinates which denies that liberal democracy works as the ideology says it should, which leaves a substantial minority endorsing the dominant perspective; there is no unanimity within the working-class. But the evidence itself is extremely limited and it deals directly with only a few elements of liberal democracy; it does not consider, for instance, what people believe to be the purpose or function of welfare policy and economic intervention, whether these redress inequality or promote the interests of capital, or what role the Labour Party has in liberal democracy. It does not even try to find out what sense of alternatives subordinates possess. There do not appear to be any immediately obvious *practical* consequences of denying the ideology, in the way that those who reject property rights endorse squatting and factory sit-ins (and perhaps even participate), or in the way that the rejection of managerialism is manifest in concrete industrial activity. There is very little active political protest that occurs outside the existing political framework or that attempts to subvert this framework.

Some recent discussions of working-class culture have questioned the view that it is irremediably permeated by a bourgeois culture that expresses the dominant ideology. Swingewood (1977, pp. ix–x) argues that working-class culture is not a simple and direct expression of the bourgeois one, because the working class receives bourgeois values after they have been mediated by the institutions of civil society, which include family, peer and occupational groups, and those institutions which represent subordinate interests, trade unions and social democratic political parties, which flourish rather than decay as capitalism matures. Content analysis of working-class novels reveals a complex, contradictory and changing popular consciousness which is not a simple transformation of bourgeois thought into working-class consciousness, but contains 'a definite historical trend towards independent collectivist institutions and ideology while at the same time emphasising the persistence of individualistic bourgeois values' (Swingewood, 1977, p. 119). This analysis rests on the familiar methodology of indirect evidence from literature and *a priori* assumptions about institutions, in this case subordinate literature and institutions, but provides no direct evidence of what values people in practice hold.

Recent ethnographical accounts of different working-class groups, one of assembly-line workers at Ford (Beynon, 1973) and another of teenage pupils in a midlands school (Willis, 1977), are therefore valuable sources of information about beliefs. They show the continuity, at least among these two groups, of that autonomous culture which we identified in nineteenth-century England and which Hoggart and Klein documented in the 1950s and 1960s. Ford workers, particularly the shop stewards, shared a culture that was clearly oppositional and collectivist, the institutional embodiment of which was to be found in trade unionism (Beynon, 1973, pp. 187–208). Expressed in the workplace, this culture promoted a 'factory class consciousness' which perceived the conflict of interest between labour and capital, treated industrial relationships between workers and managers as inherently oppositional, and provided the stimulus to a continuing series of battles over the issue of control. Factory consciousness did not lead to any radical political activity beyond the factory gates. Beynon emphasises the significance of historical tradition for the perpetuation of non-incorporated beliefs, as do other commentators. Among Ford workers, the tradition of labourist and socialist ideologies inherited from older generations informed their appraisals of employment (Beynon, 1973, pp. 190–1). Moorhouse and Chamberlain (1974) argue a similar case when they account for the rejection of property rights and the principle of accumulation. The impact of socialist thought so permeated working-class culture between 1880 and 1939 that residual elements of socialist theory have been inherited by the contemporary working class and still have a force, despite the absence of any major radical political party at the present time. Nichols and Armstrong (1976, pp. 145–6) emphasise what they term 'less direct experience', the transmission through working-class culture of the experience of earlier generations of workers who were engaged in the more naked class conflicts of the prewar period.

Willis's (1977) account of a group of teenagers shows how the school regarded the boys in this group as difficult pupils, because, unlike many of their contemporaries, they rejected the values embodied in the educational system. Instead, they had a well-developed and self-contained culture which was barely integrated with the dominant value system, and which was transmitted by their families and peers. The school emphasised individualism, which included several different components. These are a belief in self-fulfilling and creative activity, the need for people to make choices which reflect their own personalities rather than being imposed, and the desirability of individual achievement, defined as success within the existing prestige hierarchy which rewards non-manual rather than manual occupations. It also tried to inculcate a respect for hierarchy and deference to authority. The boys instead emphasised an 'us' versus 'them' view of school and society. This was concretely manifest in various ways: a refusal to submit to authority; the value of solidaristic collectivism and the rejection of the various elements of the individualistic ethos; a glorification of manual labour and the devaluation of mental work; and an awareness that labour has only a commodity status in the modern economy, coupled with the acceptance of this fact.

All the elements of the school culture were therefore neatly inverted. Paradoxically, this inversion may well have made the boys more, rather than less, suitable for post-school employment. Values such as self-fulfilment, individual job choice on the basis of matching job and personality attributes, achievement, are all dysfunctional for the economy when low-level employment does not *offer* much in the way of fulfilment, choice or achievement opportunities. Satisfaction in work is a fairly important bourgeois value (Anthony, 1977, pp. 230–68) and, together with the other elements of individualism, it forms an area of the dominant culture which workers ought not to absorb if their expectations are to be matched to employment opportunities. The crucial fact about working-class integration that emerges from this account is the boys' acceptance of the commodification of labour. They correctly penetrate the ideological mystification of work which the individual-istic, dominant culture disseminates, the function of which is to *conceal* commodification, to appreciate the reality that they are only labour-power and that work can only offer them a commodity status. They accept this reality. It is sometimes assumed that this understanding, that capitalism creates alienated labour-power, is one of the crucial developments in the growth of 'true' class consciousness. But in this case understanding fosters acceptance. Indeed, the glorification of manual against mental labour allows the boys to feel that they are rejecting the dominant ideology, even at the moment in which they accept the nature of the economic system and their place in this.

There has been a significant change between early and late capitalism in the power of the agencies of transmission. Mass education and the mass media of communication provide for the first time the means of transmitting dominant values on a universal scale. How effective are these institutions in this role? The empirical evidence presented so far in this chapter in a sense answers the question and shows that their efficacy is somewhat limited, since so many subordinates reject dominant values. But it is still appropriate to treat the agencies of transmission in a little more detail.

Mass media studies are agreed that the content of the media is based on 'a limited and recurring range of images and ideas which form rather special versions of reality' (McQuail, 1977, p. 81). Commentators on the left assert that these represent the values of the groups which are dominant in society. The dominant class is directly manipulative of the content of the press and television because large corporations and wealthy individuals own large chunks of the media (Cohen and Young, 1973, pp. 16–17). Even those who disagree that there is direct manipulation on the basis of class interests present a picture of the determination of content which produces the same set of values: Burns, for instance, suggests that it is the market place which restricts the content of the press, because newspapers compete for readers with high spending-power in order to maximise revenue from advertisers and are therefore obliged to follow the consensus line that is based on what the 'well-heeled professional and managerial middle classes' want to read (Burns, 1977, p. 66). The media fulfil their role of promoting a consensus based on the view of the world that is held by dominant groups by propagating a particular view of specific issues and also by fixing the agenda of what may be considered. Agenda-setting involves the establishment of an order of priorities and a scale of values that is determined elsewhere, usually in the political arena, which does not directly determine people's beliefs but may limit what they can believe (McQuail, 1977, p. 84).

The issue, of course, is not to prove that the media for one reason or another are partial, but to establish that the media have a significant influence on what people believe. Here we move into the realm of conjecture, where the facts are 'so scarce, open to dispute and often puny in stature' (McQuail, 1977, p. 87), that the issue is usually resolved by cerebration. It is probable that beliefs are influenced by the media in some way when people have *no* other basis on which to form an opinion (McQuail, 1977, p. 80), for instance, by reference to their own experience, that of others, or their cultural tradition. Such a state of affairs is in fact rarely encountered, but it may apply when subordinates evaluate alternative social forms of which they have no direct knowledge; the media may account, for example, for the unpopularity of Soviet-style socialism which we note below. The evidence of media influence is so thin and subject to so many caveats that our conclusion must be that the media are not significant except in the most isolated instances.

Education might reasonably be expected to be more important, because, after the family, it is the major influence on childhood socialisation. Once again, the content of school curricula and the values of the teaching staff can without difficulty be shown to be largely 'middle class', that is, those of the dominant groups. There are good reasons for suggesting, however, that this content is not universally absorbed. On the one hand, the literature regarding working-class achievement within the educational system suggests that the degree to which children have come to terms with the demands of the system – for instance, the bourgeois culture of teachers and the elaborated codes of language which form the universe of educational discourse – is highly variable and largely accounts for differences of attainment. Moreover, one of the determinants of this outcome is the prior compatibility of the home environment with the values of the school. On the other hand, studies like that of Willis show how children may quite clearly reject school culture even after many years within the educational system, and that the basis of this rejection is prior socialisation into an alternative set of beliefs and values. Education undoubtedly does have an effect, but the realisation of its potential for disseminating dominant beliefs varies widely.

We have suggested that both Marxist and functionalist sociologies have created false problematics for the study of subordinate beliefs and culture. Both have an over-socialised conception of society, which leads them to exaggerate the extent to which subordinate classes are ideologically incorporated. Two conclusions emerge from this chapter which challenge these orthodox perspectives. The major conclusion must be that Britain is *not* in fact a cohesive society. Sociologists have overestimated the degree of social integration. This can most clearly be demonstrated in the economy, where social relations are anomic, conflict-laden, and reflect hostilities between social classes and between the interests of capital and labour. Two sociologists outside the Marxist and functionalist perspectives have convincingly demonstrated that the reality of the social relations of production in modern Britain is such as to destroy any notions about the efficacy of value integration (Fox, 1974; Goldthorpe, 1974). The second conclusion, which is in fact an elaboration of the first, is that value dissensus can be found throughout the working class and concerns, in varying degrees, most of the range of ideological elements which we identified earlier. Anomie does not appear to lead to activity outside the economy which overtly destroys social integration, but its prevalence suggests that social order cannot be explained primarily by ideological incorporation and value consensus. We may speculate about the various ways in which social order and integration are maintained in the absence of powerful consensual values.

Subordinates have not formulated a radical belief system which contains a model of an alternative society along the lines that some sociologists have demanded as evidence of 'true' class consciousness. This obviously reduces the threat to social order that would have resulted should subordinates have developed such an oppositional ideology. This state of affairs need not be accounted for in terms of the indoctrinating power of dominant ideology, and can satisfactorily be explained in other ways. The most obvious is that reformism has produced real, tangible benefits for the working class, with the result that, for many, it no longer appears necessary that existing institutions, including capitalism, should be destroyed. Radical transformation by revolutionary means would lead inevitably to disruption, exchanging the hope of better things to come at some moment in the future for the almost certain loss in the short and medium terms of the benefits already enjoyed. Capitalism has revolutionised the means of production and increased the sum total of wealth, with the consequence that the lot of the working class has improved dramatically and regardless of inequalities in the distribution of the fruits of this wealth. Subordinates obviously do question the way in which rewards and power are distributed within society, but this distribution can in principle be modified substantially without destroying the capitalist mode of production. In comparison with early capitalism, the trade union organisation of the contemporary economy and the liberal democratic political system which gives citizenship rights to all in late capitalism, have already increased the influence of the organised working class on the dominant class. Cumulatively, reformist gains may even threaten the interests of the dominant class (Offe, 1975).

The other explanations of the absence of radical beliefs are negative in character, and depend on the absence of certain conditions rather than the positive benefits which accrue from the existing order. Briefly, these include the familiar and well-documented observations that subordinate classes are riven by internal stratification which reduces homogeneity and shared interests, and that class agencies such as trade unions and the Labour Party have chosen a reformist path which prevents them from providing a revolutionary leadership. Both factors inhibit radicalism. One might add the less frequently noted phenomenon, that the currently available alternatives are hardly likely to attract the British working class. Soviet-style socialism discredits the Marxist-Leninist alternative, which is both the most clearly formulated and the one to which the working class has been most exposed in this century. The demonstration effect of Russian communism may promote aversion rather than endorsement.

Integration is maintained in other ways which are unrelated to the values and beliefs of subordinates as these affect social order and social cohesion. *System integration* is important, in the sense that a complex division of labour establishes interdependencies which must be realised, and which are indeed usually realised. There is no necessary coherence between social and system integration (Lockwood, 1964). System integration, in so far as it affects subordinates and relies on their activities, is the result of self-interest and various forms of external constraint. Workers may perform their roles in the division of labour simply because this is necessary for the continued survival of the system on which they themselves depend. The integration of the system is in their own self-interests. There is no need, in fact, for workers to endorse the values of the system. They need not, for example, accept the managerial ideology which justifies economic privilege and superior power. There is nothing to stop them acting in ways which testify to the collapse of social integration and social cohesion, provided that they perform their roles within the division of labour with some degree of effectiveness. It is this awareness of system integration which Mann encapsulates in his phrase that workers have an 'experience of (largely economic) interdependence with the employer at a factual, if not a normative level' (1973, p. 68).

The appraisal of self-interest which leads subordinates to the pragmatic acceptance of system constraints, including some sort of compliance to managerial decisions in the economic realm, is not of course entirely voluntary and uncoerced. In late capitalism, as in the early variety, compulsion remains an important condition of system integration and of pragmatic apathy as an element of the subordinate culture. Compulsion is most obviously founded in the structure of economic relations, which oblige people to behave in ways which support the status quo and to defer to the decisions of the powerful if they are to continue to work and to live. But economic force is not the only form of compulsion, since the state's coercive potential also has a significant role. An example can be drawn from the economic realm, where management has always been able to rely on the legal system to support its claims to power and control, and to use the sanctions of the law to this end. Liberal democracy has to some extent eroded this support over the last two decades, but it remains true that legal force is exercised primarily in the interests of management, for instance, in the assumption that managers give orders and that workers obey. In a celebrated description, Weber (1964) referred to the state as the legitimate user of physical force. This force, which is given effect by means of law and assumes a concrete expression in the activities of the police and military agencies, must be seen as a powerful buttress to the maintenance of system integration. The essence of this sort of compulsion, of course, is that it need rarely be manifest in action, since it is the *potentiality* of physical force which serves to maintain order for the most part.

In short, the agencies of ideological transmission are well developed in late capitalism and potentially have a substantial part to play in the process of incorporation. However, this potential is not properly realised for a variety of reasons. One is the incoherence of the dominant ideology itself, which reflects the internal differentiation of the dominant class into separate economic interest groups and the changing functional importance of this class as a bearer of productive property in late capitalism. Another is the continuing autonomy of working-class culture.

We claim that notions such as incorporation via ideological hegemony or integration via common culture need not in any case enter the explanation of why late capitalism survives. There are other satisfactory explanations which make no reference to the ideology of dominant or subordinate classes, nor to the indoctrination of one by the other. One major weakness of the dominant ideology thesis which emerges in our examination of the factual basis of the theory is that sociologists know scarcely anything about the ideology of the dominant class, and take on faith a variety of unsubstantiated generalisations which are derived from their theoretical preconceptions rather than any real evidence. A similar criticism can be levelled at common culture theorists who take for granted a shared value system.

Chapter 6

The End of Ideology?

There has been a very general agreement that all class societies have to have either a dominant ideology or a dominant culture. Apparently finding support in historical data, Giddens claims (1968, p. 269):

> The fact that subordinate groups in society, even if they are subjected to what to an outsider might appear to be extreme exploitation and degradation, accept their subordination is evident to any student of society with even a cursory knowledge of history.

A sharply different view is presented by the historian Wallerstein in his *The Modern World-System* (1974, p. 143):

> It is doubtful if very many governments in human history have been considered 'legitimate' by the majority of those exploited, oppressed, and maltreated by their governments . . . governments tend to be endured, not appreciated or admired or loved or even supported.

In our consideration of the dominant ideology thesis we have provided empirical evidence which supports Wallerstein's view. Specifically, our arguments in the preceding three chapters can be summarised in terms of answers to the four questions which we posed in Chapter 1.

What is the dominant ideology? While it is often assumed that the dominant ideologies are clear, coherent and effective, we show that, on the contrary, they are fractured and even contradictory in most historical periods. However, the ideological structure is relatively more coherent in feudalism and early capitalism than in contemporary society. In feudal society the dominant ideology was religious, or at least deeply informed by religious considerations. In early capitalism it was united by a set of beliefs describable as individualism. In late capitalism the limited ideological unity of previous periods has collapsed. The scope and effectiveness of the dominant ideology, despite improvements in the apparatus of transmission, have been curtailed because of major changes in the economic and political organisation of society.

What are the effects of the dominant ideology on the subordinate classes? The dominant ideology has had little effect on subordinate classes. In feudalism there was a widespread cultural separation between social classes, and the peasantry had a culture quite distinct from the dominant one. In early capitalism there was little penetration of dominant conceptions into the working class. However, in late capitalism that situation again differs since now there is some limited ideological incorporation of subordinate classes. But this incorporation is only partially effective, there being a duality of consciousness and culture. We should stress at this point that we are arguing against the claim that there is ideological incorporation of subordinate classes by a dominant ideology. Nevertheless, we do not want to suggest that ideology or culture *cannot act* as a cohesive force. There is, for example, the real possibility that elements of the culture of subordinate classes, which develop autonomously from the culture of dominant classes, will have the effect of dampening down oppositional activity. This should not, however, be mistaken for ideological incorporation.

What is the effect of the dominant ideology on the dominant classes? If subordinate classes are not normally incorporated by the dominant ideology, dominant classes on the contrary *are* incorporated, at least in feudalism and early capitalism. In late capitalism, however, there is considerable uncertainty as to whether dominant classes do hold the dominant ideology. To some extent, this lack of ideological incorporation of dominant classes is due to the lack of definition and unity of the ideological structure which we have already noted. It is also due to the changing nature of the dominant class itself, which derives from changes in the economic structure of capitalism.

What is the apparatus of transmission of the dominant ideology? Any theory of ideology requires an account of the apparatus of transmission. In fact, many Marxist theories of ideology have identified the 'means of mental production'. However they have failed to recognise that these means do not have uniform consequences for all social classes. The differential effects of the dominant ideology on subordinate and dominant classes are partly explained by the variable efficacy of this apparatus. Dominant classes are more exposed to the means of mental production than are subordinate classes. In the feudal period, religious practices were often organised in such a way that they were not fully meaningful to the peasantry. Similarly, in early capitalism, the ideological aspects of the church, the education system and even the workplace did not result in any mass involvement. In late capitalism, however, the apparatus of transmission becomes potentially more efficient with the development of the mass media and a mass compulsory education system. This creates the paradox that, at the same time as the apparatus becomes more forceful, the coherence of the dominant ideology becomes weaker. Our basic thesis is that for feudalism and early capitalism there is a fairly coherent dominant ideology which, partly because of the character of the apparatus of transmission, incorporates the dominant classes but not the subordinate classes. Social stability and coherence cannot therefore simply be attributed to ideological incorporation or to the existence of value consensus. However, late capitalism is paradoxically different from both feudalism and early capitalism in that its dominant ideology is relatively less well defined, the dominant classes are relatively less incorporated, and the subordinate classes are relatively more incorporated, though only partially so. Despite this last feature, one still cannot argue that the stability of late capitalism is mainly produced by any form of ideological or value coherence.

Our arguments are plainly intended to have critical force, in that we are suggesting that the theories outlined in Chapters 1 and 2 are, at the very least, seriously misleading. Both the Marxist dominant ideology theorists and their sociological counterparts make assumptions that are often unexamined. For example, the relation between dominant ideology and the dominant classes is not considered, the apparatus for the transmission of ideology and values is not investigated in detail, and incorporation via ideology or integration by shared values is all too often taken for granted once the existence of a dominant ideology or value system is demonstrated. These weaknesses are essentially failures to investigate satisfactorily the conditions of the theories themselves. More radically, we have also argued that many versions of the dominant ideology thesis are simply false, especially the essential assumption that subordinate classes are ideologically incorporated.

The Coherence of Class Societies

We now attempt to broaden our discussion away from the mainly critical arguments directed against the dominant ideology thesis. If these arguments are correct, we have to answer two further questions. First, if class societies are not held together by a dominant ideology, how do they cohere? Secondly, what is the relationship of economy to ideology, if relations of domination are not underpinned by ideology?

There is a sense in which it is foolish to ask how societies cohere, for the answer is that they do not. This is a weakness inherent in the dominant ideology thesis, for it tends to produce an over-integrated view of society, in which ideology forges a seamless whole. It is obvious that societies are fractured in all sorts of ways which are manifested in anything from rick-burning to peasant revolts, and from industrial sabotage to general strikes. In the view of both Marxist and Weberian theory, there are essential political and economic contradictions within societies which will issue in conflict. However, given the theory, which we share, that there are such contradictions, there is still a question to be answered as to how the societies that we have described have *any* stability.

In previous chapters we have identified a number of factors which are involved in the quiescence of subordinate classes, some much more important than others. It is obvious that military force is the ultimate sanction available in all societies. As Moore (1978) says: 'Until decay overtakes the apparatus of repression no revolutionary movement stands a chance.' Similarly, the forceful exercise of the criminal and civil law may work to the disadvantage of subordinate groups. Our earlier discussion, and that of many authorities, indicates that these are significant factors, particularly in feudalism and early capitalism. However, it is undoubtedly true that military and judicial force are much less present in the every-day life-experiences of the working class in late capitalism than they were for the subordinate classes of early capitalist or feudal societies. Law in capitalist societies has progressively attenuated the rights of capital and occasionally strengthened those of workers.

Military or judicial force cannot, therefore, be a major factor in the coherence of capitalist societies. Economic compulsion, however, is significant, being mediated in a variety of ways. In capitalism the essence of the relations of production is that the worker is both controlled by management and separated from the means of production. Both Marx and Weber made similar points here and the emphasis on control and separation is found in both *Capital* and *Economy and Society*, although developed more fully in the former. The conventional Marxist account of the concept of the relations of production suggests that it includes two kinds of relationships between the labourer and the non-labourer and the means of production (Poulantzas, 1973, 1975). The first, economic ownership, refers to the control over the allocation of the means of production to particular uses and the power to dispose of the product. This economic ownership is analytically separable from legal ownership although, clearly, the two are closely related in fact. In class societies of all kinds, the non-labourer economically owns the means of production and is able to assign them to various uses, and has the power to appropriate the product. The non-labourer is, in this sense, separated from the means of production.

The second relationship, that of possession, refers to the power of putting the means of production into operation. Concretely, possession implies control over a specific labour process. We have argued in Chapter 3 that in feudal societies the peasant did have control over the labour process, while in capitalist societies the worker does not. In capitalist societies, therefore, the worker is doubly separated from the means of production, in terms of both economic ownership and possession.

Wright (1976) clarifies Poulantzas's account of the relations of production by displaying those relations as involving three kinds of control, over labour-power, over the physical means of production and over the allocation of resources. The first two of these correspond to different aspects of the relation of possession, while the third corresponds to economic ownership.

Typically, the management of labour involves the direct subordination of the workforce to managerial control. It is a sociological commonplace that efficient capitalism is possible 'only where the workers are subjected to the authority of business management' (Weber, 1964, p. 248). It is also argued that, as capitalism has progressed, managerial techniques have improved and the management structure has become increasingly differentiated and refined. Braverman, for example, suggests that the history of capitalism is a history of the increasing subordination of worker to management (Braverman, 1974; also Wright, 1976). In the early history of several industries there was no real 'problem' of management since production was organised on a subcontracting or 'putting-out' basis (Pollard, 1968). This was true, not only of trades that could be followed in the homes of the craftsmen, but also in such industries as metal-working, mining and cotton spinning. However, the lack of control over the workers by the manufacturer had numerous drawbacks, including irregularity of output, uncertainty over the quality of the product, inability to increase output readily and, most important of all, inability to change the process of production. The factory system did not have these deficiencies since it enabled much greater control over the labour-force, a control often exercised harshly in a legal and moral environment which favoured the manufacturer.

From its earliest days, capitalism has developed by refining the division of labour. Besides giving a competitive advantage, increased division of labour also gives management greater control by lessening the opportunities for worker resistance. Each individual worker, once in control of several phases of the production process by virtue of his craft skill, now knows only one small segment. By breaking down the method of production into a very large number of steps, management is able to specify even the physical movements that a worker will make. There is thus a radical distinction between conception of the whole work process by management, which involves minute planning, and *execution* by the worker, which has become a simply prescribed task. The worker has therefore become more like a machine, closely controlled. Indeed the increased use of sophisticated machinery also favours increased management control, since, plainly, a programmable machine is more easily directed than even the most 'deskilled' worker.

The increased need, and opportunities, for management have bred a corresponding stress on management technique. In Braverman's view the scientific management school, particularly as pioneered by Taylor, elevated the principles of managerial control to new heights. Before Taylor, management had sought to control labourers in a fairly general way, including, for example, 'the supervision of workers to ensure diligent, intense, or uninterrupted application; the enforcement of rules against distractions (talking, smoking, leaving the workplace, etc.) that were thought to interfere with application . . .' (Braverman, 1974, p. 90). None the less, there would be little direct interference in the actual tasks performed by the worker. 'But Taylor raised the concept of control to an entirely new phase when he asserted as an absolute necessity for adequate management the dictation to the worker of the precise manner in which work is to be performed.' Needless to say, since the principles of scientific management involved the widening of customary managerial rights, their introduction met with considerable resistance and still does.

If the significance of management derives from such sources as changes in the labour process, it is also related to changes within the patterns of ownership in capitalist enterprises. Not only is it impossible for an individual owner to oversee all aspects of his business, but the growth of joint-stock companies has meant that managers have replaced owners as effective controllers. Early capitalism may have been characterised by the concentration of legal ownership, economic ownership and possession all in the same hands. In late capitalism these three elements have become separated from one another to give a chain of managerial authority, with economic ownership vested in those at the top, and possession in those at the bottom.

It is therefore possible to see control by management over the worker as a fundamental process, if not *the* fundamental economic process of capitalism. As the preceding discussion has indicated, it is also closely related to the other two features of the relations of production identified by Wright, control over the physical means of production and control over the allocation of resources, both of which are aspects of the *separation* of the worker from the means of production.

This concept of separation, expressed by the term expropriation, also occupies an important place in Weber's economic sociology (Weber, 1964). One of the ways in which he classifies economic systems is by the mode of appropriation of economic advantages. The objects of appropriation can be either returns from labour, or material means of production, or opportunities for profit from the exercise of managerial functions. Capitalism is characterised by, amongst other things, the appropriation of the means of production by owners, which means 'the expropriation of the workers from the means of production, not merely as individuals, but as a whole' (Weber, 1964, p. 240). Weber further makes clear that the workers thus expropriated are free in the sense that they can offer their labour to whomsoever they choose, where they can make the best wage bargain. Capitalism has developed this form of appropriation of the means of production in response to the competitive edge given to enterprises which realise the high levels of efficiency given by autocratic managerial control.

The similarities between Weber's position, as sketched here, and that of many Marxist writers, is striking. However it is difficult to map his concepts on to those employed so far in this discussion. In particular, Weber's work does not so easily permit the distinction between economic ownership and possession which is important to Marx. There is an apparently similar distinction in Weber's analysis of socialism. He separates economic ownership from the control of the labour process, when he suggests that bureaucratic and centralised economic decision-making would continue the alienation of workers despite the abolition of capitalist forms of economic ownership. This distinction was less central to his analysis of capitalism, and in any event the terms possession and control are not synonymous. For Marx the non-labourer has both economic ownership and possession in the capitalist mode of production, while in the feudal mode he only has economic ownership, the labourer remaining in possession.

In capitalism the non-labourer (and this may not necessarily be an individual owner) has economic ownership. That is, he has control over such matters as the distribution of the enterprise's resources to given uses, the distribution of profit or the kind of product made. In effect we have already discussed the relationship of possession when reviewing the control of labour-power, for the latter is but one aspect of possession, the other being control over the physical means of production. Control over the physical means of production is really the other side of the coin of control over labour-power. Marx's discussion in the second part of Volume 1 of *Capital* illustrates this point, and Braverman's treatment of the same topic is essentially an elaboration of Marx's earlier work. It is control over physical plant, over the labour process, that enables the worker to resist managerial authority. As soon as the owner or manager has effective possession, whether by increased division of labour or the introduction of machinery, he has control.

In sum, control over the labour process and control over the allocation of resources give management its authority over the labourer. As Marx observes: 'From a social point of view, therefore, the working class, even when not directly engaged in the labour-process, is just as much an appendage of capital as the ordinary instruments of labour' (Marx, 1970, Vol. 1, p. 573). It should be clear, however, that, although to some extent these managerial prerogatives are 'given' by changes within the processes of capitalism itself, for example, by technical change, they can be, and are, 'politically' resisted. There is therefore no *necessity* in the expansion of managerial authority.

The claim that it is economic compulsion in the form of the separation of the worker from the means of production which gives control to management is not on its own a satisfactory account of social coherence, for it does not explain why that authority is *accepted*. Marx provides a solution to this problem which has found favour with Marxists and non-Marxists alike. 'Capitalist production, therefore, of itself reproduces the separation between labour-power and the means of labour. It therefore reproduces and perpetuates the condition for exploiting the labourer. It incessantly forces him to sell his labour-power in order to live . . .' (Marx, 1970, Vol. 1, p. 577). It is in this sense that 'the dull compulsion of economic relations' (1970, Vol. 1, p. 737) completes the total structure of control and acquiescence. The labourer, deprived of any claim to the means of production, only has his labour-power to sell and is therefore dependent on the individual capitalist or corporation to buy his services in exchange for the necessities of life. However, such a situation can only arise if the labourer is 'free', that is, unencumbered by any feudal ties, for the capitalist has to be able to purchase labour-power in a free market. Capital and free labour are conceptually and actually bound together. 'Capital presupposes wage-labour, and wage-labour pre-supposes capital. One is a necessary condition to the existence of the other; they mutually call each other into existence' (Marx, 1970, Vol. 1, p. 578). For the labourer this is a paradoxical freedom, since he also no longer has access to any means of production on his own account, an access that would give him a measure of independence.

In contrast to the worker in industrial capitalism, the feudal peasant does have some degree of effective possession of the means of production, although economic ownership is vested with the lord. The extent of this possession and control should not be exaggerated because, as both Weber and Hindess and Hirst have pointed out, the feudal landowner plays a crucial role in organising the labour process in as much as this extends beyond the individual peasant, as in the provision of flour mills and drainage schemes (Weber, 1964, p. 242; Hindess and Hirst, 1975).

But to the extent to which the peasant does have substantial control over the labour process, he has some independence of the landowner's authority. This, in turn, means that force, both military and judicial, plays a more central role in feudal societies than in capitalist ones. Force and economic compulsion are thus inversely related; less of one means more of the other.

The history of industrial capitalism in Britain has been marked by a move from the direct use of force in the transitional period (the use of the state directly to regulate wages, for example), to a less coercive regime which depends more on the workings of economic dependence. This is not to say that force is absent or that acquiescence is total, merely that the relative balance of force and economic compulsion has changed. The history of trade unionism is of the continuing effort by labour to organise in such a way as to reduce the impact of economic compulsion, and of changes in the law (the mobilisation of judicial force) in response to this pressure. Legal changes do not, of course, work entirely in the direction of increasing the force available to management, because the workings of social democracy may lead to less coercive laws. The main point is that force and economic compulsion are found together in both feudal and capitalist societies, even if inversely related. As far as feudal societies are concerned we have to reject the view found in Anderson (1974) that force alone is responsible for stability, and that advanced by Cutler et al. (1977) that force is irrelevant.

Weber's general characterisation of the structures of the capitalist economy of contemporary society bears a very close similarity to Marx's definition of capitalism. In Weber, the rationality of capitalist production is given, not by the nature of the beliefs of individuals, but by the objective requirements of profit-making in a formally competitive context. Thus, Weber declares: 'It is only in the modern western world that rational capitalistic enterprises with fixed capital, free labour, the rational specialization and combination of functions, and the allocation of productive functions on the basis of capitalistic enterprises, bound together in a market economy, are to be found' (Weber, 1964, p. 279). In the same passage, Weber goes on to treat the separation of the worker from productive means as the essential requirement of capitalist production where 'voluntary' labour is 'the typical and dominant mode of providing for the wants of the masses of the population, with expropriation of the workers from the means of production and appropriation of the enterprises by security owners' (Weber, 1964, p. 279). Thus, it is not Protestant asceticism as the ideological belief system of workers and capitalists which provides ideal conditions for capitalist development, but the political and economic organisation of capitalist society. Indeed, Weber goes so far as to say that 'free labour and the complete appropriation of the means of production create the most favoured conditions for discipline' (Weber, 1964, p. 248). The consequence of these economic structures for coercive authority relationships is that workers who are deprived of independent control over the means of production are compelled to submit to managerial authority in order to live. In Weber's economic sociology we possess a detailed account of how the coherence of capitalist societies is produced by the 'dull compulsion of economic relations' without recourse to a theory of the role of a dominant ideology.

There are two further comments that we need to make on the question of economic compulsion. Many Marxist writers make a distinction between the forms of separation from, or possession of, the means of production and the ideological and political conditions of existence of that separation or possession. For example, it is argued that 'Capitalist forms of possession are equally dependent on definite legal and political conditions of existence. In particular, they presuppose legal definition and sanction of private property in the means of production' (Cutler *et al.,* 1977, p. 246). We have argued throughout this book against the view that conditions of existence are ideological, if this means that the rights of property are accepted as just by all members of a society. We have also argued against a conception of the ideological as sets of real social relations which comprise the conditions of existence of the economy (which includes relations of possession), on the ground that this is an unwarranted extension of the concept of ideology (see Appendix). Although we reject the notion of an ideological condition of existence for relations of possession, we do hold that there are legal, political and military conditions, which should be seen as coercive rather than ideological; the less labourers are separated from the means of production, the more they are legally, politically and militarily coerced.

Secondly, Marx argues that, even if 'the dull compulsion of economic relations completes the subjection of the labourer to the capitalist', these relations become natural and taken-for-granted, so that 'the advance of capitalist production develops a working-class, which by education, tradition, habit, looks upon the conditions of that mode of production as self-evident laws of nature' (Marx, 1970, Vol. 1, p. 737). Miliband interprets this passage as evidence of *ideological* incorporation (1969, pp. 262 ff.). Again, we cannot accept arguments like these, if they mean that the working class comes to accept the *justice* of capitalist relations through the educational system or any other apparatus of the transmission of dominant ideology.

However, there is an important distinction between the acceptance of social arrangements because they appear just, and acceptance simply because they are there, or because they appear as a coercive external fact. Mann makes a similar distinction between *normative acceptance,* 'where the individual internalises the moral expectations of the ruling class and views his own inferior position as legitimate', and *pragmatic acceptance,* 'where the individual complies because he perceives no realistic alternative' (1970, p. 425). We do not understand this kind of pragmatic acceptance as entailing the possession of any set of beliefs, attitudes or 'false-consciousness'. Instead pragmatic acceptance is the result of the coercive quality of everyday life and of the routines that sustain it. There is, of course, a well-developed line of argument about the 'solidity' of everyday life within phenomenological and ethnomethodological sociology. Berger and Luckmann (1967), for example, argue that everyday life represents the 'paramount' reality. It is a powerful, constraining environment that appears entirely natural to social actors. It is essentially ordered and objectified. 'The reality of everyday life is taken for granted *as* reality. It does not require additional verification over and beyond its simple presence. It is simply *there,* as self-evident and compelling facticity' (Berger and Luckmann, 1967, p. 37, original emphasis). The massive and constraining quality of everyday life resists change or challenge, and if actors wish to transform it in any way they have to engage in prolonged struggle. Similarly, accidental disruptions of everyday life appear as quite terrifying. The routines of everyday life are therefore a powerful constraint in *themselves.*

People live out their lives within them and resist stepping outside them. It requires a massive disruption to break the reality of everyday life. The same point is illustrated by Garfinkel's famous experiments (1968). In these, students deliberately disrupted everyday routine in various ways. Some, for example, behaved as lodgers in their parents' homes, while others responded to normal conversational gambits like 'How are you?' with detailed descriptions of their bodily states. The reaction of those whose everyday lives had been thus disturbed was unexpectedly fierce. The suggestion is, again, that everyday life is taken as a solid, unvarying routine and disruptions to it are extremely worrying.

A similar argument, from within quite a different theoretical tradition, is advanced in Moore's recent book on the nature of injustice (1978). Moore is interested in the nature of moral outrage and the conditions in which a sense of injustice develops and issues in some form of radical action. For Moore, revolt is an exceptional circumstance, for 'I strongly suspect that doing nothing remains the real form of mass action in the main historical crises since the sixteenth century' (1978, pp. 156-7). It is the routines of everyday life which are the norm and which 'in ordinary times hold society together' (p. 365). Even in times when there is some mass participation in revolutionary events, as in Russia in 1917, the routines of everyday life break through. 'Very soon the imperatives of ordinary life, getting food, exchanging at least some goods and services, reassert themselves. In an urban society it is impossible for each individual to take care of his or her own requirements without the help of others. For that reason the imperatives of co-operation reassert themselves rapidly . . .' (p. 480). Indeed, in Moore's view, so important is the solidity of everyday life to people that it is disruption of common routines, such as the simple ability to buy food, rather than a sense of injustice engendered by deprivation, that is responsible for mass revolutionary participation.

In the quotation above, Moore clearly connects the imperatives of everyday life with the imperatives of co-operation. It has been argued that the likelihood of revolutionary protest is greatest in early capitalism where contradictions are more intense than in late capitalism (Mann, 1973). An alternative hypothesis is that late capitalism is characterised by a more extensive social and technical division of labour which heightens the interdependence between workers and their dependence on existing social arrangements. Revolutionary dissent in societies with a high division of labour has a higher and more immediate cost, in that the economic dislocation of everyday life will appear all the more sharply and all the sooner. This point is put more generally by Durkheim in *The*

Division of Labour. Here, as we have shown in Chapter 2, Durkheim explains the coherence of industrial society not in terms of common values but by reference to the interdependence of members of a society. The structure of social relations compels individuals to depend on each other, thereby promoting a solid form of integration. There is a similarity between *The Division of Labour* and *Capital,* since both Durkheim and Marx recognise the way in which inter-dependence is generated by increasing division of labour. We do not, of course, wish to argue that the *overall* theories of Marx and Durkheim are in fundamental agreement. For example, Durkheim regards the ultimate cause of the division of labour as an increase in population, whereas Marx locates its origin in the mechanisms of the capitalist mode of production.

Our position is that the non-normative aspect of system integration provides a basis of a society's coherence, irrespective of whether or not there are common values. Social integration and system integration can vary independently. Social classes do have different and conflicting ideologies but are, nevertheless, bound together by the network of objective social relations.

Many writers have noted that another factor making for quiescence in subordinate classes is that most economic systems, and particularly capitalism, do provide a stream of rewards. As Habermas suggests, 'The system of advanced capitalism is so defined by a policy of securing the loyalty of the wage-earning masses through rewards' (1971, p. 208). The pursuit of such rewards is not the result of 'ideological manipulation', as members of the Frankfurt school have argued; they are not illusory rewards. After all, a washing machine is a machine for washing clothes which has real advantages. A very concrete reward is that late capitalism creates the conditions whereby the expectation of life is extended. The possibility of such rewards provides an impetus to labour, even if, in welfare capitalism, it is no longer a question of labouring to live. The more rewards an economic system gives, the higher is the cost of replacing it. Conversely, any reduction in the level of reward is likely to accentuate the social conflicts already present in any society. In this context, we may note that the political struggle of labour is channelled into the maximisation of economic rewards through institutionalised wage bargaining. This 'economism' is not false consciousness. It is rooted in the workers' experience of capitalism; it is the only thing that they can get (Mann, 1973, p. 32). In our view, these arguments have some merit and are compatible with the more important features of social order described earlier.

We have provided a number of grounds for supposing that the stability of class societies need not be attributed to ideological coherence or value consensus. We make one qualification to this proposition. In Chapter 5 we argued that there is a measure of what we might call 'secondary incorporation' in late capitalist societies, because of the relative efficiency of the means of ideological transmission. In addition to this, as the evidence of Chapters 4 and 5 shows, some elements of working-class culture may perhaps impede opposition and thereby favour integration. It should be clear, however, that this form of restraint on dissent is not systematically related to the dominant ideology nor to the interests of the dominant class. Of course, in any case, active political opposition does not follow automatically from opposed class interests. Articulated opposition requires organisation and, particularly in capitalist societies, this is crucially impeded by the very division of labour on which we have commented earlier.

The Function of Ideology

In discussing the second question raised by our earlier arguments, we start with the concept 'ideological condition of existence'. This concept can have two meanings. First, it may indicate that ideology functions as a condition of existence in the sense that it conceals or obscures real social relationships. Secondly, it can mean that ideology intervenes in the working of the economy, so that the economy literally could not work without it. We have already argued against the use of the notion of ideology in the first sense. We turn now to a discussion of the second sense.

In much of the recent literature, the notion that ideology functions as a condition of existence of the economy makes a frequent appearance. It implies a particularly strong kind of relationship between ideology and economy, with ideology being a dominant feature. To some extent, such a view of the importance of ideology is an understandable reaction to economistic interpretations of Marxism, although it is often unclear just who embraces such an interpretation. Of course, neither Marx nor Engels were straightforward economic determinists. Engels, particularly in his correspondence, stressed the manner in which the ideological sphere not only develops autonomously, but can also influence the economy. Marx, in *Capital,* also gave plenty of examples of the way that ideological features are necessary to a ʼcapitalist economy.

The phrase 'condition of existence', however, suggests a very much more intimate relation between the two terms. G. Cohen, for example, argues that 'production relations, for maximum order and efficiency, *require* a legal expression in property relations' (1970, p.

138, our emphasis). It is still not clear what *kind* of claim this is, for the phrase 'maximum order and efficiency' might well permit a fairly radical disjunction between economy (production relations) and ideology (legal expression). None the less, Cohen seems to believe that this proposition is equivalent to 'the further claim that property relations have the character they do because actual or envisaged production relations *require* them to have that character', a much stronger statement of the relation between economy and ideology (1970, p. 138, our emphasis).

The most notable attempt to conceptualise the economy and its conditions of existence is that of Althusser, particularly in his early work. We will not attempt to review his position since we have discussed much of it in Chapter 1. However, we do need to reiterate some points, particularly concerning the relationship that he adduces between ideology and economy. Althusser is strict on this question. The economy *must* have ideological and political conditions of existence. Thus 'certain relations of production presuppose the existence of a legal-political and ideological superstructure as a condition of their peculiar existence . . . the relations of production cannot therefore be thought in their concept while abstracting from their specific superstructual conditions of existence' (Althusser, 1970, p. 177). Althusser is insistent on this point; the economy simply cannot be separated from ideology and politics even at the abstract level. 'In no sense is this a formal demand; it is the absolute theoretical condition governing the definition of the *economic* itself' (Althusser and Balibar, 1970, p. 178, original italics). Modes of production are totalities, consisting of structures (economic, political and ideological) whose relations are overdetermined; any one structure 'is inseparable from its formal conditions of existence, and even from the instances it governs; it is radically affected by them, determining, but also determined in one and the same movement . . .' (Althusser, 1969, p. 101).

Generally considered, therefore, economy and ideology are intimately connected in a very tight relationship. Althusser speaks of it as a conceptual or definitional relation. However, it is not just that economies require ideologies in general; they have to have *specific* ideologies as conditions of existence. Here it is a little less clear how strict the relationship has to be between a specific economy and a specific ideology. Thus Althusser says the whole of the economic structure of the capitalist mode of production, from the immediate process of production to circulation and the distribution of the social product, presupposes the existence of a legal system, the basic elements of which are the *law of property* and the *law of contract* (Althusser and Balibar, 1970, p. 230; see also pp. 177–8).

Althusser's discussion certainly implies that fairly strict specific ideological conditions of existence have to be met for capitalism to flourish.

This raises a fresh problem of Althusser's use of the concept of 'ideological practice'. He wishes to get away from the notion of ideologies as sets of ideas in people's heads. Thus, for him, the relevance of 'bourgeois freedoms' to capitalist economic practice is that these freedoms represent real relations which agents have to live out. It might therefore be argued that Althusser's use of 'ideology' is not similar to ours. However, Althusser does not maintain the notion of practice exclusively, but does consistently ascribe a role to 'beliefs' and he also tends to make the notion of an ideological practice so wide as to collapse it into other kinds of practice.

Althusser, of course, believes that one can conceive of a mode of production, being a totality of structures which are the conditions of existence of each other, in the abstract, without any necessary reference to concrete societies. Such societies are characterised by an articulation of more than one mode of production, each of which has its ideological structure modified by relationships of domination and subordination between modes. In addition, the domination of any one mode may ensure the survival or re-activation of older ideologies. The analysis of ideology in concrete societies is thus a complex and contingent matter, and therefore, in these circumstances, it is not clear how precise a relationship there has to be between ideology and economy.

There is not a similar uncertainty in the early work of Hindess and Hirst because they propose a rather different set of relationships between economy, ideology, analysis of the 'pure' mode of production and analysis of concrete societies (Hindess and Hirst, 1975). Thus they say: 'the relation between the concepts of mode of production and social formation may be understood in terms of the conditions of existence of particular modes of production . . . The concept of each particular mode of production defined certain economic, ideological or political conditions that are necessary to the existence of that structure of economic social relations.' In sum: 'A particular mode of production exists if, and only if, its conditions of existence are present in the economic, political and ideological levels of a determinate social formation. If these conditions are not secured then the mode of production cannot continue' (Hindess and Hirst, 1975, pp. 13–14). Hindess and Hirst want to establish a tight and intimate relationship between ideology and economy. As a methodological strategy, the attempt to form an abstract model of the economy, whose political and ideological conditions of existence can only be secured in actual societies, seems to us more sensible than Althusser's alternative strategy of formulating relations between economy, politics and ideology in the abstract as a theoretical construction which takes place prior to the analysis of the social formation. However, this strategy does tend to produce an unwarranted further constriction of the relations between economy and ideology. Indeed, Hindess and Hirst generally argue that ideological elements have to be specified very precisely to serve as conditions of existence. For example, 'it is clear that the capitalist and the slave modes of production require that certain forms of monetary calculation are performed by particular agents of production. The existence of these modes therefore depends on the maintenance of the ideological social relations in which these forms of calculation are developed and individuals are trained in their use' (Hindess and Hirst, 1975, p. 14). At the same time they argue, both programmatically and in their more specific analyses, that a certain variation is permissible within conditions of existence, although the range of variation is limited 'if the mode of production is to survive'. Similarly, Hindess gives a number of examples of the connection between relations of production and political and legal phenomena. He argues that 'capitalist relations of production do require definite political-legal and ideological or cultural conditions of existence, but they do not determine the precise form in which their conditions of existence will be secured' (1977b, p. 105). Thus, the wage-labour relation must receive legal recognition in the form of a wage-contract. Capitalism requires the enterprise to be recognised by legal definitions of various kinds which 'clearly affect the scale of operation that is possible'.

In sum, we have argued that the Althusserian tradition has drawn the relationship between economy and ideology very tightly, whatever variations exist between particular writers, and however much some of their accounts lack clarity. There have to be ideological conditions of existence, and these have to be of a closely specified character. The very phrase 'condition of existence' suggests a strong and tight relationship. Even Hindess's argument that the *precise* form of the legal conditions of existence is determined by class struggle, while not indicating exactly what range of variation in legal forms is permissible, suggests to us that the relations of production do circumscribe legal conditions fairly closely. In a sense, Althusser's occasional lapses into saying that the concept of the economy includes ideology, or that the economy is defined in terms of ideology, are revealing. Such claims clearly will not do, since they rule out causal relations between the terms. None the less, they indicate a craving for a relation of economy and ideology which will dispose of economic determinism once and for all.

We wish to argue that the conception of the ideology–economy relation depicted in the last few pages is far too strict. Very often there is no good reason, either theoretical or substantive, for adopting it, with the result that one is often presented with arbitrary constructions. For example, Hindess and Hirst offer an analysis of the slave mode of production in which ideology is given an important role. However, it is unclear why the functions assigned to the ideological structure could not equally well be performed by the political instance. Part of the difficulty is created when the relations between ideology and economy are theorised at an abstract level, at the level of the *concept* of the economy. We will in fact wish to argue that the ideology–economy relation can only be conceptualised at the level of concrete societies and that there is no such thing as a relation between ideology and economy at the level of the abstract mode of production.

The major conclusion of these considerations is that it is better to see ideology as more or less functionally useful, with the range of utility being set widely. The economy can take a variety of very different ideological forms; there is a wide range of functional alternatives. We have to take into account the limiting case of an economy which does not need ideology at all, and it is our contention that late capitalism is very nearly such a case. We should emphasise that it is the role of *ideology* that is in question. We have already suggested that the economy may require *political* forms of some kind, particularly in class societies, and that in this case late capitalism is significant because of the importance of the state in the functioning of its economy.

The test of a strict ideology–economy relation is to consider in what ways an economy is conceivable without *particular* ideological forms or, indeed, without ideological forms at all. It is useful to mention Weber's work in this context as he effectively comes near to performing such a test. As is well known, Weber argues that there is an 'elective affinity' between the kinds of beliefs and behaviour, especially rational action, which underpin capitalism and the kinds of belief and behaviour involved in the Protestant religions. He suggests that certain varieties of Protestantism were crucial in organising their adherents' lives into rational wholes. This was achieved by a variety of religious prescriptions, in favour of hard work and against the 'spontaneous enjoyment of life', in favour of man having a 'calling' and, in its more Calvinist manifestations, encouraging men to organise their lives so that their every action was a demonstration of their being one of God's elect. The 'Protestant ethic' so formed matched the kinds of behaviour required for capitalist activity and provided thereby one of the essential preconditions for the emergence of capitalism.

In advancing these arguments, Weber rejects what he refers to as a 'naive historical materialism', which would 'deduce the Reformation, as a historically necessary result, from certain economic changes', a rejection similar to the opposition to economism voiced by Althusser, Gramsci and Habermas. At the same time, Weber does not want to fall into an idealist position, in which religious changes of themselves gave rise to capitalism.

Just as Weber stresses that Protestantism is relevant to capitalism in the period in which capitalism has its origins, so he also argues that Protestantism is not important as a continuing condition of existence, once it is firmly established. Once started, the *economic* structure of capitalism has a logic of its own which propels it along. 'The capitalistic economy of the present day is an immense cosmos into which the individual is born, and which presents itself to him . . . as an unalterable order of things in which he must live. It forces the individual, in so far as he is involved in the system of market relationships, to conform to capitalistic rules of action' (Weber, 1930, p. 21). Any person who tries to escape this 'unalterable order of things' cannot function as an entrepreneur or worker. He is eliminated from the capitalist economic scene, not necessarily because of his beliefs, but because he does not conform to the logic of the economic system.

One could, therefore, draw the conclusion that Weber is arguing that ideology in *any* form is unnecessary in developed capitalism, and such a conclusion might be justified by Weber's repeated stress on the coercive power of the purely economic relations which keep capitalism going. In this respect, as in his discussion of the importance of 'free' labour, Weber's account bears a similarity to Marx's notion of the 'dull compulsion of economic relations'. Weber is then made the prophet of historical contingency. The relationship between ideology and economy is made comparatively loose, so that a variety of ideological forms could help capitalism into being and, similarly, a variety of forms, or none at all, could keep it in being. It just so happened that the logic of Protestant rationalisation coincided with the logic of capitalist accumulation.

Unfortunately, although Weber can assist our argument to some extent, particularly in his emphasis on the economy as against ideological elements, this general interpretation of his work cannot be conclusive. The chief difficulty is that Weber's employment of various categories of belief bears an uncertain relationship to our use of the concept of ideology. For example, Weber stresses the importance of rationality (possibly a category of ideology) to current capitalist economic practice. Further, there are occasional indications that he did think that the 'spirit of capitalism' was a continuing necessity. Thus he says 'the capitalistic system so needs this devotion to the calling of making money, it is an attitude toward material goods which is so well suited to that system, so intimately bound up with the conditions of survival in the economic struggle for existence . . .' (Weber, 1930, p. 72). However, later in the same passage he clearly states that in established capitalism 'Men's commercial and social interests do tend to *determine* their opinions and attitudes' (our emphasis).

We now attempt to take our arguments about the function of ideology further by considering in more detail the role of particular elements of the dominant ideology.

Regions of the Dominant Ideology

In deploying our critical arguments we have not attempted to identify the strategic significance of *particular* elements of the dominant ideology. Our method so far has been to rely on others' definitions of the dominant ideology in any society or to identify ruling ideas simply as those most widely available (though not necessarily 'believed'). The net result has been to produce the dominant ideology as a 'list' of features, more or less related to one another. We do not apologise for this method.

However, it should be plain from our discussion that we believe that particular elements of the dominant ideology have particular functions in different modes of production, and that different modes may be related in different ways to these elements. Poulantzas advances an apparently similar argument when he identifies different regions of a dominant ideology: 'ideology itself is divided into various regions which can be characterized, for example, as moral, juridical and political, aesthetic, religious, economic, philosophical ideology . . . it must also be said that in the dominant ideology of a social formation it is generally possible to decipher the dominance of one region of ideology over another' (Poulantzas, 1973, p. 210). It is not pure accident that one region of the ideological is dominant, for it is always the case that that region best fulfils the function of masking the role of the economy. For example, Poulantzas holds that the juridico-politico region is dominant, colouring the conceptions of other regions, because it constitutes individual subjects as free and equal and essentially isolated. Though interesting, Poulantzas's account is very thin and it will be clear that we cannot accept his fundamental claim that ideology has the general function of concealing exploitative social relations. None the less, we want to borrow the notion of regions of the dominant ideology, while giving it a quite different interpretation and theoretical context. We suggest that these regions are separable, that they can be analysed over time, and that they may have different functions towards the economy in different modes of production. In effect, in the earlier substantive chapters of this book we have identified a number of such regions. Of particular significance are conceptions of family and personal morality, conceptions of private property and conceptions of the just distribution of resources.

Family and personal ideology occupies a strategic place in the dominant ideologies of very different societies. It obviously relates to the transmission and accumulation of private productive property and will be functionally important to the extent that an economy operates by means of the *private* ownership of productive resources.

Essentially the issue resolves itself into three questions. (1) What is the significance of private property in particular modes of production? Put differently, this is the question: what is the economic subject? (2) What is the role of the family in relation to property, either as it involves inheritance customs, or as wider kin are involved in the financing of the acquisition of productive property? (3) What is the role of those elements of the dominant ideology stressing family and property in relation to private property and its transmission?

Property, as many have noted (Thompson, 1976*b*) refers to a bundle of rights and privileges which varies in character considerably from society to society. In the following argumentative sketch we restrict our discussion to *productive* property, mostly in the form of enterprises which will produce an income in various ways. Private productive property is then productive property legally owned by identifiable persons. Such private property is important in feudalism and early capitalism, but very much less so in late capitalism. By 'important' we mean that productive resources are not only legally owned but are also economically owned and possessed (or partially possessed in the case of feudalism) by identifiable persons. That is, the private legal ownership of property has an economic function in that it allies ownership with control. Some modes of production may well function by the institution of private property, but it is important to note that they do not necessarily do so. That is, economic agents do not have to be individual persons. It is perfectly possible for other entities to hold relations of economic ownership and possession and to make economic decisions. For example, in feudal Europe it was possible for religious communities or colleges to be the possessors of the land and, in more recent times, the joint-stock company is a non-individual economic agent which can occupy the place of capital and exercise its powers in a manner quite distinct from any of the qualities of its shareholders.

However, despite the *possibility* of economic agents not being individual persons, the prevailing tendency in feudal and early capitalist England was towards the private ownership of productive property. The feudal lord had effective personal ownership, deriving his revenues from control over his tenants' labour-services and his rights to their produce. However, as we have already argued, these rights of ownership were limited by the lord's relationship to the king and also by the tenants' immediate control over their own land. Indeed, such was the resistance of English peasants towards the end of the fourteenth century that villein land tenure was transformed into copyhold, which, in turn, became indistinguishable from free tenure (Hilton, 1978).

However, these transformations of tenure had paradoxical consequences in that they, in turn, eventually enlarged the rights of private property in the period from the fourteenth to the late eighteenth centuries, a transitional period which, as Perkin (1969) says, was different both from feudalism and from the capitalism of the Victorian period. The transition from a feudal economy was marked by the appearance of capitalist relations of production in the countryside, in merchant activities and eventually in extractive and manufacturing industries. Demesnes were run in a commercial way, producing for a market, and lords began to find it convenient to commute the labour services of their unfree tenants into money rents and to depend on hired labour for their own land, or even to rent out their estates to tenant farmers. By the end of the seventeenth century the majority of estates were run by permanently renting out the land. The very freedom of the new tenure made the tenants vulnerable, and the result of these and other changes was the creation of a landless proletariat and a group of successful tenants farming for the market.

The intrusion of capitalist relations into the countryside was associated with a new conception of private property. While the feudal lord's ownership of his land was to some extent circumscribed, the landowner of the transitional period enjoyed his property absolutely. He was able to do with it as he wished, unfettered by the customary or legal claims of others; property had become an aggregate of economic privileges, not a responsible office. He had the freedom to sell or to rent. The transformation of the conception of property was not achieved without a struggle. As Perkin says: 'Not by philosophical argument but by a political, legal and some-times physical struggle lasting from the high middle ages until the seventeenth century, the English landowners shook off the claims of crown, church and peasants, and transformed lordship into ownership' (1969, p. 53).

> Thus the institution of property in the sense it came to have in bourgeois law posits a person (*persona*) and a thing (*res*), joined by a legal norm called property or ownership. Human society is dissolved into isolated individuals, and the world of goods split up into discrete items. One can no longer speak of a duty to use property or behave towards others in a certain way: all such duties as may be imposed by law are prima facie derogations from the fundamental 'right of property'. (Tigar and Levy, 1977, p. 197)

This conception of property did not inform only the holding of land. As is well known, the landed interest played a substantial part in the industrial revolution, partly by the development of extractive industries and transport, the 'preconditions' of the industrial revolution (Perkin, 1969). The exploitation of natural resources and the creation of a transport network lay in the hands of entrepreneurs, not always landowners, who often formed partnerships, frequently with members of their own family (Gough, 1969). The partnership continued to be a common legal form of the ownership and management of enterprises until well into the nineteenth century. Payne suggests that the notion of the single entrepreneur as owner-manager is probably rather misleading and 'probably more common were small, often family-linked, partnerships, reliant in varying degrees on capital provided by sleeping partners, whose active members concentrated on different entrepreneurial functions' (1978, p. 18).

In sum, there is a fairly close relationship between the individual economic subject and the productive enterprise in feudalism, the transitional period and early industrial capitalism. In the feudal period the relationship is less close because there was no concept of absolute rights over private property. None the less, in all these societies, private property has a distinct function within the mode of production.

This is not so in late capitalism. The shift is symbolised by the passage of the Joint Stock Companies Act in 1844 although some trading companies had taken this form a long time before the passage of the Act and the private or partnership form of ownership continued long afterwards. Even by the 1880s, the majority of firms were still in private hands (Payne, 1978). However, the new form began to be more common in the early part of the twentieth century, carrying with it the very important potential for the dispersal of ownership of an enterprise among a wider group of persons than before. The response of families owning firms privately to the possibilities of limiting their liability was not to continue to own large blocks of shares in their old firm, but to spread their risks by diversifying their shareholdings among different firms (Hannah, 1976, pp. 64 ff.). The well-documented trend in the present century towards the great increase in size of firms has led to a further separation of ownership from control. As Poulantzas (1975) indicates, the net effect of these changes is to separate legal and economic ownership on the one hand, and economic ownership and possession, by the differentiation of management functions, on the other. In addition, the role of financial institutions, including insurance companies and pension funds, in the financing of firms, and the increased intervention of the state, all diminish the significance of the individual holdings of shares.

The net effect of all these changes is to separate the ownership of property from its economic function. Late capitalism works without the institution of privately-owned productive property. It should be noted that we do not hold that there is no private property in late capitalism, or that the distribution of economic resources is not unequal. These phenomena are, however, *effects* of the capitalist economy, not its *preconditions*.

In circumstances in which the individual's holding of private property has an economic function, one might expect the family also to have a role. The productive unit will not stand being split up indefinitely, and there is therefore a need to conserve and transmit it over time. Further, in capitalism, there is a requirement not just to conserve, but also to *accumulate* capital within the enterprise. The family is the device whereby the conservation and accumulation of productive property is effected. Consequently, one should treat the family as the locus of private property just as much as the individual. This is the case even in very diverse economic conditions. For example, Stone, writing of the landed aristocracy of the fifteenth, sixteenth and seventeenth centuries, says that 'the central concern of the individuals under study was – or was supposed to be – the prosperity and continuity of the family . . . The prime responsibility of the current head of the family was to preserve, or perhaps increase, the family inheritance, and to ensure its continuity by producing a healthy male heir' (1973, p. xvi). Foster, discussing capitalist industrial production in the nineteenth century, makes a similar point: 'The employer saw himself as son and grandson to an estate and judged himself within this familial (still almost peasant) perspective. He was successful if he increased the inheritance. The pattern of industry itself made wealth more familial than personal. The capital requirements of high-profit production meant that a firm's assets could not be divided up every generation' (1974, p. 180).

These considerations direct attention, in the first place, to the law and customs of marriage, inheritance and family finance, a realm of relatively formalised ideology, and, in the second, to family, sexual and personal morality, a less definite area.

As far as inheritance is concerned, the first and most obvious consideration is the diversity of the customs involved, over time, between different regions of the country, and between different social classes. None the less, we believe some generalisations can be formulated. Discussion of peasant inheritance customs is outside the scope of our present work, though it is of relevance (see Howell, 1976; Spufford, 1976; Macfarlane, 1978). The basic problem in the inheritance of either land or a capitalist enterprise is the tension between parental duties to all children and the necessity for preserving the economic unit intact. There is a conflict between partibility and primogeniture. Excessive generosity to all children could mean long-term disaster. There are difficulties in producing too many children, and burdening an estate by providing for all of them, and producing too few, in which case the estate might not be conserved for lack of a suitable heir (Stone, 1973; Mingay, 1976).

This tension is resolved in different ways at different times. Some forms of property might make resolution easier. For example, if an estate has liquid funds available these can be used to provide for younger children. In contemporary capitalism shares are more easily distributed equally than land. Basically, however, in feudalism, the transition period and early capitalism, inheritance worked in such a way as to keep the productive unit intact, and this tendency became more pronounced the more capitalist social relations intruded. In the feudal period there was a diversity of inheritance practices, but by the late thirteenth century some form of primogeniture had been established. Nevertheless, primogeniture was associated with attempts to provide for all children, either in money or land (Stone, 1973), and, as indicated above, this form of generosity had its price. The result was often that estates became burdened with debts. However, the balance shifted rather more to primogeniture, and hence to the more systematic conservation of property, in the seventeenth century with the increasing use of the practice of strict settlement which eventually became codified into law. Under this practice, the current owner of an estate was made a tenant for life. He could not sell the land and could only mortgage it for particular purposes and only up to a particular sum. In addition, a proportion of the estate was reserved to pay for marriage settlements, jointures and portions. These legal requirements very effectively tied the hands of owners and represented an interesting restriction of the individual's claim on property, while enlarging those of his family. Despite the fact that some estates found it difficult to meet the expense of providing for children and widows in the stipulated manner, the net effect was to tighten the grip of a family on the ownership of a productive enterprise. One index of this was the rising tide of complaints on behalf of younger sons that they were hard done by (Thirsk, 1976). Indeed, younger sons might often be provided for, not directly by gifts of money, but by being placed in a government office, or other career, via patronage or family connection. Evidence of the inheritance practices of the owners of capitalist manufacturing enterprises is scanty. The indications are, however, that here too the unity of the productive unit was preserved intact, partly by the legal devices of joint tenancy and tenancy-in-common. Similar problems of evidence attend the analysis of inheritance in late capitalism, but we would be very surprised if this was generally anything other than by equal shares among offspring.

In sum, we argue that inheritance practices, while attempting to provide for all children, have the effect of preserving private productive property intact. With the development of capitalist social relations, the pressure for unimpeded inheritance was increased and has only died away in late capitalist societies which no longer function by the institution of private property. However, inheritance is not the only means by which the family intervenes in the functioning of private property. In many circumstances marriage is important, not only in that it may represent an outflow of funds in making marriage settlements on daughters, but also in that it can result in the inflow of much-needed finance from the dowries of daughters-in-law. The result was a close interest in, and regulation of, marriage practices. At least until the nineteenth century, a successful and permanent marriage could make a good deal of difference to the viability and preservation of a landed estate or family firm. Marriages were then a matter of negotiation and contract, with both families involved having an interest in the careful disposition of estates and money. In an extreme form, families would arrange marriages with particular individuals, but by the eighteenth century, and on into the nineteenth, the choice of marriage partner could be largely dictated by the feelings of the sons or daughters concerned, in the confident expectation that the resultant marriages would naturally be between members of the same social class (Simpson, 1961; Mingay, 1963 and 1976; see Trumbach, 1978, for a slightly different view). However, again, the regulation of marriage is not nearly so significant in late capitalism, a fact reflected not only in the attachment to the ideals of romantic love but also in the laws and customs relating to divorce.

Historically, family connections have also been important in the provision of finance for meeting debts or for the acquisition of land or property. Accounts of individual landed families show a constant exchange of short- or long-term loans or gifts. The family was well placed to be a lender of first resort. When the seventeenth-century merchant Thomas Cullum entered into partnership with his master, an association that was to make his career, he lacked £600 and he turned naturally to his brother and sister for help (Simpson, 1961). Banks were unlikely to help the thrusting entre-preneurs of the late eighteenth and early nineteenth centuries and again they often went to their wider families or connections through marriage as a source of capital (Perkin, 1969; see also the account of the Peel family in Hobsbawm, 1969, pp. 62–3). In a process of assistance almost the reverse of this, it was not uncommon for established family firms in the nineteenth century to extend the family commitment by taking in impecunious relatives as employees or managers.

In short, in modes of production in which private property has a well-defined economic role, it is probable that the family will be deeply involved in the conservation, transmission and accumulation of that property, in a variety of ways. It is therefore proper to speak of family estates and family firms. As we have tried to show, family involvement in private productive property is buttressed not only by family loyalty, but also by custom and law.

However, besides the relatively formalised areas of belief associated with marriage and inheritance, wider considerations are also relevant to the involvement of the family in economic life. As is often argued, attitudes to children and parents, personal conduct as it affects the stability of the family unit and marriage prospects, and sexual morality all have a bearing. We have discussed the region of family and personal morality in the previous three chapters and, as it is a very large subject, we can do no more than indicate the main areas of interest here.

We can start by distinguishing two polar types of social control, repression and permissiveness. Each of these represents control – or lack of control – over a whole bundle of personal behaviours and attitudes, not just sexual relations and relations between spouses and children and parents, but also habits of dress and behaviour, manners and opinions. Repressive moral regimes will prescribe fairly closely the acceptable norms of behaviour in these areas and will punish significant deviations. Permissive regimes, on the contrary, will allow the individual to follow his inclinations in matters of personal morality. No society conforms exactly to either of these types. Further, some societies will be permissive in some respects and not in others. Eighteenth-century upper-class England, for example, was a society of sexual libertinism yet rigid etiquette. With these qualifications in mind, it is none the less possible to use the very general categories of repression and permissiveness to organise the discussion.

It is consistent with the general drift of our argument so far to suggest, as many others have done, that repressive moral regimes are associated with societies which depend on the conservation of private property. In addition, we have implied that a permissive regime is likely to be associated with a mode of production in which private property does not have a productive function, this being the case in late capitalism.

On a superficial acquaintance, such an argument appears plausible. In Chapter 3, we have argued that the feudal moral regime was repressive, especially in relation to the behaviour of women. The nineteenth century is notoriously also a period of moral repression (Hobsbawm, 1977, pp. 273–83; Stone, 1977, pp. 666 ff.), equalled in ferocity only by the seventeenth century (although all repressive regimes have some difficulty in controlling male sexuality). Contemporary capitalist societies, on the other hand, appear as good examples of permissive moral regimes, in which individuals can indulge themselves as they choose in matters of sex, marriage, dress and all other aspects of personal behaviour (see Chapter 5). A difficulty is created, however, by consideration of the period from the end of the seventeenth century to the end of the eighteenth. This 'ought' to have been a time in which the comparatively repressive regimes of earlier times were continued, or even accentuated, given what we have described as the tightening grip of the family on landed estates by the device of the strict settlement. However, it was not a repressive century. On Stone's (1977) account, for example, the period's domestic arrangements were dominated by the 'closed domesticated nuclear family' whose main characteristics were: mate selection largely by free choice, declining authority of parents over children and husbands over wives, a trend to the legal and educational equality of the sexes, adultery by both sexes and a general sexual liberation.

Stone's description of eighteenth century mores is part of a wider argument concerning the relationship between repressive and permissive moral regimes and family structures. He suggests that from the fifteenth century there have been marked swings, first repressive (1450–1650), then permissive (1650–1860), then repressive in the late Victorian period and finally permissive in the twentieth century. In his view these swings are not directly attributable to economic causes. Rather, repressive regimes and moral panics were due to prevailing feelings of social insecurity generated by a 'fear that the whole structure of social hierarchy and political order were in danger' (1977, p. 677). Such feelings were common between 1450 and 1650, and in the nineteenth century, and less so in the eighteenth and twentieth centuries. Such an account is not totally inconsistent with the more conventional one, connecting moral regimes with the transmission of property, that we have more or less supported hitherto. First, in the eighteenth century, that being the point of contention, there was permissiveness only in certain respects; customs directly to do with property were largely unaffected. Secondly, there is no reason why we should not super-impose Stone's 'swings' of moral fervour on to an underlying relationship of morality to property.

The function of this sketch of the relationship between ideology in the form of family and personal morality and the transmission and accumulation of private productive property has been twofold. First, we have illustrated our more general arguments about the manner in which ideology can function as a condition of existence of the economy. Secondly, we have provided part of an explanation for our descriptive findings about the dominant ideology, particularly as these findings indicate the uniqueness of late capitalism.

We could have investigated other regions of the dominant ideology which have been touched on in previous chapters. Thus one might ask how social class relates to modes of production which function by the mechanism of private property. That is, social classes, as collections of economic agents functioning by means of their possession of private productive property, may well have a functional role in feudal and early capitalist societies. Dominant social classes assist in the conservation and transmission of private property. The same will not be true of economies which do not specify individual persons as economic agents. One might expect corresponding shifts in ideology. In societies in which classes are functional for the economy, one finds dominant ideologies stressing the legitimacy of hierarchy and the unequal distribution of rewards of all kinds. In societies, like late capitalism, in which classes do not have a similar role, these aspects of ideology are correspondingly attenuated. Again, the notion that certain 'bourgeois freedoms', particularly as they are expressed in the concept of individualism, are essential to capitalism, in that they necessarily constitute the individual as the economic subject, could bear re-examination. The ideology of individualism is not necessary to capitalism, since late capitalism can function perfectly well without it.

By way of summary we will review the theoretical part of our analysis of family and personal morality. We have found that, although in previous modes of production the dominant ideology is relatively coherent, in late capitalism it is losing definition. In feudalism and early capitalism the dominant class, *not* the subordinate class, is incorporated by the dominant ideology, mostly because the apparatus of ideological transmission only has an effect on that class. It is our contention that ideology does not function as a *necessary* condition of existence of an economy. As dominant ideology, it may or may not be functionally useful, depending on historical circumstances. For example, in the case of family ideology, it does have functions towards the economy, but *only* in societies in which certain conditions are met, particularly that private property has an economic role and that there is a family structure. In these societies the dominant ideology works via the dominant class, which is the economically active class. However, in late capitalism the dominant ideology is relatively attenuated because there is no economic requirement for it, or at least for some of its regions, in the institution of private property. Other regions of the dominant ideology may be present, ideologies of distribution, for example, although we suspect that these too are relatively diminished. It should be noted that our contention that late capitalism operates largely without ideology is not similar to the arguments of the 'end of ideology' theorists (see Waxman, 1968) since, amongst other things, we cannot accept their explanation of the nature of late capitalism.

The functional relation of ideology and economy is therefore a contingent one, specifiable only at the level of concrete societies. There cannot be a general theory of ideology. This is not to suggest, however, that economies do not have requirements that have to be met outside the economy. For example, in both feudalism and capitalism there has to be some means of maintaining the separation of the labourer from the means of production. These requirements can, however, be met by a wide range of functional alternatives, political and ideological, the precise character of which is not specified by the economy. Indeed, modes of production will vary in the degree to which they require *any* extra-economic support and in the degree to which their economic logic is self-sustaining. The net effect of the various arguments throughout this book has been to suggest that ideology does not have the importance ascribed to it in a great deal of recent sociological work on the subject, which has broken with the classical sociological tradition of Marx, Weber and Durkheim.

Appendix: The Concept of Ideology

In this study of the dominant ideology thesis, we have quite deliberately concentrated on substantive issues rather than on secondary matters of a methodological or technical nature. In our view, this empirical focus is the most effective route along which the sociology of knowledge or ideology can move forward. Much of the contemporary discussion of ideology in Marxism and sociology has been merely a sterile and derivative review of existing theoretical literature. We recognise, of course, that any debate within this area must partly depend on what meaning is attached to the concept of ideology. Therefore, having stated our general position in some detail through the medium of historical illustration, we now turn in this appendix to state briefly our views on certain technical and theoretical problems.

It is widely agreed that the notion of 'ideology' has given rise to more analytical and conceptual difficulties than almost any other term in the social sciences. The term has suffered many demolitions and reconstitutions. One issue in particular has bedevilled theoretical debate, namely, whether to understand the term in a special or in a general sense. In the first, 'ideology' is taken to refer to distinctive *kinds* of belief which are produced by particular social structures. 'Ideology' understood in this sense typically refers to *false* beliefs, although there is considerable room for dispute as to the precise way in which they are false. At this stage in the argument, the question of the falsity of beliefs is often confused with the problem of the rationality with which those beliefs are held. In order to avoid the trap of relativism, this conception of ideology must entail the existence of a class of true beliefs (that is, not ideological beliefs) which can generically be called scientific. However, such a rigid distinction between science and ideology gives rise to the familiar difficulty of identifying what is to count as science. This, of course, is a difficulty not just for Marxism but for a wide range of alternative methodologies and approaches. By contrast, to employ the term 'ideology' in the general sense means that it can refer to any set of beliefs regardless of its social causation or its truth or falsity. Many commentators have assumed that this position leads straight to a relativist impasse in that it appears to have removed any independent basis for judging the truth or falsity of ideologies.

In our view these are not serious problems because they are founded on an elementary mistake. Part of the conceptual difficulty is generated by the assumption that the identification of the social origins of beliefs and the demonstration of their truth or falsity are logically connected in such a manner that the discovery of the social basis of belief entails its falsification. This assumption is incorrect. For example, the discovery that most members of the Frankfurt school had a Jewish parentage is not a demonstration of the falsity of their beliefs about the importance of Freudian psychoanalysis or of their beliefs about the effects of instrumental rationality in late capitalism. This discovery might, however, sensitise us to problems in their approach to Freud and to capitalism. Thus a particular kind of social determination may give the researcher *clues* as to the validity of beliefs but it cannot *establish* their validity. There are no beliefs which do not have social causes. One can therefore regard all beliefs, including scientific ones, as the rightful province of the sociology of ideology without thereby committing the relativistic sin. At the same time, one can argue, following Marx and Engels, that certain social situations are *likely* to generate false beliefs, without thereby arguing that one has proved the beliefs to be false. Following our stance in the middle sections of this book, we want to argue for a certain flexibility or looseness between belief and structure: it *may be* that social determination points in the direction of falsity. Of course, such a position must ultimately require the identification of the proper procedures of sociology or of the rules of sociological science. But then so must all work in sociology; the problem of specifying the methods of sociological science is not one that is especially prominent in the sociology of ideology.

In our argument we have so far equated 'ideology' with beliefs. It could be argued that this equation is mistaken in two different ways. First, there is a definite tendency in the sociology of knowledge to concentrate attention and analysis only on articulate, theoretical or systematic beliefs. There is, as a consequence, an emphasis on beliefs which are codified and written down. This tendency is most obvious in the research of sociologists who have worked within the tradition of Mannheim and Goldmann. We do not want to suggest that this tendency is the result of a deliberate methodological policy. The concentration on written material may be inevitable, given the lack of evidence that is not presented in a literate form. Clearly, however, the net effect of such a methodological strategy will be on the one hand to avoid consideration of less well-defined, and perhaps more subtle, intellectual forms, such as language itself, while on the other it concentrates attention on the intellectual stratum to the neglect of other groups in society.

To some extent, this difficulty is implicit in the kind of sociological problem that we have tried to tackle in this study, as we have already indicated in our introductory chapters. Within these methodological and theoretical limitations, we believe that we *have* investigated the various subtler ways in which a dominant culture might incorporate subordinate classes. We have not found evidence, or any compelling theoretical reasons, for supposing that there is any such incorporation, subtle or otherwise. On the contrary, we have established that the everyday discourse, epistemology, or way of life, of subordinate classes is largely formed outside the control and domain of the dominant class and its culture. Against the evidence we have presented, there may be clear, persistent attempts to preserve the validity of the dominant ideology thesis which involve the suggestion that the dominant ideology has its effects in primarily indirect, undercover, even unseen, ways. However, we would require *concrete* evidence for changing our position in favour of the argument that ideology must take this covert form. All that has been established so far is the *possibility* of such subterranean ideological incorporation. The fetishism of commodity argument in writers like Lukács and Sohn-Rethel is often used to suggest the presence of an all-pervasive, but disguised and secretive, ideology. In this book and elsewhere (Abercrombie, 1980), we have argued that the fetishism theory is a particularly inadequate and inappropriate version of the dominant, covert ideology thesis, because it is difficult to formulate the argument in a coherent fashion and the evidence for it is invariably flimsy.

A second, more fundamental objection to our equation of ideology and beliefs is that ideology cannot be treated *purely* as a category of consciousness. In part, this objection is based on the supposition that ideologies are not entirely illusory. Althusser's treatment of ideology would be an example of this particular approach. This supposition, and the antipathy to the Marx and Engels of the *German Ideology* that goes with it, is correct. However, the proponents of this view wish to go on to argue that ideologies, even if they are not illusory, *are* misleading. The question then becomes: in what way is ideology simultaneously misleading and socially effective? The solution is to see ideologies as sets of practices, or as 'real' social relations, which are necessary to the functioning of class societies, but which nevertheless conceal the nature of such societies from human subjects. It can be argued, for example, that certain bourgeois freedoms are necessary for the capitalist mode of production. Freedom of contract is, for instance, essential to the buying and selling of labour-power in a market which is, in turn, constitutive of capitalism. These bourgeois freedoms are, therefore, not simply a question of individual beliefs; they are also practices or lived experiences which are nevertheless misleading, since they conceal the actually exploitative character of capitalist relations of production. The formal freedom of labour in the market-place masks the unequal nature of economic power in capitalism which compels the worker to sell his labour-power.

In our view these theoretical proposals constitute a worthy and important attempt to remove and overcome the conceptual muddle of earlier formulations of ideology as false beliefs or mental aberrations. However, we cannot accept their substantive import, namely, that ideology does successfully incorporate subordinate classes by the process of disguising their real condition or by misleading them. In addition to this problem, the methodological conclusions of this approach are suspect, if they are pressed so far that they collapse the distinction between ideology and other categories. In particular, it is difficult to avoid the conclusion that ideology must be seen as a category of consciousness in order to make a discordance between belief and practices theoretically possible. Not to make this distinction merely robs ideology of any theoretical autonomy by collapsing it into other practices, particularly into the political category. We observed this difficulty in theoretical and empirical terms in our discussion of the feudal mode of production. Ideology must be distinguished both from political coercion and from what we have called the 'economic logic' of a mode of production.

In referring to ideology as a category of consciousness we are making assumptions about the relationship of ideology to the human subject, a topic of recent debate. It should be clear, however, that the question of the 'location' of ideology in human beings is very different from the question of the origins of the ideological structure. In our view, ideology and the human subject *are* conceptually linked together, but that is not to say that the origins of ideology lie in the autonomous human spirit. Any valid theory of ideology must treat human beings as the bearers or carriers of beliefs. This assertion is not, furthermore, dependent on regarding ideology as beliefs rather than practices. This claim about the linkage between structure and agent is bound up with our view that ideology cannot be theoretically located and elaborated at the level of the mode of production. The conceptualisation of relations and forces of production simply does not require, and could not have, 'ideology' as a condition. In 'spatial' terms, we have attempted to think about ideology in the interstice between 'social formation' and 'mode of production'. However, while human beings are the carriers of beliefs, we have also argued that ideological beliefs cannot be simply and directly reduced to the class position of their human carriers. In part, this position follows from the argument that social classes are themselves the complex effects of modes of production. In part, whether or not social beliefs can be connected with class interests is an empirical question, however difficult the formulation of its methodology might be. All beliefs, scientific and ideological, are socially determined or socially caused; it is not possible to identify a belief or set of beliefs which does not emerge and survive as the result of social determination. This does not mean, however, that we have to produce a simple mechanism, such as class interest or the function of a mode of production, to justify that claim.

We also recognise the irony of our argument. In neo-Marxism and contemporary sociology the social role of dominant ideologies has been greatly exaggerated. Since the real task is always to understand the economic and political forces which shape people's lives, too much has been said about ideology in recent decades. Perhaps more erudite sociologists would be tempted to conclude with some witty observation on Wittgenșteinian silence.

Bibliography

Aaronovitch, S., and Sawyer, M. C., *Big Business* (London, 1975).

Abercrombie, N., *Class, Structure and Knowledge* (Oxford, 1980).

Abercrombie, N., *et al.*, 'Superstition and religion: the God of the gaps', in *A Sociological Yearbook of Religion in Britain*, ed. D. A. Martin, Vol. 3 (London, 1970), pp. 93–129.

Abercrombie, N., and Turner, B. S., 'The dominant ideology thesis', *British Journal of Sociology*, vol. 29, no. 2 (1978), pp. 149–170.

Adam, P., *La Vie paroissiale en France au XIVe Siècle* (Paris, 1964).

Adler, M., 'Ideology as appearance', in *Austro-Marxism*, ed. T. Bottomore and P. Goode (Oxford, 1975), pp. 253–61.

Althusser, L., *For Marx* (Harmondsworth, 1969).

Althusser, L., 'Ideology and ideological state apparatuses', in *Lenin and Philosophy and Other Essays* (London, 1977).

Althusser, L., and Balibar, E., *Reading Capital* (London, 1970).

Anderson, M., *Family Structure in Nineteenth-Century Lancashire* (Cambridge, 1971).

Anderson, M., 'Sociological history and the working-class family: Smelser revisited', *Social History*, vol. I, no. 3 (1976), pp. 317–334.

Anderson, P., 'Origins of the present crisis', *New Left Review*, no. 23 (1964), pp. 26–53.

Anderson, P., 'Socialism and pseudo-empiricism', *New Left Review*, no. 35 (1966), pp. 2–42.

Anderson, P., *Lineages of the Absolutist State* (London, 1974).

Anderson, P., *Considerations on Western Marxism* (London, 1976).

Anderson, P., 'The antinomies of Antonio Gramsci', *New Left Review*, no. 100 (1976/7) pp. 5–80.

Anthony, P. D., *The Ideology of Work* (London, 1977).

Arnold, T., and Guillaume, A. (eds), *The Legacy of Islam* (London, 1961).

Austin, J., 'The province of jurisprudence determined' (1832), in M. Warnock (ed.) (1962), pp. 322–42.

Baldwin, J. W., *Masters, Princes and Merchants: The social views of Peter the Chanter and his Circle* (Princeton, NJ, 1970).

Barber, R., *The Knight and Chivalry* (Ipswich, 1970).

Bates, T. R., 'Gramsci and the theory of hegemony', *Journal of the History of Ideas*, vol. 36 (1975), pp. 251–366.

Behrend, H., *et al.*, *Incomes Policy and the Individual* (Edinburgh, 1967).

Behrend, H., *et al.*, *Views on Income Differentials and the Economic Situation* (Dublin, 1970).

Bellah, R., 'Religious evolution', *American Sociological Review*, vol. xxix, no. 3 (1964), pp. 358–74.

Bendix, R., *Work and Authority in Industry* (New York, 1956).

Bentham, J., 'Introduction to the principles of morals and legislation' (1789), in M. Warnock (ed.) (1962), pp. 33–77.

Berger, P. L., *The Social Reality of Religion* (London, 1969).

Berger, P. L., 'On the obsolescence of the concept of honour', *European Journal of Sociology*, vol. xi, no. 2 (1970), pp. 339–47.

Berger, P. L., Berger, B., and Kellner, H., *The Homeless Mind* (Harmondworth, 1974).

Berger, P. L., and Luckmann, T., *The Social Construction of Reality* (London, 1967).

Best, G., *Mid-Victorian Britain* (London, 1971).

Beynon, H., *Working for Ford* (London, 1973).

Bieler, L. (ed.), *The Irish Penitentials* (Dublin, 1963).

Birnbaum, N., 'Monarchs and sociologists: a reply to Professor Shils and Mr Young', *Sociological Review*, vol. 3, no. 1 (1955), pp. 5–23.

Birnbaum, N., *Toward a Critical Sociology* (London, 1971).

Black, M. (ed.), *The Social Theories of Talcott Parsons* (Englewood Cliffs, NJ, 1961).

Bloomfield, M. W., *The Seven Deadly Sins* (Michigan, 1952).

Blumler, J. G., Brown, J. R., Ewbank, A. J., and Nossiter, T. J., 'Attitudes to the monarchy: their structure and development during a ceremonial occasion', *Political Studies*, vol. 19, no. 2 (1971), pp. 149–71.

Bocock, R., *Ritual in Industrial Society* (London, 1974).

Bottomore, T., *Marxist Sociology* (London, 1975).

Braverman, H., *Labor and Monopoly Capital* (New York, 1974).

Briggs, A., *The Age of Improvement* (London, 1959a).

Briggs, A. (ed.), *Chartist Studies* (London, 1959b).

Briggs, A., 'The language of "class" in early nineteenth century England', in *Essays in Labour History*, ed. A. Briggs and J. Saville (London, 1960), pp. 43–73.

Briggs, A., Introduction to *Chartist Portraits*, by G. D. H. Cole (London, 1965).

Burke, P., *Popular Culture in Early Modern Europe* (London, 1978).

Burns, T., 'The organisation of public opinion', in *Mass Communication and Society*, ed. J. Curran *et al.* (London, 1977), pp. 44–69.

Callinicos, A., *Althusser's Marxism* (London, 1976).

Chaucer, G., *The Pardoner's Tale*, ed. Carleton Brown (London, 1935).

Chenu, M. D., *L'Eveil de la conscience dans la civilisation médiévale* (Paris, 1969).

Child, J., *British Management Thought* (London, 1969).

Clegg, H., *How to Run an Incomes Policy* (London, 1971).

Cohen, A. K., 'The sociology of the deviant act: anomie and beyond', *American Sociological Review*, vol. 30, no. 1 (1965), pp. 5–14.

Cohen, G. A., 'On some criticisms of historical materialism', *Supplementary Proceedings of the Aristotelian Society*, vol. 44 (1970), pp. 121–41.

Cohen, S., and Young, J., *The Manufacture of News* (London, 1973).

Cole, G. D. H., *Chartist Portraits* (London, 1941).

Coxon, A., and Jones, C., *The Images of Occupational Prestige* (London, 1978).

Crossick, G., 'The labour aristocracy and its values', *Victorian Studies*, vol. 19, no. 3 (1976), pp. 301–28.

Cuming, G. J., and Baker, D. (eds), *Popular Belief and Practice* (Cambridge, 1972).

Cutler, A., Hindess, B., Hirst, P., and Hussain, A., *Marx's 'Capital' and Capitalism Today* (London, 1977).

Dahrendorf, R., 'Out of utopia', *American Journal of Sociology*, vol. 64, no. 2 (1958), pp. 115–127.

Davies, R. T., (ed.), *Medieval English Lyrics* (London, 1963).

Delumeau, J. (ed.), *Histoire de la Bretagne* (Toulouse, 1969).

Diamond, Lord, *Report No. 1 of the Royal Commission on Distribution of Income and Wealth* (London, 1976).

Dickinson, J., *The Statesman's Book of John of Salisbury* (New York, 1927).

Donovan, Lord, *Report of the Royal Commission on Trade Unions and Employers' Associations, 1965–1968* (London, 1968).

Downes, D., *The Delinquent Solution* (London, 1966).

Duby, G., *Medieval Marriage – Two Models from Twelfth-Century France* (Baltimore and London, 1978).

Duncan, G., *Marx and Mill: Two Views of Social Conflict and Social Harmony* (London, 1973).

Durkheim, E., *The Elementary Forms of Religious Life* (New York, 1961).

Durkheim, E., *Socialism and Saint-Simon*, with an introduction by A. W. Gouldner (New York, 1962).

Durkheim, E., *The Division of Labour in Society* (New York, 1964a).

Durkheim, E., *The Rules of Sociological Method* (New York, 1964b).

Durkheim, E., *Suicide* (London, 1970).

Durkheim, E., and Mauss, M., *Primitive Classification* (London, 1963).

Elliott, J., *Conflict or Co-operation?* (London, 1978).

Engels, F., *Anti-Dühring* (Moscow, 1959).

Engels, F., *The Peasant Wars in Germany* (New York, 1966).

Engels, F., *The Condition of the Working Class in England in 1844* (London, 1968).

Engels, F., 'Auguste Comte' (letter from Engels to Ferdinand Tönnies), in *Marx and Engels, Basic Writings on Politics and Philosophy*, ed. L. S. Feuer (London, 1969), pp. 486–7.

Erritt, M. J., and Alexander, J. C. D., 'Ownership of company shares: a new survey', *Economic Trends*, no. 287 (September 1977), pp. 96–105.

Femia, J., 'Hegemony and consciousness in the thought of Antonio Gramsci', *Political Studies*, vol. 23, no. 1 (1975), pp. 29–48.

Fenn, R. K., 'Max Weber on the secular: a typology', *Review of Religious Research*, vol. 10, no. 3 (1969), pp. 159–69.

Finer, S. E., *The Life and Times of Sir Edwin Chadwick* (London, 1952).

Foster, J., *Class Struggle and the Industrial Revolution* (London, 1974).

Fox, A., 'Industrial relations: a social critique of pluralist ideology', in *Man and Organization*, ed. J. Child (London, 1973), pp. 185–233.

Fox, A., *Beyond Contract: Work, Power and Trust Relations* (London, 1974).

Friedman, W. G., 'The function of property in English law', *British Journal of Sociology*, vol. 1, no. 3 (1950), pp. 240–59.

Galbraith, J. K., *The New Industrial State* (London, 1967).

Gamble, A., *The Conservative Nation* (London, 1974).

Garfinkel, H., *Studies in Ethnomethodology* (Englewood Cliffs, NJ, 1967).

Gay, P., *The Dilemma of Democratic Socialism* (New York, 1962).

Geertz, C., 'Ritual and social change: a Javanese example', *American Anthropologist*, vol. 61 (February 1959), pp. 991–1012.

Geertz, C., 'Ideology as a cultural system', in *Ideology and Discontent*, ed. D. Apter (New York, 1964), pp. 47–76.

Geras, N., 'Fetishism in Marx's *Capital*', *New Left Review*, no. 65 (1971), pp. 69–85.

Gerth, H. H., and Mills, C. W. (eds), *From Max Weber* (London, 1948).

Giddens, A., ' "Power" in the recent writings of Talcott Parsons', *Sociology*, vol. 2, no. 3 (1968), pp. 257–72.

Giddens, A., 'Durkheim's political sociology', *Sociological Review*, vol. 19, no. 4 (1971), pp. 477–519.

Giddens, A., 'Four myths in the history of social thought', *Economy and Society*, vol. 1, no. 4 (1972), pp. 357–385.

Giddens, A., *The Class Structure of the Advanced Societies* (London, 1973).

Giddens, A., *Durkheim* (London, 1978).

Gilbert, A. D., *Religion and Society in Industrial England: Church, Chapel, and Social Change, 1740–1814* (London, 1976).

Glasgow University Media Group, *Bad News* (London, 1976).

Goldmann, L., *The Hidden God* (London, 1964).

Goldmann, L., *The Philosophy of the Enlightenment* (London, 1973).

Goldthorpe, J. H., 'Industrial relations in Great Britain: a critique of reformism', *Politics and Society*, vol. 4, no. 3 (1974), pp. 419–52.

Goldthorpe, J. H., Lockwood, D., *et al.*, *The Affluent Worker: Industrial Attitudes and Behaviour* (Cambridge, 1968a).

Goldthorpe, J. H., Lockwood, D., *et al.*, *The Affluent Worker: Political Attitudes and Behaviour* (Cambridge, 1968b).

Goldthorpe, J. H., Lockwood, D., *et al.*, *The Affluent Worker in the Class Structure* (Cambridge, 1969).

Goodridge, R. M., 'The ages of faith – romance or reality?', *The Sociological Review*, vol. 23, no. 2 (1975), pp. 381–96.

Goody, J., 'Inheritance, property and women: some comparative considerations', in J. Goody, J. Thirsk and E. P. Thompson (eds) (1976), pp. 10–36.

Goody, J., 'Against "ritual": loosely structured thoughts on a loosely defined topic', in *Secular Ritual*, ed. S. F. Moore and B. G. Myerhoff (Assen, 1977), pp. 25–35.

Goody, J., Thirsk, J., and Thompson, E. P. (eds), *Family and Inheritance* (Cambridge, 1976).

Gough, J. W., *The Rise of the Entrepreneur* (London, 1969).

Gouldner, A. W., *The Coming Crisis of Western Sociology* (London, 1971).

Gramsci, A., *Selections from the Prison Notebooks*, eds Q. Hoare and G. Nowell-Smith (London, 1971).

Gray, R. Q., *The Labour Aristocracy in Victorian Edinburgh* (Oxford, 1976).

Groethuysen, B., *The Bourgeois, Catholicism vs. Capitalism in Eighteenth Century France* (London, 1968).

Habermas, J., *Toward a Rational Society* (London, 1971).

Habermas, J., 'What does a crisis mean today? Legitimation problems in late capitalism', *Social Research*, vol. 40, no. 4 (1973), pp. 643–67.

Habermas, J., *Legitimation Crisis* (London, 1976).

Halévy, E., *The Growth of Philosophic Radicalism* (New York, 1928).

Halévy, E., *A History of the English People in the Nineteenth Century*, Vol. 1 (London, 1949).

Han, W. S., 'Two conflicting themes: common values versus class differential values', *American Sociological Review*, vol. 35, no. 5 (1969), pp. 679–90.

Hannah, L., *The Rise of the Corporate Economy* (London, 1976).

Hannah, L., and Kay, J. A., *Concentration in Modern Industry* (London, 1977).

Harris, N., *Competition and the Corporate Society* (London, 1972).

Harrison, J. F. C., *The Early Victorians, 1832–1851* (London, 1971).

Harrison, J. F. C., 'A knife and fork question?: some recent writing on the history of social movements', in *Victorian Studies*, vol. 17 (1974), pp. 219–24.

Hayward, J. E. S., 'Solidarity: the social history of an idea in nineteenth century France', *International Review of Social History*, vol. IV, no. 2 (1959), pp. 261–84.

Hearn, F., *Domination, Legitimation and Resistance* (Westport, Conn., 1978).

Herberg, W., 'Religion in a secular society', *Review of Religious Research*, vol. 3, no. 4 (1962), pp. 145–58; vol. 3, no. 6 (1962), pp. 33–45.

Hewitt, M., *Wives and Mothers in Victorian Industry* (London, 1959).

Hick, J., *Evil and the God of Love* (London, 1966).

Hill, S., *The Dockers* (London, 1976).

Hilton, R. H., *A Medieval Society: the West Midlands at the end of the thirteenth century* (London, 1966).

Hilton, R. H., *The English Peasantry in the Later Middle Ages* (Oxford, 1975).

Hilton, R. H., Introduction in *The Transition from Feudalism to Capitalism* (London, 1978).

Hindess, B., *The Decline of Working-Class Politics* (London, 1971).

Hindess, B., *Philosophy and Methodology in the Social Sciences* (London, 1977*a*).

Hindess, B., 'The concept of class in Marxist theory and Marxist politics', in *Class, Hegemony, and Party*, ed. J. Bloomfield (London, 1977*b*), pp. 95–108.

Hindess, B., and Hirst, P. Q., *Pre-Capitalist Modes of Production* (London, 1975).

Hinton, J., *The First Shop Stewards' Movement* (London, 1973).

Hirst, P. Q., 'Althusser and the theory of ideology', *Economy and Society*, vol. 5, no. 4 (1976), pp. 385–412.

Hobsbawm, E. J., 'Methodism and the threat of revolution', *History Today* (February 1957), pp. 115–24.

Hobsbawm, E. J., *Primitive Rebels* (London, 1959).

Hobsbawm, E. J., *Labouring Men* (London, 1964).

Hobsbawm, E. J., *Industry and Empire* (Harmondsworth, 1969).

Hobsbawm, E. J., *The Age of Capital 1848–1875* (London, 1977).

Hoggart, R., *The Uses of Literacy* (London, 1958).

Hollis, P., *The Pauper Press* (Oxford, 1970).

Horkheimer, M., and Adorno, T., *Aspects of Sociology* (London, 1973).

Howell, C., 'Peasant inheritance customs in the Midlands, 1280–1700', in J. Goody, J. Thirsk and E. P. Thompson (eds) (1976), pp. 112–155.

Hyman, R., and Brough, I., *Social Values and Industrial Relations* (Oxford, 1975).

Inglis, K. S., *Churches and the Working Class in Victorian England* (London, 1963).

Jeanroy, A., *La Poesie lyrique des troubadours*, 2 vols (Paris, 1934).

Jeanroy, A., *Les Chansons de Guillaume IX, duc d'Aqitaine* (Paris, 1927).

Johnson, R., 'Barrington Moore, Perry Anderson and English social development', in *Working Papers in Cultural Studies*, No. 9 (1976), University of Birmingham Centre for Contemporary Cultural Studies, pp. 7–28.

Kay-Shuttleworth, J. P., *The Moral and Physical Condition of the Working Class* (London, 1832).

Kautsky, K., *Foundations of Christianity* (London, 1925).

Kidron, M., *Western Capitalism Since the War* (Harmondsworth, 1970).

Kolakowski, L., *Positivist Philosophy: from Hume to the Vienna Circle* (Harmondsworth, 1972).

Kumar, K., *Prophecy and Progress* (Harmondsworth, 1978).

Laqueur, T. W., *Religion and Respectability: Sunday Schools and Working Class Culture, 1780–1850* (London, 1976).

Lea, H. C., *A History of Auricular Confession and Indulgences in the Latin Church*, 2 vols (London, 1896).

Le Bras, G., 'Déchristianisation – mot fallacieux', *Social Compass*, vol. X, no. 6 (1963), pp. 445–52.

Lecoy de la Marche, A., *La Chaire française au moyen âge* (Paris, 1886).

Le Roy Ladurie, E., *The Peasants of Languedoc* (Urbana, Ill., 1974).

Le Roy Ladurie, E., *Montaillou, village occitan de 1294–1324* (Paris, 1975).

Lemert, E. M., *Human Deviance, Social Problems and Social Control* (New York, 1967).

Lewis, C. S., *The Allegory of Love* (London, 1936).

Lewis, C. S., *Studies in Words* (Cambridge, 1961).

Lockwood, D., 'Some remarks on *The Social System*', *British Journal of Sociology*, vol. 8, no. 2 (1956), pp. 134–46.

Lockwood, D., 'Social integration and system integration', in *Explorations in Social Change*, ed. G. K. Zollschan and W. Hirsch (London, 1964), pp. 244–58.

Lovejoy, A. O., *The Great Chain of Being – a Study in the History of an Idea* (Cambridge, 1938).

Luckmann, T., *The Invisible Religion – the Problem of Religion in Modern Society* (London, 1957).

Lukes, S., 'Political ritual and social integration', *Sociology*, vol. 9, no. 2 (1975), pp. 289–308.

Lukács, G., *History and Class Consciousness* (London, 1971).

Macfarlane, A., *The Origins of English Individualism* (Oxford, 1978).

MacIntyre, A., *Secularization and Moral Change* (London, 1967).

MacIntyre, A., *Marxism and Christianity* (Harmondsworth, 1971).

MacIntyre, A., and Ricoeur, P., *The Religious Significance of Atheism* (New York and London, 1969).

Macpherson, C. B., 'Democratic theory: ontology and technology', in *Political Theory and Social Change*, ed. D. Spitz (New York, 1967), pp. 203–20.

Malcomson, R. W., *Popular Recreations in English Society, 1700–1850* (Cambridge, 1973).

Mann, M., 'The social cohesion of liberal democracy', *American Sociological Review*, vol. 35, no. 3 (1970), pp. 423–39.

Mann, M., *Consciousness and Action Among the Western Working Class* (London, 1973).

Mannheim, K., *Ideology and Utopia* (London, 1966).

Marcuse, H., *One Dimensional Man* (London, 1964).

Markham, F. (ed.), *Social Organization, the Science of Man and Other Writings* (New York, 1964).

Marshall, T. H., *Citizenship and Social Class* (Cambridge, 1950).

Martin, D., *A Sociology of English Religion* (London, 1967).

Martin, D., *The Religious and the Secular* (London, 1969).

Martin, D., 'The secularization question', *Theology*, vol. 76 (February 1973), pp. 81–7.

Martin, D., *A General Theory of Secularization* (Oxford, 1978).

Marx, K., *Capital* (London, 1970).

Marx, K., *Grundrisse* (Harmondsworth, 1973*a*).

Marx, K., *The Revolutions of 1848* (Harmondsworth, 1973*b*).

Marx, K., and Engels, F., *German Ideology* (London, 1965).

Marx, K., and Engels, F., *Selected Works* (London, 1968).

Marx, K., and Engels, F., *On Religion* (Moscow, n.d.).

Mather, F. C., *Public Order in the Age of Chartists* (Manchester, 1959).

McCarthy, T., *The Critical Theory of Jurgen Habermas* (London, 1978).

McKenzie, R., and Silver, A., *Angels in Marble* (London, 1968).

McLennan, G., Molina, V., and Peters, R., 'Althusser's theory of ideology', *Working Papers in Cultural Studies*, No. 10 (1977), pp. 77–105.

McLeod, H., *Class and Religion in the Late Victorian City* (London, 1974).

McLeod, H., 'Recent studies in Victorian religious history', *Victorian Studies*, vol. 21, no. 2 (1978), pp. 245–55.

McQuail, D., 'The influence and effects of mass media', in *Mass Communication and Society*, ed. J. Curran *et al.* (London, 1977), pp. 70–94.

Mepham, J., 'The theory of ideology in *Capital*', *Radical Philosophy*, no. 2 (1972), pp. 12–19.

Merton, R. K., *Social Theory and Social Structure* (Glencoe, Ill., 1957).

Miliband, R., *The State in Capitalist Society*, (London, 1969).

Mills, C. W., *The Sociological Imagination* (New York, 1959).

Mingay, G. E., *English Landed Society in the Eighteenth Century* (London, 1963).

Mingay, G. E., *The Gentry* (London, 1976).

Mitzman, A., 'Tönnies and German Society 1887–1914: from cultural pessimism to celebration of the *Volksgemeinschaft*', *Journal for the History of Ideas*, vol. 32, no. 4 (1971), pp. 507–24.

Moore, B., *The Social Origins of Dictatorship and Democracy* (London, 1968).

Moore, B., *Injustice: The Social Bases of Obedience and Revolt* (London, 1978).

Moore, D. C., 'The Corn Laws and high farming', *Economic History Review*, vol. 18, no. 3 (1965), pp. 544–61.

Moore, R., *Pitmen, Preachers and Politics* (Cambridge, 1974).

Moore, S. F., and Myerhoff, B. G. (eds), *Secular Ritual* (Assen, 1977).

Mollat, M., and Wolff, P., *The Popular Revolutions of the Late Middle Ages* (London, 1973).

Moorhouse, H. F., 'The political incorporation of the British working class: an interpretation', *Sociology*, vol. 7, no. 3 (1973), pp. 341–59.

Moorhouse, H. F., 'The Marxist theory of the labour aristocracy', *Social History*, vol. 3, no. 1 (1978) pp. 61–82.

Moorhouse, H. F., and Chamberlain, C., 'Lower-class attitudes to property', *Sociology*, vol. 8, no. 3 (1974), pp. 387–405.

Morse, C., 'The functional imperatives', in M. Black (ed.) (1961), pp. 100–52.

Murray, A., 'Religion among the poor in thirteenth century France: the testimony of Humbert de Romans', *Traditio*, vol. XXX (1974), pp. 285–324.

Musson, A. E., 'Class struggle and the labour aristocracy 1830–1860', *Social History*, vol. 1, no. 3 (1976), pp. 335–56.

Nairn, T., 'The English working class', *New Left Review*, no. 24 (1964), pp. 43–57.

Nichols, T., *Ownership, Control and Ideology* (London, 1969).

Nichols, T., and Armstrong, P., *Workers Divided* (Glasgow, 1976).

Nordlinger, E. A., *The Working-Class Tories* (London, 1967).

Obelkevich, J., *Religion and Rural Society: South Lindsey, 1825–1875* (New York, 1976).

Offe, C., 'The theory of the capitalist state and the problem of policy formation', in *Stress and Contradiction in Modern Capitalism*, ed. L. N. Lindberg *et al.* (Lexington, Mass., 1975), pp. 125–44.

Ossowski, S., *Class Structure in the Social Consciousness* (London, 1963).

Owst, G., *Literature and Pulpit in Medieval England* (Oxford, 1967).

Painter, S., *French Chivalry* (Baltimore, 1957).

Panitch, L., *Social Democracy and Industrial Militancy* (Cambridge, 1976).

Parkin, F., *Class Inequality and Political Order* (London, 1972).

Parsons, T., 'The place of ultimate values in sociological theory', *International Journal of Ethics*, vol. 45 (1935), pp. 282–316.

Parsons, T., *The Structure of Social Action* (Glencoe, Ill., 1937).

Parsons, T., *The Social System* (London, 1951).

Parsons, T., *Working Papers in the Theory of Action*, in collaboration with Robert F. Bales and Edward A. Shils (New York, 1953).

Parsons, T., 'Durkheim's contribution to the theory of integration of social systems', in *Essays on Sociology and Philosophy*, ed. K. H. Wolff (New York, 1960), pp. 118–53.

Parsons, T., 'The point of view of the author', in M. Black (ed.) (1961), pp. 311–63.

Parsons, T., 'On the concept of influence', *Public Opinion Quarterly*, vol. 27 (1963a), pp. 37–62, 87–92.

Parsons, T., 'On the concept of political power', *Proceedings of the American Philosophical Society*, vol. 107 (1963b), pp. 232–62.

Parsons, T., 'Systems analysis: social systems', in *International Encyclopedia for Social Science*, ed. D. L. Sills (New York, 1968), pp. 458–73.

Parsons, T., 'Emile Durkheim', in D. L. Sills (ed.), *op. cit.* (1968), pp. 311–20.

Parsons, T., 'On building social system theory: a personal history,' *Daedalus* (Fall 1970), pp. 826–81.

Parsons, T., and Shils, E. (eds), *Towards a General Theory of Action* (Cambridge, 1951).

Parsons, T., and Smelser, N. J., *Economy and Society* (London, 1956).

Patterson, O., 'The cricket ritual in the West Indies', *New Society*, no. 352 (26 June 1969), pp. 988–9.

Payne, P. L., *British Entrepreneurship in the Nineteenth Century* (London, 1978).

Perkin, H., *The Origins of Modern English Society* (London, 1969).

Pollard, S., *The Genesis of Modern Management* (Harmondsworth, 1968).

Poulantzas, N., *Political Power and Social Classes* (London, 1973).

Poulantzas, N., *Classes in Contemporary Capitalism* (London, 1975).

Redlich, J., *The History of Local Government in England* (London, 1903).

Remmling, G. W., *The Sociology of Karl Mannheim* (London, 1975).

Ricardo, D., *Principles of Political Economy and Taxation* (London, 1891).

Roberts, K., *et al., The Fragmentary Class Structure* (London, 1977).

Robinson, R. V., and Bell, W., 'Equality, success and social justice in England and the United States', *American Sociological Review*, vol. 43, no. 2 (1978), pp. 125–43.

Rocher, G., *Talcott Parsons and American Sociology* (London, 1974).

Rodman, H., 'The lower-class value stretch', *Social Forces*, vol. 42, no. 2 (1963), pp. 205–15.

Rogally, J., *Grunwick* (Harmondsworth, 1977).

Rose, N., 'Fetishism and ideology; a review of theoretical problems', *Ideology and Consciousness*, no. 2 (1977), pp. 27–54.

Rosenwein, B. H., and Little, L. K., 'Social meaning in the monastic and mendicant spiritualities', *Past and Present*, no. 63 (1974), pp. 4–32.

Runciman, W. G. (ed.), *Max Weber: Selections in Translation* (Cambridge, 1978).

Schlaugh, M., *English Medieval Literature and its Social Foundations* (London, 1967).

Schumpeter, J. A., *History of Economic Analysis* (New York, 1954).

Scott, J. F., 'The changing foundations of the Parsonian action scheme', *American Sociological Review*, vol. 28, no. 5 (1963), pp. 716–35.

Seideman, S., 'The Durkheim/Weber "unawareness problem" ', *European Journal of Sociology*, vol. XVIII, no. 2 (1977), p. 356.

Shils, E., *Center and Periphery: Essays in Macrosociology* (Chicago and London, 1975).

Shils, E., and Young, M., 'The meaning of the coronation', *Sociological Review*, vol. 1, no. 2 (1953), pp. 63–82.

Shiner, L., 'The concept of secularization in empirical research', *Journal for the Scientific Study of Religion*, vol. 6, no. 2 (1967), pp. 207–29.

Simpson, A., *The Wealth of the Gentry 1540–1660* (Cambridge, 1961).

Smelser, N. J., *Social Change in the Industrial Revolution* (Chicago, 1959).

Spufford, M., 'Peasant inheritance customs and land distribution in Cambridgeshire from the sixteenth to the eighteenth centuries', in J. Goody, J. Thirsk and E. P. Thompson (eds) (1976), pp. 156–76.

Stedman-Jones, G., *Outcast London* (Oxford, 1971).

Stone, L., *Family and Fortune* (Oxford, 1973).

Stone, L., *The Family, Sex and Marriage in England 1500–1800* (London, 1977).

Struik, D. J. (ed.), *Marx, 1844 Manuscripts* (London, 1973).

Swingewood, A., *The Myth of Mass Culture* (London, 1977).

Tawney, R. H., *Religion and the Rise of Capitalism* (Harmondsworth, 1938).

Taylor, L., *Deviance and Society* (London, 1971).

Tentler, T. N., 'The Summa for confessors as an instrument of social control' in C. Trinkaus and H. A. Oberman (eds) (1974), pp. 103–26.

Thirsk, J., 'The European debate on customs of inheritance 1500–1700', in J. Goody, J. Thirsk and E. P. Thompson (eds) (1976), pp. 177–91.

Tholfsen, T. R., *Working-Class Radicalism in Mid-Victorian Britain* (London, 1976).

Thomas, K., *Religion and the Decline of Magic* (London, 1971).

Thompson, E. P., *The Making of the English Working Class* (London, 1963).

Thompson, E. P., 'Peculiarities of the English', in *The Socialist Register 1965*, ed. R. Miliband and J. Saville (London, 1965), pp. 311–62.

Thompson, E. P., 'On history, sociology and historical relevance', *British Journal of Sociology*, vol. 27, no. 3 (1976a), pp. 387–402.

Thompson, E. P., 'The grid of inheritance: a comment', in J. Goody, J. Thirsk and E. P. Thompson (eds) (1976b), pp. 328–60.

Tigar, M. E., and Levy, M. R., *Law and The Rise of Capitalism* (New York, 1977).

Tiryakian, E., 'A problem for the sociology of knowledge: the mutual unawareness of Emile Durkheim and Max Weber', *European Journal of Sociology*, vol. VII, no. 2 (1966), pp. 330–5.

Tönnies, F., *Gemeinschaft und Gesellschaft: Abhandlung des Kommunismus und socialismus als empirische Kulturformen* (Leipsig, 1887).

Towler, R., *Homo Religiosus* (London, 1974).

Trevor-Roper, H., *Religion, the Reformation and Social Change* (London, 1967).

Trinkaus, C., and Oberman, H. A. (eds), *The Pursuit of Holiness in Late Medieval and Renaissance Religion* (Leiden, 1974).

Trojel, E. (ed.), *Andreae cappelani regii Francorum de amore*, 3 vols (Copenhagen, 1892).

Trumbach, R., *The Rise of the Egalitarian Family* (New York, 1976).

Turner, B. S., *Weber and Islam: a critical study* (London, 1974).

Turner, B. S., 'Confession and social structure', *Annual Review for the Social Science of Religion*, vol. 1 (1977a), pp. 29–58.

Turner, B. S., 'Class solidarity and system integration', *Sociological Analysis*, vol. 38, no. 4 (1977b), pp. 345–58.

Turner, R., 'Value conflict in social disorganisation', *Sociology and Social Research*, vol. 38, no. 5 (1953–4), pp. 301–8.

Ullmann, W., *Principles of Government and Politics in the Middle Ages* (London, 1965).

Veness, T., *School-Leavers: Their Aspirations and Expectations* (London, 1962).

Wallerstein, I., *The Modern World-System* (New York, 1974).

Ward, W. R., *Religion and Society in England, 1790–1850* (London, 1972).

Warnock, M. (ed.), *John Stuart Mill: Utilitarianism* (Harmondsworth, 1962).

Waxman, C. I. (ed.), *The End of Ideology Debate* (New York, 1968).

Weber, M., *The Protestant Ethic and the Spirit of Capitalism* (London, 1930).

Weber, M., *The Methodology of the Social Sciences* (New York, 1949).

Weber, M., *The Theory of Social and Economic Organization* (New York, 1964).

Weber, M., *The Sociology of Religion* (London, 1965).

Weber, M., *The Agrarian Sociology of Ancient Civilizations* (London, 1976).

Westergaard, J. H., 'The rediscovery of the cash nexus', in *The Socialist Register 1970*, ed. R. Miliband and J. Saville (London, 1970), pp. 111–38.

Westergaard, J. H., and Resler, H., *Class in a Capitalist Society* (London, 1975).

Willis, P., *Learning to Labour* (Oxford, 1977).

Wilson, B., *Religion in Secular Society* (London, 1966).

Wilson, B., *Contemporary Transformations of Religion* (London, 1976).

Wolff, K. H., 'The sociology of knowledge and sociological theory', in *Symposium on Sociological Theory*, ed. L. Gross (New York, 1969), pp. 567–602.

Wood, T., *English Casuistical Divinity during the Seventeenth Century* (London, 1952).

Wright, E. O., 'Class boundaries in advanced capitalist societies', *New Left Review*, no. 98 (1976), pp. 3–41.

Young, M., and Willmott, P., 'Social grading by manual workers', *British Journal of Sociology*, vol. 7, no. 4 (1956), pp. 337–45.

Zeldin, T. (ed.), *Conflicts in French Society* (London, 1970).

Index

Leibniz, G. W. 20, 73–4
Lemert, E. M. 55
Lewis, C. S. 81, 87–8
Liberal Government(s) 132
liberalism 95, 100, 102, 104, 111–12
literacy 124
Lloyd, H. 93
Locke, J. 74
Lockwood, D. 46, 50, 154
Lovejoy, A. O. 73
Luckmann, T. 66
Lukács, G. 31, 56, 189
Lukes, S. 53
Luther, M. 80

Macfarlane, A. 180
MacIntyre, A. 60, 67–8
   and Ricoeur, P. 68
Macpherson, C. B. 98–9
Magna Carta 79–80
Malcolmson, R. W. 104
Malthus, T. 97, 107
Malthusianism 97–8
management 135–6, 145, 146, 155,
   159, 161–2, 164, 178
   of labour 160
   scientific 161
   managerial power 136
   managerialism 137, 148
Mann, M., 141–3, 148, 154, 166–8
Mannheim, K. 30–2, 34, 53, 188
Marcilhacy, C. 69
Marcuse, H. 1, 10, 126
market(s) 17, 97, 107–8, 131, 134–5,
   137–8, 146, 163, 177, 189
Markham, F. 37
marriage 86–8, 90–1, 104, 180–3
   bond 93
   contract 91
   feudal 89
   lay system of 89–90
   strategy 90
   (see courtly love)
Marshall, T. H. 136
Martin, D. 69
Marx, K. 2, 6, 8, 14, 19, 21, 24, 27–8,
   30–5, 39–40, 45–6, 50, 53–4, 56–
   62, 65, 92, 108, 159, 162–4, 166,
   168–9, 174, 185
   and Engels, F. 1, 7, 8, 30–2, 54, 56,
   59–63, 71, 169, 188–9
Marxism 7, 9, 12, 15, 28–34, 37–8, 54,
   59, 62, 126, 169, 187

Althusserian 30, 65
Second International 9
vulgar 36
mass media 124, 130, 132, 145, 151,
   158
   schooling 124, 158
materialism, historical 63, 174
Mather, F. C. 123
Mauss, M. 39
McCarthy, T. 20
McKenzie, R. and Silver, A. 145, 147
McLennan, G. et al 20
McLeod, H. 103, 108, 118, 120–1,
   125
McQuail, D. 151–2
Mepham, J. 27
Merton, R. 31, 36, 46, 55
Methodism 100–2, 109–10, 121–2
Middle Ages 21, 59, 69, 72, 76, 78–9,
   81–2, 84–5, 87–8
Miliband, R. 24–5, 55, 166
Mills, C. Wright 49
Milton, J. 81
Mingay, G. E. 180, 182
Mitzman, A. 66
mode of production 20, 51, 56, 60, 62,
   129, 144, 166, 170–1, 175–6, 178,
   183–4, 190–1
   capitalist 4, 9, 21, 59, 138, 153, 162,
   168, 170, 172, 189
   feudal 59, 64–5, 92, 162, 190
   pre-capitalist 62
   slave 61, 172–3
   (see social formation, society)
Mollat, M. and Wolff, P. 72, 75
monarchy 148
monogamy 89–91
Moore, B. 92, 106–7, 159, 167
Moore, D. C. 107
Moore, R. 102, 109, 120
Moore, S. F. and Myerhoff, B. G. 53
Moorehouse, H. F. 43, 119
   and Chamberlain, C. 131, 143, 144,
   149
moral(s) 43, 68
morality 71, 105, 108, 138, 176, 180,
   182, 184–5
   Christian 104, 108
   familial 94, 104
   traditional 138
Morse, C. 54
Murray, A. 69, 75
Musson, A. E. 119, 123